I0818987

By Nicole Gonzalez Van Cleve

*Crime Fictions*

*Crook County*

# Crime Fictions

Nicole Gonzalez Van Cleve

RANDOM HOUSE
NEW YORK

# Crime Fictions

## How Racist Lies Built a System of Mass Wrongful Conviction

Random House
An imprint and division of Penguin Random House LLC
1745 Broadway, New York, NY 10019
randomhousebooks.com
penguinrandomhouse.com



Hardcover ISBN 9780593447086
Ebook ISBN 9780593447109

Printed in the United States of America

1st Printing

FIRST EDITION

BOOK TEAM: Managing editor: Rebecca Berlant • Production manager: Katie Zilberman • Copy editor: Martin Schneider • Proofreaders: Melissa Churchill, Ruth Anne Phillips, Claire Maby

Title-page image: de-nue-pic/Adobe Stock

The authorized representative in the EU for product safety and compliance is Penguin Random House Ireland, Morrison Chambers, 32 Nassau Street, Dublin D02 YH68, Ireland. https://eu-contact.penguin.ie

*To my beloved boys,*
*Dylan Salvatore Van Cleve and*
*Micah Gonzalez Van Cleve*

*In this world, remember what is required of us: To act justly, to love mercy, and to walk humbly with God.*

# Contents

# Introduction

In 2015, I was finishing a study on Chicago's criminal justice system when I met Trevon Yates. One of Trevon's attorneys, Laura Nirider, worked upstairs from me, along with some of the top exoneration attorneys in the country. Trevon was one of many Black boys she represented at the Center on Wrongful Convictions of Youth at Northwestern University.

Trevon Yates's story never made national news. The accusations made against him were so incriminating that the local media and the public accepted them as fact, even though they proved to be fiction. Police accused the boy of committing an armed robbery near his hometown of East St. Louis, Illinois, in St. Clair County.[1]

Trevon was only seventeen years old, but his disabilities were so pronounced that his cognitive ability was that of an average nine- or ten-year-old child.[2] When the officers came to his home, Trevon's dad stood guard between his son and the armed men, asking a flurry of questions as they handcuffed his son and put him in the police car. In desperation, his dad begged to follow the car to the station, but the police would not allow it. Without obtaining a warrant, police detained Trevon from his home and against the will of his father. In any other context, this chain of events would be considered an abduction.

The police had little evidence in this case. A tipster had pointed to "Trayvon," a man who lived in the neighborhood and had bragged about the crime. He was described as having gold teeth, big earrings, a box haircut, and a sleeve of tattoos and weighing about 160 pounds.[3] The Trevon in their custody looked nothing like the description they had received. No gold teeth, no earrings, no box haircut, no tattoos, and he weighed only 105 pounds.[4] There was only the unfortunate coincidence that his name resembled the supposed suspect's, albeit spelled differently.

There was a whole team of officers handling Trevon. But two officers, Scott Weymouth and Kenneth McHughes, conducted a choreographed, tag-team interrogation.[5] The purpose of such interrogations is to create an admission of guilt.[6] That process required intimacy with the suspect, built in small rooms and close proximity, with fluorescent lights and endurance tests.

Detective McHughes read Trevon the Miranda warnings, but Trevon was not able to understand his right to remain silent nor his right to an attorney.[7] Trevon never explicitly waived his rights, but the officers proceeded as though he had. Due to his disability, he struggled to understand the Miranda warnings, but the officers chose to continue nonetheless.

Trevon faced a barrage of questions, with officers rotating in and out of the room and then leaving him for periods of isolation. Trevon prayed out loud for deliverance.[8] "Lord, you know me. You know me, Lord," he wailed, all the while rocking in his chair.[9] His hands wrung his shirt tight, and he collapsed from the stomach down as though an invisible fist were sucker punching him slowly to the gut. Propped up against the wall of the interrogation room, he cried toward the empty wall as if it might cradle him back. He twisted in his chair when the police came close and hid his head under his shirt to wipe his tears. Thirty-five times, he begged for his mother, but because he didn't ask for an attorney, the police simply continued with their questioning. Between the sobs and gasps for air, Trevon hit his head on the table as he maintained his innocence again and again, but the officers did not relent. Over at least two hours, police repeatedly told Trevon that if he did not confess, he would be viewed, in their words, as a "thug and a hard-core" who needed to come clean because "all the evidence" pointed toward him.[10] But this was a lie; there was no evidence, which one of the officers, Scott Toth, later admitted under oath.[11] This was one of over forty-two lies Trevon was told, in a process designed to deceive and confuse him, according to a civil complaint that he would later file.[12] But Trevon still upheld his innocence. Indeed, he did it at least thirty-five times in two hours.[13]

"I did not rob nobody," Trevon pleaded to a detective. "I swear to God. I'm being honest with you, sir. I'm being so, so honest. I try to do right. I'm going to school to get my GED."[14] Trevon was begging the officers to see him the way God saw him. He was a good kid who was truthful and trying to do right. He was bettering himself, going to school, and swearing to God so that they would believe him. And, despite his pleas, it was clear that the police did not see Trevon as a boy, nor as an innocent kid. And that lens—a way of seeing suspects—was so entrenched that the officers ignored the fact that the Trevon weeping at the table in front of them looked nothing like the real suspect. But none of that mattered; what they had was a Black child who shared the same name as their alleged suspect.

Two hours of coercion, and it was all too much. Trevon threatened to kill himself. He collapsed to the floor in guttural anguish. According to Trevon's civil complaint, Detective McHughes provoked Trevon during the interrogation with saying, "Man up!" Lieutenant Weymouth dug in as well, challenging Trevon, "Let's see what kind of a man you're going to be."[15] All of this difficulty frustrated the officers because, in the view of law enforcement, some criminals are so inept, they aren't even good at being criminals, which meant that the police had to do all the work.[16] Before getting a full confession, Weymouth stepped in again:

> I'm not gonna spoonfeed you what I know. . . . I want to see if what you have to say matches up to the evidence that I'm talk-

ing about, because then I can prove to people that you're telling the truth.[17]

The police convinced Trevon that the only way out—to see his parents, to get out of the interrogation room, to possibly get free—was to say what the police wanted him to say. So he did just that. He gave up. And against everything he knew to be true, he gave them a confession peppered with all the information the police fed to him. Trevon would sit in an adult jail for nine months awaiting trial. Prosecutors would eventually review his case for procedural abuses and decide to drop the charges.[18] What I would learn from Laura Nirider was that most kids in these situations are convicted rather than released.

Many police interrogations of kids and young adults happen in the depths of police departments: no videos, no parents, no witnesses except for another officer and a prosecutor[19] who would eventually walk in to memorialize the confession that would seal the child's fate. All of this is legal because there are few safeguards protecting minors when police take them into their custody. Police can lie and deceive suspects, including children, and literally confuse or terrify them into falsely confessing.[20] Luckily, in Trevon's case, Laura Nirider had a recording of his interrogation, and at her suggestion, I watched it.

I was embarrassed to admit to Laura that her office, the Center on Wrongful Convictions of Youth, did not make much sense to me as a scholar who studied the adult criminal justice system. *What could these kids be wrongfully convicted of?* I thought. *Shoplifting? Stealing rims? Being out after curfew?*

Laura told me that there were many other "Trevons" out there charged with serious crimes, like murder and sexual assault. So many kids were being arrested, in fact, that the center didn't have the financial resources to fight for them all. And for the boys it could represent, the fight to exonerate them took so long that many of the innocent "kids" were now middle-aged men behind bars.

I was stunned. How did the world not know about Trevon and all the other boys like him who had been abducted, interrogated, accused, and even convicted of crimes they did not commit? Surely this was another form of racial violence, like police shootings or vigilante injustice, but it wasn't one I'd seen up close.

Not long after I learned about Trevon, I got a call from Laura Nirider's mentor and colleague, Steven Drizin, who was a clinical professor of law and co-founder of Northwestern University's Bluhm Legal Clinic's Center on Wrongful Convictions of Youth. Steven told me that in thirty years of litigating wrongful conviction cases, he had noticed a disturbing pattern.

As in Trevon's case, the police would engage in an invasive interrogation of a suspect, create a "contaminating narrative" to demonstrate their guilt, and then manipulate them into making a false confession. Though these narratives were often built upon racist dog whistles that defied logic and even DNA evidence, juries believed them and had convicted hundreds of innocent people based on police fictions. Steven's theory was that false confessions were the engine of wrongful conviction. Because these tactics were used mainly to incriminate Black boys and teens, race and racism clearly played a role in these cases. He wondered what I, as a social scientist trained to see empirical patterns across cases, might be able to uncover by looking at the data through a racial lens.

Initially, I agreed that false confessions were the problem and gathered a sample of them to examine. After many years of research and a lot of data, however, I have come to a different conclusion. False confessions are just one of many tools that police use to *create* wrongful convictions, practices so pervasive that they have built an entire "shadow system" of justice for Black people in America. This is part of what the visionary sociologist and criminologist W.E.B. Du Bois called America's "double system of justice."[21]

We have all seen stories of innocent people exonerated after years in prison: formerly incarcerated people hugging their attorneys or walking out of prison with their arms raised to the heavens. These images create a false sense that there is some hope for vindication, truth, and justice even after things in our criminal justice system go wrong. But wrongful convictions of Black boys and men are not glitches in an otherwise well-functioning machine, nor are they misfires in a system of supposed color-blind due process protections. We cling to the mythology that the innocent will go free and court processes will allow the truth to be exposed. Indeed, wrongful conviction, framed as some kind of aberration, is its own lie.

The systemic patterns across many cases must lead us to ask whether wrongful conviction is an intentional act or an extension of the broader criminal justice system, and whether it is a system that operates with racist intent.

Before I began this study, I never considered myself an expert on wrongful conviction. I specialized in racism's impact on everyday legal practices in the criminal courts. In 2016, I published a book called *Crook County: Racism and Injustice in America's Largest Criminal Court,* that explored the results of my decade-long investigation of Chicago's Cook County Criminal Courts, the largest unified court system in the United States. As a young law clerk and researcher embedded in the courts, I had a front-row seat to blatant violations of due process: prosecutors pushing plea bargains or sometimes barely opening their case files; sloppy compliance with the *Brady* disclosure rules. The 1963 Supreme Court decision *Brady v. Maryland* required prosecutors to disclose evidence that is favorable to the accused, material to the case, and in the possession of the prosecutor or their law enforcement partners. However, despite the decision, it was clear that prosecutors were expected to look away from egregious violations of law and prosecute with blinders on—never questioning the veracity of police officers and their cases.

Beyond the proximity to legal practices, I had proximity in another way. I am Chicana but light-skinned; during the course of my research, the attorneys generally assumed me to be White. With that privilege came access. There was no shortage of judges, lawyers, and officers justifying abuse by using racism, in its subtle and overt forms. They mocked Black defendants in bastardized Ebonics or Black English vernacular; used coded racial slurs to refer to defendants, victims, and their families; and used the court as a forum to degrade and humiliate Black and Latino people, even those sitting in the public gallery.

For years, I took field notes as Black and Latino defendants took plea bargains—waiving their right to trial in the hope of leniency from the court. The expectation among attorneys was that the accused would just plead guilty without protest or participation. When the time came for the prosecutor to read the factual basis of the defendant's conviction "for the court record," defendants would often look confused, whispering to their attorney that the facts were wrong. Some would say, *That's not what happened.* A few would raise their hands, obediently, as if they had objections. Public defenders were expected to "control them" into compliance. In one case, the prosecutor read the police report and detailed the facts of the case for the record. The judge asked: *Are those the correct facts?* And the defendant interjected quickly, "That's what the police say . . ." His private attorney leaned toward him with a biting whisper, telling his client to just say "YES!" Immediately, the defendant complied: "Yes, Judge."[22]

At first, I dismissed these moments of dissonance as the defendants' confusion or even anger at having to plead guilty to a crime. Maybe I was conditioned by the lawyers, who had trained me to see these mostly Black and Latino defendants as inherently blameworthy. What I now realize is that many of these defendants were trying to tell the court they were innocent, but we had all been conditioned to ignore them.

Once I realized that the prosecutors and judges in my study knew that police lied on cases and on the stand, the protests of Black and Latino defendants led me to another conclusion, one I had never seen represented in pop culture, nor taught in my law, criminology, or policing classes: The police intentionally fabricated criminal cases against Black defendants from poorer areas of the city, and their lies were embedded throughout the legal process—from the arrest to the investigation to the inevitable conviction.[23] One judge admitted to me that police created "epidemics" of bogus cases in Black neighborhoods.[24]

They were able to weaponize wrongful conviction against Black people because they had a monopoly on the truth.

The police's word is a type of indisputable evidence for judges and juries. Insidiously, police know what they say will be accepted as truth, *the* truth, the kind of truth that has thirty-, forty-, or fifty-year consequences. Imagine that world, where you are so powerful that lies don't exist because you own the truth. Merely an accusation can crush a childhood, a person, a future; this is the world the police create and inhabit. This underground system of justice is reserved for those imagined without a childhood, a personhood, or a future. And that system, that double system of justice, has been built for Black people in America.

At the end of *Crook County,* after documenting systemic violations of due process, I ended with a question: What if the numbers that we understand as mass incarceration are, in actuality, mass wrongful convictions?

Mass wrongful conviction is a persistent error built into the system on a scale that is largely unknown. What we know is that nationwide, nearly 3,800 people have been exonerated since 1989.[25] That amounts to over thirty-five thousand years that those exonerated people spent in prison—for crimes they did not commit.[26] Similar to the racial disparities seen in the larger criminal justice system, Black men and boys are astoundingly overrepresented in the statistics concerning wrongful conviction. The likelihood of being wrongfully convicted of serious crimes like murder and sexual assault is 7.5 times higher for Black people than for White people.[27]

The workhorse technique of wrongful conviction is forcing people to confess to crimes they did not commit. But these statistics reflect only the exonerated. Many people languish decades behind bars, waiting an average of two years just to have a pro bono attorney read an application to review their case.[28] Some firms are so overwhelmed with requests that the letters just get dusty in old file cabinets. Most letters are thrown out, and the innocent are left either to represent themselves or to accept the fate of being innocent and in prison for decades.

While the problem of wrongful conviction is national in scale, I came to realize that Chicago is the wrongful conviction capital of the United States, convicting more innocent people than any other jurisdiction.[29] As of January 2026, of the 3,767 national cases of wrongful conviction that we do know of, 576 are from the state of Illinois, and 148 of those convictions included false confessions.[30] Here it was, the largest unified court system in the U.S. with the second-largest prosecutors' office in the nation, the system that I had access to for so many years, being the most fruitful place to understand wrongful conviction. Sadly, Chicago, my hometown, was the workhorse of this clandestine double system of justice.

I assumed that the easiest cases for the police to rig would be low-grade crimes such as drug possession or possession with intent to sell—charges that people plead guilty to all day long. What I did not anticipate was that the big cases—the high-stakes "heater" cases warranting life in prison or even death—were just as tainted.[31] These were the cases Steven and Laura worked on.

Criminal cases generally take two paths through the courts. There are cases that end in a plea bargain, and there are other cases that are resolved via trial; spread across the two groups is a subset of innocent people going to prison who are the victims of wrongful convictions, both big and small. Our society's faith in due process and in the protective role of the police has made us blind to the people who are forced down this path, living within this unknown and unseen error.

Wrongful conviction is a system produced—actively—by police. In this system, police officers have such a monopoly on what constitutes truth that their lying is redefined as "building a case."[32] Police investigations are not about fact-finding but about persuasion. Where there is no physical evidence linking a person to a crime, police can extract a confession and place *their* words in the suspect's mouth; they can ignore or bury exonerating evidence and threaten witnesses with arrest in order to convince them to offer the "right" details. Then, they call the testimony of these supposed witnesses "corroboration." All of these tactics—in varying doses—create the illusion of a spontaneous eruption of guilt instead of the product of police fiction that it is. Police know that courts give significant weight to officers' testimony over the suspect's word, which allows this system to remain unseen and unchecked.[33]

The United States has deep mythologies about police as competent crime fighters, the "thin blue line" that protects us.[34] But from what, specifically? The answer is often racially tinged with lies about the supposed looming threat of Black boys. The mythology of "fighting crime" is often code for the surveilling and targeting of Black people.

Rather than crime fighters, police are more like "crime fiction writers" crafting narratives for cases all over the system—stories that prosecutors then help present to judges and juries in order to secure convictions.[35] Certainly, each case in this book is unique, but if you take the cases as a whole, damning patterns emerge that show the wrongful conviction system at work.

First, we meet Romarr Gipson and Elijah Henderson, the youngest boys known to be targeted by these practices. At seven and eight years old, they are among the youngest people to be charged with murder in the U.S., despite it being physically impossible for children of such a young age to commit these heinous crimes. In this case, the racist imagination of the police, the court, and the media defied science to cast these boys as "superpredators."

The wrongful conviction of fourteen-year-old Lee Hester in 1961, a disabled child accused of killing his teacher, opened the door for Black schools to be surveilled and for Black children to be targeted. We meet George Jones, the middle-class honors student who was framed for a rape and murder despite resisting a confession. There are the cases of the Roscetti Four, the Dixmoor Five, the Englewood Four, and the Marquette Park Four—all resembling the manhunt that targeted New York's Central Park Five in 1989. These cases show how the techniques of wrongful conviction can be weaponized against not just one Black child but many, in a preemptive strike on Black children.

A significant amount of time and effort in the wrongful conviction movement is spent on examining the most prevalent technical errors in order to identify the causes of wrongful conviction.[36] Some scholars even conduct a "sentinel event review," treating wrongful conviction like a plane crash or isolated disaster.[37] Rarely do we look at the system itself—examining how supposed outliers are actually patterned, persistent, and essential to our justice system. Only by looking at the commonalities among cases can we see the "shadow system" at work, one that firmly targets Black and Brown children *en masse,* much like our prison system as a whole. Black people have disproportionately borne the brunt of this wrongful conviction system, but all people—especially those who are poor or disabled or possess a trait that makes them vulnerable to such targeting—can find themselves in this wrongful conviction nightmare. As sociologist Reuben Miller has pointed out—speaking as a Black father and scholar—"the system built for my children could someday harm some of yours."[38]

We have to ask ourselves why we, as Americans, have such blind faith in police and the cases they create. What is it about our culture that so readily believes that innocent young people—even seven-year-olds—are capable of monstrous acts? Why is a police officer's word always reason enough for us to take away the liberty and lives of so many young Black people?

These questions drove my investigation into the "evidence of things not seen," the racism that fills the gaps between the accusations made by the police and the incriminating narratives they create to make it all seem real.[39] It required forcing myself to see the holes and the lies up close, rebuilding iconic wrongful conviction cases from the ground up. I had to walk the old crime scenes, talk to those who had lived through these tragedies, and weed through dusty archives, false confessions, legal documents, and civil case files. It required searching through and analyzing hundreds of pages of media coverage on each of these cases and tracing how police lies became entangled with the reporting of "facts" and how those "facts" triggered a gruesome racial animus. And finally, it required following a handful of officers and their accessories, from case to case, to see how clandestine practices developed over time and across precincts and were passed down like an inheritance to new generations of officers for a new generation of boys. It was through these data, through rebuilding cases and seeing these practices that were meant to be buried like the dead, that I could see the mechanics of the shadow system of justice. So, this book—a how-dun-it of policing in America—is an attempt at a new way of seeing . . . for all of us.

In a court of law, we would hold a trial for the accused perpetrators of a crime. We would do a deep investigation and put forth the evidence. I've tried to do the same for the police, and this is my opening statement: Police are not the crime fighters you think they are. They are the perpetrators of wrongful convictions, meting out a type of vigilante justice that just so happens to be woven into the fabric of our criminal justice system. Rather than uncovering evidence, they create crime fictions about the perceived guilt of the accused. These fictions narrate guilt and almost always lead to conviction. They steal decades from the lives of innocent people.

And the majority of these people have one thing in common. They are Black.

# Crime Fictions

# 1

# The Question We Must Ask

*Therefore, justice must satisfy the appearance of justice.*

**—Supreme Court decision, *Offutt v. United States,* 348 U.S. 11 (1954)**

If summer in Englewood in the 1990s had a sound, it would be the slow build of Al Green's "Love and Happiness," a wistful memory sung like a regret and a joy. Soulful, slow, pensive, but laced with small layers of happiness and rhythm that come with Chicago in the summer and the Englewood neighbors on their stoops.

Groups of boys and girls rode their bikes back and forth, skipped rope, talked smack, made plans, taunted, laughed, and looked around for small change to buy penny candy at the store across from the elementary school. Getting that money took work: planning with friends, asking adults, offering to do chores, and promising to be good.

There was a lot happening on Normal Avenue. It was near Paul Robeson High School, where the local kids could parade their bikes, showing off new reflectors and streamers and the like. They rode back and forth and sometimes in circles, legs straight, back flat, and coasted with the momentum. Adults sat on the stoops, watching and supervising the circus of love and happiness on Normal Avenue, two worlds, together but apart.

Eleven-year-old Ryan Harris was part of this crowd, balancing on a blue Road Warrior bike that had some splendor to it. Ryan was the new girl on the block, visiting her godmother and heading to camp along with many of the kids riding around. Ryan had a tall and slender frame, her hair often in those rubber bands bound with plastic balls that looked like little candy jawbreakers. Ryan was summer, dressed in a white shirt, popsicle green shorts, and white Nikes.[1]

Seeing Ryan bike toward Marquette Road was expected. Almost every child would eventually go down that road. The momentum of Normal Avenue pulled toward Marquette Road. The convenience store was the ever-coveted destination for all the kids, because that place offered the promise of not just candy but also BBQ chips and cheese-flavored popcorn.[2]

But to see her turn left and not right—toward the railroad tracks—that was something only a few folks saw, and that was strange for her because Ryan had always been told to stay in sight of her godmother. She was a particle jumping its orbit.

Some would say they last saw Ryan place her bike in the trunk of a car and get in. Others insisted they saw her with a man, walking calmly. Others didn't notice her missing at all; they only remembered her riding the bike, a new face in the neighborhood, an older kid with confidence and beauty. A crush—that was the way Romarr Gipson remembered Ryan.

Romarr was only seven. He had a crown of braids like his dad, tight to his head. Romarr had energy and charisma as well as a big grin. He had severe language delays—when he tried to say "Batman," it would sound like "Bam Bam"; so, his mom was a constant translator.[3] Romarr often went to the Wash Factory laundromat right near the convenience store.[4] There, he would sweep and earn extra change. He was so tiny that the broom would stretch above his head, and his "work" was like Snow White, pushing the dirt back and forth on the floor, whimsical but ineffectual. Shirley Blanton, who ran the Wash Factory, was inclined to say "yes" to such a boy. He was to be protected and cared for, and that was exactly what neighbors did.

Romarr's friend was eight-year-old Elijah, who lived near his grandmother's house. They played dump trucks in mud and then got inventive and built themselves a basketball hoop out of a plastic crate. And in the yard, they would live in that imaginary space for hours on end, close to their families. But they also rode bikes, navigating their way through the crowd of older kids.

For a boy Romarr's age, there was one draw that could pull him away from the backyard, the candy store, and the Wash Factory. It was the lure of the train that roared high over Marquette Street on an overpass.

For a child, it was a fantastic spectacle. Like watching construction workers or dump trucks or garbage trucks. Not the toys that ignited their backyard world but *real* ones, with real men doing big things. For little guys like Romarr and Elijah, a train overhead was one of the perks of living so close to Normal Avenue and Marquette Road. There was safety, happiness, and joy in Englewood. When Romarr grew up, he could tell you the exact moment when all of this, the Englewood they knew, their childhoods, and their dear friend, was lost. It was July 27, 1998.

## Gone Missing and Found

It was about 3 p.m. when Ryan's godmother, Diane Arrington, felt that feeling, that small panic that comes from the silence of a child who has been away for too long.[5]

At eleven years old, children are like boomerangs. They soar away but you wait, with a small tension, for their inevitable return. When they go away and do not come back with the same rhythm, a portion of your breathing stops. It is like a defiance of gravity, a misfire of nature and the rhythms that give reassurance. For Ryan's godmother, she began asking the kids of the community if they had seen her goddaughter.[6] One little girl told her about the convenience store, and so that was the first stop. Diane went to the store, likely readying some speech to scold her about "going out of sight."[7] But when Ryan wasn't in the shop, it was clear that there was no speech to give; there was now only panic and a sense of dread.

Streetlights were the curfew call, the bat signal to the kids of Englewood that it was time to head home. They didn't have to go to bed, but they had to circle and coast their bikes toward where their moms, grandmas, and aunties could see them and where they could hear their names being called. And so, one kid after another started coming, until eventually it was only Ryan's godmother who was still alone, her child unaccounted for. That was when she decided to call the police.[8] The police's response sent her further into terror. The family needed to wait twenty-four hours to file a missing person's report.[9] Like so many times before, with one of its own missing, Englewood was on its own, and the police were abdicating responsibility.

Ryan's godmother assembled a search party of friends and neighbors. That's when groups of people started searching in vacant buildings and back alleys, with concerned Romarr and Elijah tagging along in the growing darkness. All the adults started asking the kids the same questions: *Who was the last to see the baby girl? Who was with her? Where did she go?*

Englewood did the so-called detective work to find Ryan. By morning, 250 flyers were made, a grainy picture of Ryan with a big smile and a ballerina-style bun in her hair. The media would descend upon the neighborhood, and Romarr was part of the growing crowd of concerned neighbors who were searching for Ryan.[10]

What happened next was confusing. It was said that a teenage boy found Ryan's body in the high weeds and shrubs on South Parnell Avenue, adjacent to the railroad tracks.[11] Some people said that a man nicknamed "Car Wash" was one of the first to see the body and then told others in the neighborhood. Later, some would wonder if it was Romarr and Elijah who were among the earliest to find their friend behind a two-story building. Maybe the boys even saw the attack unfold.[12] But Ryan was dead and lying on the ground, and that made people run with momentum toward the unfolding tragedy.

Romarr saw Ryan's body, but it was not Ryan, not the Ryan he knew. Her clothes were pulled down and torn, part of her small frame exposed and left in the worst indignity. This was an image you could not unsee, one that doesn't go away when you close your eyes. Romarr would say that he went to his dad to tell him that he found Ryan but that no one would believe him.[13] His words were heard but not believed because even to adults, the tragedy was too much to bear.

Now that it was time to recover Ryan's body rather than help find her alive, it took police nearly fifteen minutes to descend on Englewood. In the time it took police to arrive at the scene, neighbors estimated that more than fifty people tramped through the crime scene in disbelief and horror. After one young man fainted, the people of Englewood took a green shirt and covered their lost daughter to protect her dignity, an act that should have been undertaken by police.[14]

And for Romarr, he was a boy with few words, with language delays, so to say what he saw, to put words to those images of Ryan was impossible. It was stored in his body, his wide eyes, and the erratic movements that made him run away and hide back home. The sound of his dad fixing cars in the background broke the dead silence as fear squelched any language he had. Elijah was already a quiet and hesitant boy. Unlike Romarr, he was able to talk, but what words can do justice to such unthinkable tragedy?

The *Chicago Defender,* the Black newspaper in the area, would run the heartbreaking headline about the loss of one of their own:

BODY MAY BE THAT OF BABY MISSING

"A small body found in the 6600 block of Parnell in Chicago on July 28, 1998, is feared by her family and friends to be that of an 11-year-old girl named Ryan Harris. Harris was reported missing on Jul 27."[15]

The Black community in Englewood was like a family. Ryan was their baby, a most sacred term that communicated that she was more than just Sabrina's daughter; she was Englewood's child.

## The Question

*When does a Black boy become a threat in the eyes of the police and the public?*

If you had asked me this question when I began the research for this book, I would have guessed that it was at the onset—or even the hint—of puberty, somewhere around the ages of twelve or thirteen. Sadly, I came to find out that the youngest Black children impacted by wrongful conviction were mostly this age but often had a disability that meant that their cognitive age was much younger than their prepubescent frame. For Black boys and teens, police adultified them, projecting adult-like qualities onto minors. The police imagined them as a threat to be contained and often shared a common refrain: *They may not be guilty of this crime, but they are likely guilty of something.*

For the youngest boys, those twelve- or thirteen-year-olds, police viewed their supposed criminality as a self-fulfilling prophecy. They assumed that the boys *will* be guilty of something, and because of this racist logic, Black boys are inherently labeled as blameworthy even from an early age.[16]

Despite knowing this cultural mentality, I struggled to accept that children as young as seven or eight years old could be subsumed into this narrative—where freedom and boyhood make Black children vulnerable to the police. There was a racist narrative so powerful that it was plausible for the police to suspect that two Black children like Romarr and Elijah had something to do with Ryan's disappearance. This was a reality that made grown men and women cry—including me.

The unsettling discovery made me, as a parent, study my own children's faces and small frames with awe and grief, imagining a child of similar size and frailty in an interrogation chair. I imagined their tiny legs dangling from the adult chair. I imagined them so tired that they would spontaneously nod off, head bobbing as they fought sleep and sucked their thumb. Perhaps to block out the police coming into their space, or maybe because they were so exhausted from the sheer duration of the interrogation as it extended into night. That is what seven-year-old Romarr Gipson did when he was being interrogated, when he and his friend Elijah Henderson, were accused of the murder of their neighborhood friend Ryan Harris. Romarr's lawyer still had the mug shots of Romarr, and I could not show my research assistants his picture without getting an audible gasp of shock and dismay.

In both Romarr's and Elijah's mug shots, they gaze to the side, distracted and scared. On its surface, mug shots serve a "utilitarian purpose; the pictures verify the identity" of a subject.[17] However, it is more than that. The mug shot is a pose forced upon the suspect by the police. To submit to it is to "internalize the protocols of discipline; it is to agree to act like you are already a corpse."[18] And what choice do these children have but to "agree" to this social death?

I studied Romarr's and Elijah's mug shots like my eyes were playing tricks on me. It was so clear how the police were changing these boys, making them into the monsters they imagined them to be. But I could also see their wide and terrified eyes and wondered which officer was ordering them to submit to the mug shot as though it were some kind of perverse school photo. I also saw the details of how they were loved by their families—the collared shirt that Romarr wore to church and the tiny Atari-like logos that dotted Elijah's oversized red T-shirt.

Because the police were forced to drop the charges in this case, it is not considered a wrongful conviction in the database maintained by the National Registry of Exonerations. It isn't counted in the tally of crimes committed against innocent children who have been wronged by police. But as a sociologist studying this problem, this case—which likely features the youngest children in U.S. history to be charged with murder—gives us a possible answer to questions that we must ask: How low can the Chicago Police go? At what age does a Black child—a baby—become a "brute" in the eyes of law enforcement? And how is it that we, the public, believe them to be so? In this case, I found my answers and found so many more children, teens, and young adults impacted by the same playbook.

I met Romarr Gipson when he was thirty years old, through a series of letters and phone calls. In this back-and-forth, I recognized that part of him remained traumatized, stuck in 1998's Englewood. That was the year the Chicago Police brought this innocent seven-year-old boy into a cold, fluorescent-lit room at the cross streets of 51st and Wentworth (5101 South Wentworth Avenue), separated from any grown-ups he trusted.

Ryan Harris had died, and the police needed Romarr to settle a few details. What happened next, in the ensuing hours and days, would shape much of Romarr's life and would replay in his mind forever. It involved a series of "helper" attorneys, some of whose names he knew and others who seemed unreal, the faintest of memories. His co-defendant, Elijah, would call his lawyer "the Blue Power Ranger" because he didn't understand what an attorney was, and he didn't know the difference between the police, the prosecutors, and his helpers. The police brought in a Black officer, like a lure, to play the good cop in the interrogation, a man with skin like his who could have been an uncle, cousin, or neighbor.

The boys would sleep in a cell in a mental hospital as though they were sick boys, damaged beyond repair. Romarr would cut his crown of braids from his head because it was too painful to see his own image on television, even though, previously, he liked his braids because they made him look like his dad. Elijah, the quiet soul, would collapse more into himself after the ordeal, staying closer to home as he processed the trauma.[19]

This case called me to Englewood, to see what remained in the ghosts and shadows and memories of what was and what could have been for Romarr, Elijah, and Ryan. I walked all the landmarks, from Romarr's home to the shelled-out laundromat where he swept the floor. The trees along South Parnell Avenue were tall, proud, and full of leaves, except for one tree, close to where Ryan's body was found, which stood empty and in the shadows. I saw the pristine park erected in Ryan's memory, silent and untouched while a little girl played in a third-floor apartment overlooking the park—and waved at me. I stopped to chat with older residents, and many had a memory of

Ryan's mom or godmother, Romarr's mom or grandmother. They remembered raising little girls at a time when Ryan's disappearance became the terror of the community. I spoke to mothers who reflected upon raising boys, who understood that the vanishing and violence their children could face was of a different kind. Decades passed, stores were closed and boarded up, schools were renamed, and trees were now more overgrown, but thick grief remained.

Trauma can play tricks on you. Romarr would later tell me all the stories that circled through his memories, twenty-two years after they happened. And he handwrote a letter from behind prison walls:

> *I been through alot and [in] my life time . . . my story and what I went through need to be told. I had prayed to God asking him can he send somebody my way to help me tell my story. I am so thankful for you taking time out of your day to write me that letter saying you will sit down with me and you want to hear my point of view of being falsely accused and what I went through. I know I got a important story that the world need to hear because I don't want what happen to me [to] happen to no other 7 year old child. I still to this day think about her, my angel, Ryan Harris. May she rest in heaven.*[20]

Romarr's intentions were pure. He was thinking about the future and all the kids who could be harmed the way he was. In truth, Romarr has many brothers through time, other innocent boys wrongly charged and convicted of crimes for which there was no physical evidence of guilt, only an imagination of the police—through the past and the present.

Twenty-two years after Ryan Harris had died, it was clear that Englewood still grieved. In 2021, during the writing of this book, Ryan's mom headed to court to urge the judge not to grant clemency to Ryan's actual killer, a serial rapist named Floyd Durr.[21] Trauma and tragedy on this scale can freeze time, leaving all the people who lived it replaying it in their minds like a skipping record.

Headlines would read: COPS IGNORED CLUES THAT CASE WAS WEAK, as though everything that transpired in the investigation was a mistake or the result of some Keystone Cops–style incompetence.[22] It was regrettable but run-of-the-mill, "tunnel-vision" gone wrong. Indeed, this is often the prevailing wisdom that allows such cases to be seen as anomalies and not the patterns and practices they are.

All of it obscured that what happened to Romarr and Elijah was a product of police technique and the expectation that the public would accept a familiar racist narrative about Black boys being predators-in-waiting.

And that is how two of Englewood's sacred sons were made into public enemies.

## The Investigation

Police were not in Englewood for Ryan's family. They were there to close a case. There was no shortage of neighbors willing to talk to police about what they saw or heard. Almost everyone had a story to tell. What was unknown in their grief was that the police were out to find suspects among these "witnesses." Uncles would be interviewed. Fathers. The guy known as "Car Wash." Many of the kids said that they saw Ryan with a grown man, but police stopped short of pursuing this lead because they already had a narrative that had caught their attention. With no physical evidence to go by, no fingerprints nor a bike to be found, a story—any story—was something concrete to chase.

The investigation revealed that, likely, Ryan's underwear, with all the elastic, was torn off her body with one violent pull.[23] Police had a horrible sexual assault, with Ryan's body brutalized. The type of crime denoted a type of suspect and a racial portrait. For the police, there was only ever the possibility of the suspect being Black. Ryan's bike was also missing. The theft seemed to be the motivation for the attack, and it signaled that the suspect was young.

These two aspects of the crime should have presented a fundamental contradiction. How could anyone so young commit sexual assault? The only way it could make sense is if police imagined and believed that Black children could be both childlike and small but also monstrous and violent—sexually ravenous like animals, despite such speculations contradicting medical science or even logic.

These racist beliefs led police right to eight-year-old Elijah, who was one of the first children to see Ryan's body.[24] Rumors floated around that Elijah or Romarr may have thrown rocks at Ryan a few days before her disappearance.

Police imagined that the skull fractures in Ryan's head had their origins in the strength of one of the small boys and their ability to overpower eleven-year-old Ryan. After the police identified Romarr and Elijah as suspects, officers dropped by each of the kids' houses. They asked questions—all casual—and it all made sense to the Hendersons and the Gipsons because after all, their boys had been witnesses.[25] The visits didn't raise any red flags to either family. They helped get close and build trust. The police were grooming both the boys and the adults, confident that nobody involved really understood how adept the Chicago Police were at changing witnesses into suspects.

About two weeks passed, and the case seemed to go cold. The Harris family—along with the city at large—pressured the police for answers.

Their questions were answered on August 9, 1998.

August 9 was not supposed to be an eventful day. It was a day Romarr's parents had to work, so he stayed with his grandma. Police came to the house and casually asked Romarr's grandma to bring him to the police station at 51st and Wentworth for more questions, questions that seemed intended to help solve Ryan's case under the guise of Romarr being a witness. She explained she was taking him to church but agreed to stop by the station later in the day.

Elijah's family would receive the same request. His parents were told that they wanted to ask Elijah some more questions. All of it seemed ordinary.

At the station, a detective greeted Romarr playfully: "Hey, big guy, come with me."[26] One floor below Romarr and Elijah, literally under their feet, were buried files, nearly five hundred cases filled with exculpatory evidence, purposely hidden in order to incriminate suspects just like them. Behind the detective were interrogation rooms, filled with the ghosts of other wrongfully convicted teens and boys. And waiting for them was a detective who specialized in working with kids, young kids. His name was James Cassidy. He had nearly a thousand investigations and almost thirty years of service under his belt.[27]

## The Past, Present, and Future of Policing

*We get better results than a priest does.*

—**John Reid**[28]

Detective James Cassidy was the past, present, and future of the Chicago Police. Many of Cassidy's colleagues in the police force were schooled in the tools of physical coercion associated with the third degree: swift kicks to the shin with a steel-toe boot, a punch to the body, a plastic bag over the head, an accidental fall down the stairs, or even a verbal warning that an officer could throw your head through the wall if you didn't say what the police said you did.[29] But the physical piece associated with these third-degree tactics was often messy and left evidence like bruises, blood, and other things that had to be cleaned up.

However, Cassidy was a new breed of Chicago Police. In fact, one might say he was the future.

His career began in the 1970s, and by the time he met Romarr and Elijah, he had been on the police force for nearly thirty years, a seasoned veteran.[30] Some men in the Chicago Police Department were known for their physical force with suspects. Lieutenant Jon Burge, for instance, was notorious for his torture of over 130 Black men over three decades. Burge reveled in the violence he inflicted. After work, he and his "asskickers" drank in the bars along Western Avenue, where

Burge openly bragged about torturing Black men as though they were talking sports.[31] Cassidy, however, was different; he was a man of words. And his specialty was being a trained interrogator who could extract a confession.

Confessions are like a Hollywood drama. They are actively produced and inspired by the theory of the case, rehearsed through back-and-forth intimacy, and end with a suspect reciting the incriminating words.[32] Cassidy was an imaginative puppeteer, a quiet mastermind with an unassuming demeanor, which was better for putting kids away. Prosecutors and fellow officers took notice of him and his work. It didn't hurt that his brother was a high-ranking Assistant State's Attorney. Talent ran in the family.

Chicago's police force had a significant history of using the "third degree," physical torture meant to extract a confession from an "uncompromising" suspect. Such methods fell out of favor with the public, but the Chicago Police—like many departments across the nation—simply moved these tactics to places hidden from public view: back alleys, vacant lots, interrogation rooms, and the bowels of police stations. This was the domain where officers like Lieutenant Jon Burge worked their talent. Still, police forces needed a new way to coerce and break down suspects, not physically but psychologically—quite literally breaking a person from the inside out.

Cassidy embodied those new techniques. He could wear away at suspects with words, even if they were innocent, and get them to do the unthinkable: admit to a horrendous crime they had not committed. That's how good he was.

In 1947, John E. Reid and Associates began developing interrogation and interview protocols. The Reid Technique was meant to formalize and professionalize police interrogations.[33] Indeed, the technique relied on assuming the guilt of the suspect in custody, an assumption exacerbated by racist ideas held by police and prosecutors that Black people were more criminally prone. The technique required officers to see the suspect through a guilty lens. The bias that made it natural to profile and stop and frisk Black people was now a basic premise used to psychologically manipulate suspects. The officer then deceived and isolated the suspect and eventually convinced them that they had no other alternative but to admit to guilt—even just to get out of the interrogation room.

Professor of law and psychology Richard Leo describes the adversarial model of American police interrogation as being "steeped" in "fraud" whereby detectives engage in "trickery," "role deception," and "deceit."[34] This includes "inventing or falsifying case evidence" against the suspect.[35] This barrage of tactics allows police to create the "illusion that it is in the suspect's best interest to confess."[36] Across America, when someone is brought into an interrogation room for questioning, the officer is trained to use these techniques as a mainstay of policing, much in the same way that they are trained to use a firearm.

Like other large police departments across the country, the Chicago Police fused the Reid Technique of psychological manipulation with the third degree.[37] It was a poisonous cocktail: The threat of violence that had always existed in the system was now coupled with sophisticated psychological manipulation. One didn't have to break down a suspect with a beating. One could break them psychologically. This type of abuse had the additional advantage of leaving no scars nor messy evidence.

The Reid Technique was envisioned to be used on adults, but Cassidy would twist it into something more. He started deploying the tactics on children. No doubt, he would use such techniques on "wolf pack" cases, the cases in which two or more defendants, usually Black defendants, were charged as adults in gruesome crimes.

Cassidy had mastered the delicate dance of psychological deception to lure a suspect into their own incrimination. It took patience, a back-and-forth, and a level of creativity to hold a child's hand and get them to submit to his authority. And, eventually, Cassidy would specialize in doing this with the littlest kids, the kids that were normally too young to be touched by the Chicago Police. He would work his gravitas on kids as young as ten, eight, and even seven. He strode into interrogation rooms with a gentle presence. He had a boyish look to him, his hair parted on the side and brushed carefully across his forehead like Mr. Rogers.[38]

Cassidy was the prosecutor's weapon of choice for those delicate cases, the cases that needed extra care. He began by using his soft demeanor to his advantage, talking so quietly that suspects had to lean in to hear him. His alleged victims would claim that he would hold their hands and encourage a confession with the promise of forgiveness, a pledge to see even the worst mistake as an accident. He adapted his tactics to target a child's specific needs. He would groom them. For the boys that wanted to be important, to feel seen, he would assure them that they were helping the police solve a crime. For the boys so young that they sucked their thumb and believed in make-believe superheroes and cartoons, he would befriend them with gentleness. This was an insidious intimacy built like a slow crescendo.

There were a lot of open secrets between the Chicago Police and prosecutors, open secrets that made the system an efficient conviction machine.[39] Cassidy was one of them. In the 1990s, Eileen O'Neill Burke, Chicago's current elected Cook County State's Attorney,[40] was a young prosecutor at a stage in her career where she could benefit from Cassidy's way of closing cases because such cases were virtually assured wins in the courts. Discussing Cassidy's investigative approach in the media, O'Neill stood in support of his expertise: "Officer Cassidy is the nicest, slightest man. That's why they have him interview kids."[41] O'Neill's use of the word "they" here confirmed that the strategy reflected the Chicago Police establishment; Cassidy was not some bad apple or lone miscreant.[42] An expert like Cassidy played an important role for the Chicago Police. The more overtly violent "Jon Burges" practices of the force were messy, often unhinged, and they were starting to be exposed by the media. Cassidy had a subtle, earnest, next-door-neighbor quality. He was a man with a special touch, and prosecutors came to rely on it. He was able to see the kids as guilty, and he had a skillful way of—nicely—helping the child see it too.

Police officers admitted to seeing Black children like the ones in Englewood as different from the so-called typical child. For them, "ghetto" kids were street-smart, more like adults than children. It was a refrain that traveled across time and was used to justify many wrongful conviction cases.

When officers were interviewed during the reporting of Ryan Harris's murder, they were more than happy to teach journalists and the public that Black kids were just *different* from White suburban ones. As one veteran detective said: "The 12- and 13-year-old boys you see on the West Side are going on 20. . . . With some of these kids, looking in their eyes is like looking into sharks' eyes. There's no feeling there. You got kids doing burglaries at 8 or 9 and kids who start shooting at 12 or 13."[43]

This was the rationale for why detectives interrogated Black children like adults. "Essentially, there's no difference," one detective explained. "It's just that you like to have a parent present if you can. . . . These are not suburban kids from the 1950s. These are pretty sophisticated kids."[44] And that bit about having a parent present, well, there were ways around that. You could treat the kid like a witness at first and then make them into a suspect. You could lie to the parents and imply that you were only asking a few questions to get some "help" on the case. And if the parents were uppity and insistent, you could threaten to call Child Protective Services with false claims of parental incompetence.

Cassidy was fostered in this belief system. He knew how to interrogate without touching. He had many levers to press. And Cassidy was more than a company man. He thought of himself as having a way with words; in his retirement, he became a crime fiction author, self-publishing several books.

But years before that, in 1994, he would try his hand at writing an op-ed in the *Chicago Tribune,* warning the city of a looming threat, a "different" kind of child who had the heart of a grown criminal.[45] He could not mention the suspect by name because of his tender age, but he detailed the interrogation of an eleven-year-old boy who would eventually be known to the public as "A.M."[46]

"I hated her, I hated her and I killed her." Those opening lines, according to Cassidy, were the spontaneous eruption of guilt that sent the officer "reeling," despite his decades of experience interrogating supposed calculating, cold-blooded killers. This killer, Cassidy warned, was a "baby-faced boy" of just eleven years old who lacked a conscience. A boy who could be living next to "anyone, anywhere." His article read like the talking points, narratives, and mythologies of the superpredator era, where a supposed new breed of criminals was being born, one that Chicago could not insulate itself from and that Cassidy described as the "ugliness" of childhood in the 1990s. The brutality was coded as Black. And given that he had "stared into the faces of hundreds of murders through the years," this boy, this threat, this trend, had finally gotten to him. Cassidy spelled out what it meant for the city: "The juvenile offender today is far more dangerous than the kid who 30 years ago stole a car's hubcaps. Our present-day Juvenile Code was meant for just such an offender, not for today's vicious criminals."

In Cassidy's view, leniency was meant for an earlier time. Child saving was meant for another type of kid—certainly not the monsters he was now meeting in his job. He ended his article with a final appeal to the public, deploying a superpredator logic that rationalized how the ends would justify the means of his practices on cases that were disproportionately Black: "Violent juvenile offenders should be incarcerated, locked away, if so judged by a court of law. Society must protect itself from this onslaught of juvenile crime before it gets entirely out of control."

Cassidy knew how to spin a narrative. It was about the careful selection of details and the exclusion of others. Building a case—even in an op-ed for the public—was narrating guilt through editing and omission and painting guilt through his words.

Cassidy likely believed in his moral calling to protect the city from the likes of this boy who he thought murdered an elderly White neighbor, beating her with a cane and slitting her throat in a rage. However, in true Chicago Police form, Cassidy left out the most important elements of his modus operandi—that he was manipulating and implicating these boys with *his* words, words that he softly imposed on the children. Through his skill and technique, Cassidy could turn a child from a witness or even a victim into a cold-blooded killer. He was patient, quick, and unassuming, so the child and the public would never see him coming. Sure, Burge was skilled in the use of brute force, but Cassidy was a master at creating crime fictions.

The public and the courts would know this particular child through the eyes and words of Cassidy, his tormentor.[47] A.M. was only ten years old when his neighbor, a White woman named Anna Gilvis, was killed. They lived in a mixed-race neighborhood, one that White residents had fought hard to keep segregated. This was the tinder that would ignite this case, and tinder that Cassidy would exploit mercilessly through his commentary.

Young A.M., like many children, wanted to be involved with crime fighting and wanted to be on TV. He was one of the many neighbors the police interviewed after they discovered the murder victim. A.M. was in his adjacent backyard when he talked to the first officer over the fence. He said that he had contact with Ms. Gilvis—he had helped her by carrying her grocery bags to her apartment but did not go inside. Anna would thank him, and he would head back to his home. A.M. also said that he saw a Black man, an adult, around the crime scene, which made A.M. the type of *see-something-say-something* kid that should have earned him one of those honorary police badges for being a helper. But that is not how the Chicago Police would see him.

When a year passed and the case grew cold, the Chicago Police would target A.M. to fix the problem. A.M. was brought into the police station for questioning without a guardian, parent, or lawyer present. The police had told his family that they wanted him to look at some mug shots; nothing about this request—a request to assist the police—would have given his family reason for alarm. Cassidy would question A.M. in a closed interrogation room for two hours. Throughout the interrogation, A.M. was anxious because he was missing his brother's birthday party; for a child that young, such concerns are very real.

In that room, Cassidy would wear away at A.M. with techniques and mental manipulation that could exhaust a grown man. A.M. would change his story five times, agreeing and then disagreeing to the details that Cassidy fed him. But what may have done A.M. in was a single alleged lie: A.M. claimed that Cassidy told him that the police would forgive him "like God would forgive him" and that A.M. could go home if he just told the truth.[48] The prospect of the vanishing birthday party, going home and seeing his mom, and the promise of being a good boy in the eyes of God enticed A.M. into confessing. And when he did, the best thing happened: Cassidy stopped the interrogation, and stopped getting into his face. After the confession, A.M. recanted immediately to his mom at the first chance he could. He sobbed after the interrogation: "I told them I murdered her, but I didn't do it. . . . I was scared. . . . They were hollering at me, they were cursing at me, they kept slapping their knees . . ."[49] Ultimately, A.M. would be convicted on the weight of the false confession even though the crime fiction of the confession did not match the facts of the case.

The crime scene had a fingerprint as well as the shoe print of an adult, physical evidence that could have guided police if they had been trying to solve the case rather than merely close it. In Cassidy's crime fiction, A.M. had tied up Anna with a rope from a hanging plant. But it was not a rope; it was a telephone cord that had been ripped from the wall and wound around the victim. And there was no hanging plant; in fact, the apartment had no plants that could be worked to fit this farce of a story. Cassidy also said that A.M. confessed to sneaking into the house through an open door, but the crime scene showed evidence of forced entry. Other inconsistencies should have raised red flags. A.M. was little, a boy of ten who weighed 88 pounds.[50] The victim was nearly twice his size. But the imagination of Black children as bestial and brutish allowed this fiction to be believable to a White judge.

Cassidy gave A.M. a motive and a history. By coercing the confession, Cassidy narrated A.M. into a predator who was incensed by being called a "nigger" one too many times by his neighbor, so he supposedly blurted out his hatred of Anna Gilvis, "I hated her and I killed her."[51]

Cassidy lured A.M. into a backstory that explained why elderly and helpless Anna was bound, beaten with her own cane, and found with her throat slashed.

In the police's fiction, A.M. had sought revenge for Anna's racism. One of the deep-seated fears born of White supremacy is the idea that if Black people come to power, they will enact revenge upon the White populace for all the long years of enslavement, brutal toil, sexual assault, murder, lynching, and terrorism. The idea is as old as the antebellum South. A "Black Avenger" is a historical trope where White people imagine what might happen if Black people ever realized their power.[52] The Klan was the remedy to this fictional tyranny of an avenger rising. The truth was that A.M. was a boy who regularly attended church with his grandmother and had been raised to respect the elderly.

A.M. would face a judge in this case, not a jury. His conviction would rest in the hands of a supposedly impartial figure persuaded only by reason and rule of law. One who would consider all the evidence in the case, including this incriminating confession, even though it was taken without a parent or an attorney present. But at the heart of the guilty verdict was both the skill and the reputation of Cassidy. In this case and others, he took the stand and would narrate a racist fiction from a false confession and perform it for the judge or jury. This required that Cassidy's reputation—indeed, the entire police force that he represented—was infallible, even in the absence of physical evidence and even to a judge.

A.M., now eleven, would end up being a casualty that, at the time of conviction, would go unnoticed to most Chicagoans. They would just know that the murder of Anna Gilvis had been solved, that the police had done their job, and that the justice system was working as it should.

Cassidy had pushed a significant boundary by using interrogations on children so young. He could create criminality in an eleven-year-old child. He could hold a child's hands, make promises, tell a child that God would forgive them.

In my research, prosecutors often felt that they were doing "God's work," a type of White man's burden that I often heard in my time researching prosecutors and police.[53] But Cassidy was doing more. He was elevating the Chicago Police's interrogation into a confessional where children could be absolved of their sins. And if the interrogation was a confessional, then Cassidy was the head pastor or maybe even God himself. And Cassidy was the Old Testament God—capable of mercy yet not above brutal acts of punishment and vengeance. Time and time again, Cassidy's most effective tactic was to toggle between these extremes, to kill with kindness and the illusion of mercy.

A.M. wouldn't just be another conviction or notch on Cassidy's belt. He would be a template, a case model so effective that it would be imported to other cases. Cassidy was not known for torture; he took coerced confessions to a judge who was inclined to believe police testimony.

Four years later, Cassidy and his team of officers were ready to apply these techniques to the task of closing the Ryan Harris case. Romarr and Elijah would be their youngest targets.

## The Interrogation

When Romarr and Elijah walked into the police station at 51st and Wentworth, one might imagine that they received a hero's welcome. After all, they were children who were part of the search party to find Ryan, and they were two of the first people at the scene. They were also kids who had just experienced profound trauma by seeing the brutalized body of their friend.

But the police were trained to see these boys another way—the Cassidy way.

Romarr and Elijah were escorted into separate rooms, isolated from their grown-ups and from each other. Two detectives were leading the investigation: James Cassidy, who was White, and Allen Nathaniel, who was Black. Romarr and Elijah just wanted to be helpful. That's how the interrogation began. They brought each boy into a small room and started grooming them to talk. And the grooming questions were fun to answer. Stuff about sports that they liked, favorite toys that they played with, and whether they were excited to start a new year of school. Then the real questions began.[54]

They asked Romarr the basics. "Do you know the difference between the truth and a lie?"[55] And while the officers asked him the questions, they moved closer into his space.

"You should never lie," Romarr answered.[56]

And then the Chicago Police, which had long perfected a practice of lying to suspects, began to teach Romarr the difference between telling a lie and telling the truth. They taught it to him the way most people, except the police, are held to truth-telling standards. The way parents, teachers, and pastors tell children, as though truth telling is a component of moral character.

Telling the truth is to tell "what really happened." A lie is "when someone makes up something." "To tell the truth is good," a detective said. "To tell a lie is bad. . . . Good boys only tell the truth."[57]

The police then asked Romarr a question. It wasn't about Ryan's disappearance or even finding the body. The police asked Romarr who he was.

"Are you a good boy?" a detective asked him.

"Yes," he said.

The officers then asked if they could hold his hands "because we were all friends."[58] At the time, *Barney & Friends* was one of the most popular children's shows on television; every episode ended with the purple dinosaur singing a saccharine song about friendship in a preschool world of acceptance and love. The kids hugged one another because everyone is a friend and that's what kids of this age are taught: Adults are helpers.

And so Romarr was totally disarmed. In the tiny 10-by-15-foot room, Romarr gave Cassidy his left hand and gave Nathaniel his right. And shaped like a prayer circle, they lured Romarr into insidious intimacy.

"Do you know the girl who was killed?"[59]

Romarr said that he did.

"Did you show your friend the body?"[60]

And after only a handful of questions, the police would contend that Romarr spontaneously blurted an incriminating statement that led to his arrest, a claim based on the mythology of a confession as a type of an eruption of guilt.[61] According to police, Romarr gave them specific details about the crime: a rock thrown at her head, and dragging the body by the arms. They—Romarr and Elijah—took her underwear, shoved it in her mouth, rubbed leaves on her, and put foliage in her nose. They took the bicycle and moved it to the weeds, but later, it could not be found. After it all happened, the police claimed Romarr told them he went to play with some puppies.[62]

Some medical experts would categorize Romarr as nonverbal. He could often only be understood if his mother translated. And more alarming still, he was diagnosed by a court-appointed psychiatrist with "a receptive/expressive language disorder."[63] All kids this young are particularly vulnerable to a phenomenon psychologists call "cryptomnesia."[64] This is when a person believes an idea came from them when it was suggested or generated by someone else. Of course, cryptomnesia is more common in children than adults.

Romarr's language disorder magnified this vulnerability. Romarr could not create an intelligible story from beginning to end without prompting from an adult. And the part about the puppies? He had received the pet the day before the interrogation—not at the time of the murder. He had little concept of time and sequence.[65]

Worse yet, Romarr's disability made him parrot phrases, repeating whatever adults suggested, even if it was wrong. And Romarr believed it to be true. The doctor who evaluated Romarr for the court suggested that if you sat with Romarr for ten minutes, you could convince him that he was the "Emperor of China."[66] Likewise, if you told him he had killed someone, he would have said that he was a killer.[67] And therein lies the worst part of the police's abuse of Romarr: It wasn't just being yelled at, taken from his family, or manipulated with insidious intimacy. It was that the police told Romarr, a disabled child, that what had happened to Ryan and the brutal condition of her body was his doing. This was child abuse so severe that Romarr began to see himself like the police saw him. That would follow him the rest of his life, starting with the children in his school calling him "Baby Killer."[68]

Cassidy left Romarr to attend to Elijah while Nathaniel continued talking to Romarr about sports and school. Police told Mrs. Henderson, Elijah's mom, that he was merely giving a witness statement for Ryan's case. According to police, Mrs. Henderson permitted the police to talk to Elijah so that they could "get to the bottom of this."[69] Her boy was given a soda and then put through the same routine as Romarr. Cassidy would talk about lying, good boys and bad boys, and ask Elijah to pick a side, just as he did to Romarr. Then Cassidy would claim that he gave Elijah the Miranda warnings required by law—the warnings given to those in police custody to protect their Fifth Amendment right against self-incrimination. Most Americans know this warning from pop culture:

> You have the right to remain silent. Anything you say can and will be used against you in a court of law. You have the right to an attorney. If you cannot afford an attorney, one will be provided for you.[70]

Any Miranda warning ends with the officer confirming whether the suspect understands their rights. Only then do they ask whether the suspect still wants to speak with the officer. However, Cassidy had a way with words, and he knew how to twist these warnings into a weapon. He had a version of the Miranda warning that he had adapted for children, allowing him to claim compliance with *Miranda v. Arizona,* the 1966 Supreme Court decision that made the warnings a requirement for law enforcement.[71] He could give his "kiddie" version of the warnings, manipulate the child, and guide them to where he needed them to go. He even memorialized his script in handwritten notes.[72]

*Kiddie rights to Elijah Henderson.*

*Didn't have to talk to Det. [Cassidy]—Mother could be in the room—to lie was wrong—good boys don't lie. Good boy? Said yes—Henderson's mother didn't have to be with him. Tell truth. Anything said would be brought up in court. Court described—room with people—someone would decide whether person was bad or not. Could have lawyer. Knew what lawyer was? Answer yes. What lawyer does? No. Lawyer protects people who do something bad, goes to court with them on their side and takes care of them in court. Could have lawyer now and not cost money to him or his mother. Said would talk without mother or lawyer.*

Cassidy was not just explaining or simplifying Elijah's rights. He was rigging them in his favor, making it seem like those rights were used only by "bad" or guilty people. Even adults are confused by these warnings, especially in the disorienting moment of arrest. For a child, it is far worse. It is hard to imagine a situation where a child of Elijah's age could understand the "right" to remain silent when an authority figure is talking to them and asking them questions. Children are socialized, early on, that this would be an act of defiance. As psychology professor Laurence Steinberg described, "If you ask a child what does it mean when the police officer says you have the right to remain silent, most can't explain it or are wrong. A typical answer is, 'That means you don't have to say anything until the policeman asks you a question.' "[73]

But Cassidy didn't view certain children of this era as the "typical" child. Indeed, his op-ed piece about A.M. explained quite clearly that the children he dealt with were "different," a new threat unfit for a child-saving juvenile justice system. And with Cassidy on these types of cases working the machine of incarceration in Black Chicago, the children he was describing were Black, calculating, adult-like, and dangerous. Cassidy was fighting a war, and he was going to win it by any means necessary. He was going to teach these boys the police's worldview of due process, rights, and the court system.

To Elijah, Cassidy described the entire legal system as one built for bad people. Silence was for people who didn't tell the truth. Courts were where bad people would be ruled, by a judge, to be bad. Lawyers protected bad people when they did their bad things. And for Elijah, a good boy, to exercise these rights (even if he did understand them) meant that he was the kind of kid who was bad. And that was not who he was. So Elijah, cornered, decided to talk without his mom and, certainly, without one of those lawyers for bad people.[74]

Later, Elijah's attorneys would allege in his civil lawsuit that no Miranda warnings were ever given to Elijah and that Cassidy's handwritten notes were fabricated for the case file. While police often omitted exonerating evidence from cases as a matter of practice, Cassidy did the opposite. He was a creator. As alleged in Elijah's civil lawsuit, he could write and manufacture convincing notes for the general progress reports on the case, and he could get other officers to fabricate fake supplementary reports to make the ruse feel real.[75] He understood the law and how to stage compliance with it. Other officers would participate in lockstep with the common goal of building their elaborate case against Romarr and Elijah. Indeed, as further alleged, supporting Cassidy and Nathaniel's conspiracy to fabricate notes and reports against the boys was an army of "unknown and unidentified" officers working toward the same end.[76]

Eventually, Cassidy would unleash his standard interrogation tactics on Elijah. As he did with Romarr, Cassidy would give Elijah a McDonald's Happy Meal, get in his space, build his trust, yell and scream at him in close proximity, and then do the unthinkable, according to Elijah's allegations made in his civil suit. He would force Elijah to look at the horrifying pictures of Ryan's dead body, an act of child abuse in any other context.[77] And as alleged, Cassidy would eventually write the narrative he wanted to write into Elijah's confession, a narrative that complemented Romarr's story, made Elijah an accomplice to murder and Romarr the aggressor.

As all of this transpired, Romarr's grandma and Elijah's mother were only steps away in the lobby but were never approached to be the kids' guardians in the room. Cassidy and his team had other plans. Cassidy walked down the hallway to the juvenile division and grabbed two police officers—Officers Vincent James and Anthony Powell—to act as "youth officers."[78] Cassidy told the officers and said, in Romarr's case, that his grandma did not want to be in the room while Romarr was questioned. In truth, the families had no idea that their children were being interrogated to elicit incriminating statements.

In Illinois, the law advises that a parent or "youth officer" must be present if a child is interrogated and read the Miranda warnings. Youth officers are supposed to be protective and act in the best interests of the child. However, police use "youth officers" as a loophole that can be exploited, rather than an important safeguard for children taken into police custody. Ultimately, the youth officer—who is in fact a police officer—is *aligned with the police* and often has a tendency to serve the interests of the police. At best, they will only monitor the situation and not vigorously intervene in the name of protecting the child's rights. Police know this and over time have treated the youth officer like a tool they can exploit. For the police, the presence of the youth officer can be an opportunity to circumvent parents while still remaining in compliance with the law. Detectives expect the youth officer to be a "potted plant"—to just be in the room and not interfere.[79]

For Cassidy's purposes, Powell and James were perfect for this role. They likely still had their guns on them when they were in the room during Romarr's and Elijah's interrogations, an intimidating detail even for an adult. And the part about acting like a potted plant? Officer James fit the bill perfectly; he actually fell asleep while in the interrogation room.[80] Powell and James, the two potted plants, would eventually become detectives, like Cassidy.[81]

Even though most would credit Cassidy and Nathaniel as the masterminds of the operation, these investigative practices were enabled by the work of many officers. Once Cassidy and Nathaniel had the confessions, they met with a team of detectives and supervisors. They discussed the case, the confessions, and the report from the medical examiner that had several inconvenient details: The evidence from the autopsy contradicted their theory of the crime—and now, the confessions that they had extracted. Indeed, prior to interrogating the boys, Cassidy reached out to the medical examiner, Dr. Mitra Kalelkar, who conducted the autopsy. She told Cassidy, in no uncertain terms, that his theory was wrong: It wasn't a rock thrown at Ryan's head.[82] It was a larger blunt object like a brick, thrown or smashed with great force.[83] But the police were not deterred by science.

The public often assumes that forensic science helps police revise their conclusions and theories on cases. If contradictory evidence is found, then the theory will be revised or thrown out and the investigation will continue. Certainly, this is how it should work. But the police understand the power of omission. They also understand the power of narrative as a diversion to inconvenient facts. Even when the medical examiner forewarned Cassidy that Ryan's severe injuries and other crucial details contradicted Elijah's and Romarr's statements, the police still pressed on—business as usual—in building their case against these tiny boys because the police knew that the case was going to be won with words.[84]

The police merely revised their narratives to come to the same conclusion. Romarr and Elijah were their killers, so Cassidy and Nathaniel constructed another version of events, a version they knew was impossible but was more brutal and narratively intoxicating: Elijah and Romarr bludgeoned Ryan to death with a brick. One held her down while the other struck the blow. The inconsistent confessions were not a reflection on the police; instead, the confessions showed that beyond being killers, the children were liars, another moral deficiency that the police unearthed after the interrogation.[85]

When the news came out that the boys were being charged, Dr. Kalelkar was aghast.[86] The police were twisting the case, ignoring her science and pursuing boys way too young to have ever done something so brutal. And the part of the confession that claimed that the boys supposedly "played with her softly," could not be an explanation for Ryan's sexual injury.[87]

This case was absolutely brutal; Dr. Kalelkar had the science to back up her conclusions, and she explicitly made this clear in her conversation with Cassidy. As she would later testify: "I didn't give any thought to these boys being charged or not charged. . . . I was listening to what Detective Cassidy told me and I thought . . . Ryan Harris did not die the way he was telling me the scenario occurred."[88]

Dr. Kalelkar was one of the few people to see the process of constructing a crime fiction in real time, to understand how little evidence was required to make people believe a lie. And for a woman of science and a mom who had the task of doing the autopsy for a young girl who had suffered so gravely, she now realized an additional horror of it all: The police were willing to dismiss her science to create a fiction. As she would see firsthand, the public and media were all too willing to believe the fiction.

Dr. Kalelkar went to her boss, Cook County Medical Examiner Edmund Donoghue, who dismissed her concerns. He told her to trust the process and try not to determine who was guilty or not—even though it was clear that it was the police who were guilty.[89] In the end, Donoghue would give Dr. Kalelkar an empty promise. He later reflected, "I told her there were remedies. And one of them was that the charges would be dismissed. And they were dismissed."[90]

He made it all sound so easy, so logical. Like the courts, prosecutors, juries, and judges were a reliable fail-safe switch to the wrongful conviction of the innocent. And that was another fallacy—a "sincere fiction" that made this brand of "doing justice" seem fair to police as well as those who happened to expose their clandestine techniques.[91] They could pass the buck to the courts as a way of absolving themselves from the wrongdoing.

The interrogation of Romarr and Elijah went on for several hours. And despite Dr. Kalelkar's warnings, the officers would escort the boys through the booking process, while their families in the waiting room did not have the slightest notion of what the Chicago Police were actually doing to their children. The police would take mug shots. Both kids were crying inconsolably. And when Elijah did not comply with the orders of the officer taking those mug shots, Elijah said he was scolded: "Get over there, you little bitch."[92]

By the time the Chicago Police were done, Romarr and Elijah had supposedly confessed to raping and murdering their eleven-year-old friend, making them likely the youngest murder suspects in United States history. The police had closed their case.

## The Kidnapping

Sylvia Gipson knew something wasn't right. She had gotten off work as a manager of a local fast-food chain and headed to her mother's house to reunite with her kids. She soon realized that Romarr and her mom were at the police station.

By the time she arrived, the lobby was already filled with anger and tears. She got a glimpse of Elijah's mom, who was too distraught to speak.[93] Sylvia's mom—Romarr's grandma—was incensed with anger. She had been waiting for three and a half hours in the lobby, at which point a detective came out and explained Romarr's statement. One of the detectives lied to her face, saying, "It was an accident. You can take him home. It'll be all over."[94] Grandma fought back: "That boy didn't do nothing like that. He ain't no murderer."[95]

Sylvia was also told by an officer that "it was an accident . . . he's going home," but she knew that something was wrong when the police changed their tune.[96] They required Romarr to have a police guard just to go to the washroom.

Later on, Sylvia remembered each of these scenes as she tried to piece the unfathomable together. But, when she closed her eyes, she could see the detective breaking the news to her. Her baby was charged with murder in the first degree. And she would repeat the words "first degree" when she said it out loud because the last part was the most unimaginable part to comprehend—first degree.[97] Beyond the accusation that her son had caused Ryan's death, they were charging Romarr with deliberately *planning* his crime. Premeditation. Intention. Willfulness. She couldn't accept what the police were saying. It was the type of unimaginable news that makes time slow down, where you ask people to explain things over and over, slower each time. And in that confusion she became so outraged that she began to yell back at the absurdity of it all.

"Are you out of your mind?" she said. "This is a child. Are you crazy? . . . My son can't talk. . . . If he speaks a whole sentence, you might be able to pick two words out. . . . You must be crazy."[98]

Sylvia saw her boy so clearly. She saw a baby . . . *her* baby. And the police were seeing a calculating murderer. It was gaslighting. The entire waiting room of family members, the distraught, the enraged, the grieving parents were fighting for their way of seeing their boys. The police had the power to charge their kids, but they didn't have the power to change the way they saw their children. As sons, as grandchildren, as their babies.

Grandma found Romarr holding a little car and a sucker and asleep in his interrogation chair.[99] When they let Sylvia in to see her son, she recalled his simple question:

"Hi Mom, you going to take me home?"

"Yeah, I'm coming to pick you up."[100]

But the police wouldn't let Romarr go. Elijah either.

And as the families tried to process and protest the arrest of the children, the police gave them more unsettling news. Because of their age, the police intended to take the kids to the Hartgrove Hospital, a psychiatric institution on the West Side of Chicago. Regardless of whether you called it a hospital or not, the reality was that the police were detaining and jailing their children. Now, the police had weaponized another institution meant to protect children: the Department of Children and Family Services. They gave the parents an ultimatum. Sign the kids over to the hospital or the police would give the boys to the Illinois Department of Children and Family Services (DCFS), essentially terminating their parental rights and any access to their children until a trial occurred.[101]

Sylvia didn't want to play with DCFS. "They get your child and you will never see him again," she said.[102] With such an ultimatum, the parents had no choice but to cooperate. If the police could accuse their tiny children of murder, then it would be easy to accuse the parents of "something" just to get their rights terminated. And in these cases of wrongful conviction, time and again, police dismiss Black parents and undermine their parental authority, as in the cases of A.M., Trevon Yates, and so many more to come. Police and prosecutors often cast Black families as "broken" or morally depraved, pushing involved fathers like Elijah's and Romarr's out of any realm of consideration.

As for Black mothers, they are often viewed with the most contempt.[103] Mothers of color are viewed as incapable, incompetent, and complicit in the moral failings of their children and male partners. As professor of law and sociology Dorothy Roberts explains, mothers of color, particularly Black mothers, are constructed as the vessel of the "pathological, black, urban poor family from which all ills flow; a monster creating crack dealers, addicts, muggers, and rapists."[104] It is through her body that social ills transform into supposed "criminal elements," and for that, Black mothers and grandmothers could be punished and certainly not trusted as capable and moral figures.[105] This racist view of Black families served to justify the police's lies, the seizing of the children, and the undermining of their parental rights and authority.

What Romarr's and Elijah's families didn't know in the chaos of the station (and without attorneys to help them) was that the officers were lying to them. DCFS could not legally take the children. According to filings in Romarr's civil case, the youth officers, detectives, and even the supervisors above them knew this.[106] The reality was that there were only two options available to the police: send the boys home with their parents or get the parents to voluntarily agree to placement in a hospital. The police not only concealed their parental rights but threatened and terrorized them, just as they had done to their children.[107] In plain terms, this was a kidnapping: The parents were all but forced to sign their kids away to be imprisoned in a psych ward at only seven and eight years of age.[108]

When Elijah finally saw his parents, he was awake but inconsolable. He told his parents about the officer who took his picture and swore at him and how they paraded him in front of the adult inmates. And between the tears, Elijah recanted everything that the police said he had confessed to saying. Elijah's mom would recall that Elijah said, "I did not tell him that. That's nasty."[109] And in spite of believing their son and knowing he had done nothing wrong, the Hendersons had to do the unthinkable: They had to find words to comfort their innocent boy who was going to be jailed—a boy who was terrified of being away from his family overnight for the first time.

Elijah Sr. talked to his boy with a clear face, keeping his composure so that Elijah could borrow some of his strength. He told the boy that he was just going away for some tests and would be home soon. "Soon" sounded like a manageable amount of time. "Tests" sounded familiar but not scary. These are the types of things you tell a kid when you don't want to lie but the truth is too scary to bear. And then Elijah Sr. gave his son a gift. Elijah had watched *The Lion King*. When it was released, it was Disney's highest-grossing film, and children everywhere were singing "Hakuna Matata"—which meant "no worries."

Elijah Sr. saw the film differently. It was an allegory of the falsely accused—a tale of accusation and eventual vindication. Elijah Sr. knew that his son was like the young cub, Simba, who was also misunderstood and falsely accused of a crime. And in the end, Simba was vindicated, shown for who he really was—a cub who was both brave *and* good. And for his part as a dad, he explained to Elijah Jr. that he was like Mufasa, a father who would always be with him in spirit and heart.[110]

As the police led Elijah away from his sobbing mother, it was these words that he took with him. That was the gift. Elijah Jr. was Simba and Elijah Sr. was Mufasa. And no bars could break their bond.[111]

Sylvia didn't want to wake Romarr. He was sleepy from the interrogation but still able to say that he didn't do what the police had said.[112] She held her son, readying him for the inevitable ride to the Hartgrove Hospital. She cuddled her boy in the backseat of the police car while he slept. Romarr's dad sat in the front seat, too devastated to speak. Once they arrived at Hartgrove, Sylvia laid a sleeping Romarr gently on the counter where an official from the Hartgrove Hospital was waiting. She signed the papers to relinquish her baby, and they took him from her.[113]

Elijah made it to Hartgrove in a panic. He was not only scared to be away from his parents; he was also afraid of the dark. And Hartgrove, like the police station, was a dark place. He cried, loudly and inconsolably. Hartgrove had a way of dealing with that: They isolated Elijah in a windowless room. It was a type of solitary confinement, which only made his fear and panic worse.[114]

He would cry himself to sleep, hunkered down on the floor. There, he found desperate comfort from the only source of light, which came from a small slit under the door.

# 2

# A Blueprint

*That's the thing about stories . . . they never really end, do they? We're still telling the same stories we've always told —just with different names, different faces.*

**—*The Matrix Resurrections***

## Innocence Day

I met Lee Hester through his song, a gospel song that turned a roomful of lawyers into a roomful of believers.

Lee was a gentle spirit, religious and prayerful, the type of man who walked into the room and greeted everyone with hugs rather than handshakes. He made his own peace by living a quiet life in a state of anonymity, hiding in plain sight from his past and from his trauma. He was a handyman by trade; he knew what it felt like to be broken, so he spent his years fixing things.

This modest existence lasted until three attorneys from the Northwestern Law School's Center on Wrongful Convictions of Youth convinced him to let them reinvestigate his case, which was closed in 1961. Lee had been free from prison since 1972, but the full duration of his case would take nearly sixty years and the struggles of many attorneys, witnesses, and volunteers to grant Lee a form of justice and vindication. The Cook County Circuit Court granted him a certificate of innocence on January 10, 2020, a distinction that he should have had as a boy.[1] This was his Innocence Day.[2]

After Lee was exonerated, the lawyers that had worked on the case held a ceremony, welcoming four generations of attorneys who fought the case over the course of their careers. They had passed the baton like sprinters in a relay, defending Lee as a boy and finishing as he reached his senior years. There were also special guests in attendance, those believers and witnesses who didn't need a certificate to know that Lee had been an innocent boy. His classmates were there and even one of his teachers, Dr. Joyce Clark, now in her nineties. When Lee celebrated his legal victory for his name and reputation, he broke into song, right there in the law office.

It is rare that lawyers from white-shoe law firms share a song with a client, but Lee's grace put his attorneys at ease and made them feel that something special, even spiritual, had happened. The journey to mark him as innocent had been daunting. Despite their training at top law schools, they were never taught the dark truth about the law: that the police (and, indeed, the city) could brand a child as "disposable."[3]

It was clear to everyone, including these hard-nosed litigators, that the judicial system had conspired against Lee and stolen his boyhood, decades of his time, and even his boyhood name.

When he was arrested, the media, police, and prosecutors called him "Lee Arthur Hester." It was the name his family had given him, but in this context, the three names together had a percussive quality, like John Wilkes Booth, Lee Harvey Oswald, James Earl Ray, or Chicago's own John Wayne Gacy.[4] Lee's Christian name was transformed into something nefarious; he was placed in the pantheon of society's most infamous killers.

To live a quieter life with a clean slate, he dropped the name "Arthur" and started fresh as simply "Lee Hester." He pushed the trauma and shame of his childhood far down enough that he could live above it. He never told his children what had happened in his youth and where he had spent his teenage years.

To celebrate his Innocence Day, only one song could express what he had gone through and how he had achieved peace. As he sang, some of the attendees called and responded. He began slowly, bringing the room into his world:

> I've had some weary days and lonely nights, but when I look around and I think things over,
> All of my good days, outweigh my bad days, I won't complain . . .

When his friends recognized the song, they sang quietly. A few said "Yes" and "Hallelujah," as though Lee was preaching a sermon.

> I ask, the question, Lord, why so much pain? . . . For you know what's best for me, better than the world to me, and I'll say, Thank you lord.

Here he sounded like he was starting to cry, voice cracking and loud, as though with each note he was pushing out a memory and a dream from his past.

And he spoke the lyrics one more time: *Thank you Lord. I won't complain.*

## The Man Who Lived Underground

I listened to Lee's voice on a recording shared with me shortly after he passed away in 2022. At the time, I was reading Richard Wright's *The Man Who Lived Underground,* written a few years before Lee was born.[5] In the novel, Wright tells the story of Fred Daniels, a Black man living in Chicago, an everyman.

Hustling home to his pregnant wife after a good day's work, Fred is stopped by three Chicago police officers. They encircle him, accuse him of a double homicide, and push him into a police car. The officers ignore Fred's frantic pleas for mercy, and alibis. Fred mentions his reverend, his church, and a White employer who can vouch for his character and whereabouts.

Regardless, the officers take him into custody, bring him to the station, interrogate him, beat him, and torture him until he is unconscious. Time bends. The strange is familiar; the familiar is rendered strange. Each cycle of the interrogation is a nightmare with the same ending and no resolution. None of it makes sense to Fred Daniels (or to the reader), and yet, the accusations made against him are predictable. This is the horror he has long rehearsed in his mind's eye now unfolding in front of him. In this violence, he forgets his pregnant wife, loses his identity as a joyous man delighting in the simple walk home from work, and questions his own innocence. He escapes custody and flees into the sewers of Chicago, retreating into isolation—and undergoes a reckoning with himself and the world. Through the cracks and hidden passages of the underground world, the social world above him now appears foreign and strange as his very self unravels.

Wright's novel pushed beyond social analysis of Black life to explore the madness that comes from White violence. It was a fiction born of real life, from police lies. Considered too unspeakable to publish, too close to reality to be fiction, too profane or even insane to be given a platform, it was fully buried until 2021.[6]

Wright depicted truths about policing and racism that feel bold and uncensored, even by today's standards. In its time, his work was a warning to Black people fleeing the South to the West, the Midwest, and the Northern states. They pursued new economic opportunities—but mostly, they searched for security and safety from White violence as well as a justice system that often failed to protect them from lynching and racial terror. Before the Great Migration (roughly 1910–1970), approximately 90 percent of African Americans lived in the South.[7] In the first decade of the migration, an estimated 440,000 African Americans left the South, and the pace of this exodus would accelerate with the outbreak of World War I, which created Northern demand for labor.[8]

Richard Wright was one of these migrants. Like others who fled, he traveled with his stories. He wrote about growing up destitute under the White gaze in the Deep South. When he got to the North, he contemplated the North's abundance as well as its own racial segregation that caused deprivation and hunger. The promise of comparative safety in Northern cities like Chicago wasn't the full story. There were constant threats of violence from police, and even roving White gangs that appeared terrifyingly similar to the lynch mobs that had governed the South. Even Mayor Richard J. Daley, whose family ruled Chicago for over forty years, was a member of these White gangs. Indeed, he was one of their leaders, elected president in 1924 of the gang that played a crucial role in Chicago's political machine, and that was "heavily involved in the deadliest anti-Black race riot in Chicago's history."[9]

White gangs used violence and intimidation to turn out or suppress the vote and, alongside police, were essential to enforcing racial segregation as Black people settled in the North.[10] These White gang members didn't have Klan hoods, but as recently as 1997, they acted with police support to contain Black people in overcrowded and under-resourced neighborhoods.[11]

The North prided itself on the myth that it was different from the South, that it offered Black people hope of a better life—enough hope to leave everything they knew from their hometowns for a chance at the promise of safety. But about that prevailing myth, Wright offered words of caution. According to Wright, places like the South, like Mississippi, could swallow people whole. But in Chicago, "a rat might bite you, because after all, you were made to live in slums no different from rattraps."[12] Wright's stories revealed the inconvenient truth that the lure of the North was an empty seduction, an entrée to a new kind of racism, which nonetheless had imported many ideas and tools from the South.

Wright's work reads like an eerie prophecy, a warning to other Black people, that what awaited them in the North was nothing like what they had seen in the South. It was a form of racism that would deceive Black Southerners so motivated by hope. There were no "Whites Only" signs on the doors and stores of the city, and by the 1960s, Black Chicagoans must have been astounded to see Black officers (in growing numbers) walking the beat adjacent to White officers.

But racial violence would come in different, more clandestine forms. It lurked around the corner, and it hid inside the smiles of officers who would greet neighborhood kids by day and abduct some of them by night.

Policing in the North and in Chicago would reveal that Wright's fiction was real and, more important, that many police "truths" were fictions. What Wright likely never anticipated was that the plight of his "everyman" would be weaponized against Black boys, who could be adultified as lurking predators in small form. Richard Wright passed away in 1960. He would never know that his prophecy of Fred Daniels would come true, not as an everyman but in the frail form of a disabled boy named Lee Arthur Hester. Lee's alleged crime would ignite a familiar, race-based moral panic among White Chicagoans and reveal the construction of a Northern brand of justice made especially for Black people.

## South Side Soul

The story of Lee Hester and his family is a Chicago story; indeed, they were like so many other Black families living in what South Side reporter Natalie Y. Moore has described as the "heart of Black America."[13] It was a chocolate city generations in the making.[14] There were miles of middle-class and poor Black communities living near each other. Vibrant, and with summertime stoop culture, neighbor ladies anchored the side streets and thoroughfares as a grandmotherly neighborhood watched. Backyard grills wafted smoke toward the Dan Ryan Expressway. Parks were full of family reunion–style barbecues, with house music booming through speakers that made the bass pound like a brewing percolator. Driving east on 79th Street, toward Lake Michigan, was a journey: Barber shops communing like social clubs, corner men sipping out of bottles, lines of people waiting at Harold's Chicken Shack. Bars on the windows, but people on the front sidewalks.[15] Summertime in Chicago made the frigid winters bearable.

There were churches, funeral homes, and sometimes boards on the windows. Cultural vibrancy and generations of neglect from the city. It was a place of inspiration, but a place where Muddy Waters and Buddy Guy found no shortage of reasons to sing the blues. It was through Chicago's South Side that the city's first Black mayor, Harold Washington, helped pave the way for a new generation of Black leadership, including our first Black president—a man married to a native daughter of Black Chicago.

Like other Northern cities, Chicago was a destination for Black Southerners seeking safety and opportunity, but those migrants quickly detected tears in the fabric of this dream. Black people were confined to small clusters of neglected neighborhoods—the Black Belt—on the South Side of Chicago.[16] Restrictive covenants prevented the sale of homes to Black people, leaving them unable to move freely throughout the Chicago area and into neighborhoods with the best housing, schools, and jobs. Despite this discrimination, Black migrants from the South kept the dream of Chicago intact. They were "city makers" who took those segregated spaces and transformed them into bustling cultural centers.[17]

In 1948, the Supreme Court ruled in *Shelley v. Kraemer*[18] that racially restrictive covenants could not be enforced by the courts, allowing Black Chicagoans to move into the White areas that bordered the Black Belt.[19] However, informal discrimination and violence continued to limit meaningful integration.

Roscoe and Ethel Johnson were one of many hopeful Black families who trusted that the courts would make good on this promise of equality and access. On July 25, 1949, they moved into their new Park Manor neighborhood home on 71st and St. Lawrence—the first Black family on the block. But as they moved in, a "welcome wagon" of White neighbors tried to set fire to their furniture. By night, nearly two thousand White rioters surrounded the house, hurling bricks and fuel-soaked rags through the windows. This tragedy became a trend reminiscent of lynch mobs in the South.[20]

The violence was patterned, organized, and meant to inflict terror on anyone who tried to move in—or anyone who might be planning on it. It was meant to break hope. Thousands of White people fled the city of Chicago for White suburban enclaves, effectively re-creating in Chicago the segregated structures of Jim Crow.[21]

And yet, many Black people still came to the city, believing in the promise of Chicago and fleeing the violence in the South. By 1960, Chicago was home to one of the largest populations of Black people in the United States.[22] From 1890 to 1930, the Black population in Chicago swelled from 14,271 to 233,903. By 1950, Chicago's Black population had increased to 492,265. Over the next decade, that population would balloon to 812,637.[23] If the sight of one Black family in a White community ignited mob violence and White flight, imagine the racist fears associated with entire neighborhoods of Black people.

It wasn't just the racial demographics of the city that were changing. A new wave of the police reform movement arose to clamp down on corruption and brutality, a continuation of the changes designed to professionalize policing. Reformers hoped that policing would be a type of civil service and not just physical force. Crime control would still be the centerpiece of the police's mission, but crime fighting should be seen as an effort to improve society. Policing should be driven by centralized leadership and professionalism, scientific investigation, and adherence to the letter of the law.

Richard J. Daley relied on prominent policing leader Orlando W. Wilson to modernize and reform the Chicago Police Department in 1960.[24] However, none of those reforms were targeted at protecting Black residents. Despite more Black officers being added to the police force, the orientation of policing was geared toward protecting White interests, upholding segregation, and disregarding White violence against Black communities.[25]

When Black people, like the Hester family, began to move into Englewood, specifically, in the 1960s, White people rioted, sometimes for days at a time. But eventually they gave up and moved out. By 1960, Black people made up a majority of Englewood, with 69 percent of the population. From 1960 to 1980, Englewood's White population "plummeted from 1,583 to 818."[26]

Black people were treated as a problem to be solved, a tinderbox that could ignite a city. Around the kitchen tables and in the living rooms, many White Chicagoans were having the same discussion: *If this could happen to Englewood, which neighborhood was next?*

These types of questions drove my maternal grandparents to flee Black integration in Chicago in search of a White "safe haven." There was a moral panic over neighborhoods "turning Black." My grandmother had "safety strategies"—ones that she would eventually teach me when I was a little girl. She regularly walked to the other side of the street when she saw Black men, and she gripped my hand tighter as though I might be snatched up by a Black stranger. She locked and checked her doors several times before bed. In the car, she would lock her doors when she saw a Black or Brown person, even though, in the 1970s and 1980s, that meant dropping the silver lock knob in a way that was immediately obvious to people on the sidewalk outside.

My grandfather taught me racist jokes. He died when I was seven, but he always had a doozy of a joke that didn't make sense to me as a little girl. He told this story of a Black family driving through his White neighborhood. In his telling, the Black couple would lock their car doors as *they* drove through the White space in fear of their safety. The joke was flipping the script at what he saw as the absurdity of a Black person fearing a White neighborhood.

Racism was an echo chamber for White residents like my grandparents, one that blinded them from the threats around them. The great irony of White flight and, perhaps, my grandfather's racist joke is that in the safe, White place where my grandparents relocated, they had a neighbor who lived just a half mile away named Mr. John Gacy.

Gacy was a dad known for dressing up as a clown for kids' birthday parties. He was seen as an upstanding guy, a hardworking man. He was affiliated with the Junior Chamber of Commerce and local Democratic politics and had ingratiated himself with local police unions. He even had a visit with Mrs. Rosalynn Carter, the First Lady, when she visited Chicago. He lived in a humble brick ranch that was neat and tidy and clean. Yet under that neat, tidy, clean house was a looming "odor of death," a maleficence that built and built for years.[27]

With so many White people fixated on Black people as the true threat, they missed that John Gacy was more than just the upstanding neighbor who cared about his patch of lawn or clowning at kids' parties. In the crawl space of the house and beneath the driveway and garage, were the bodies of twenty-nine young people, with four more recovered from the Des Plaines and Illinois Rivers.[28] Boys and young men, all White and mostly connected to people he knew. Gacy lived on top of his sins, a "Tell-Tale Heart" of his own creation—an echo of Edgar Allan Poe's tale, where guilt refuses to stay buried. It was as though he wanted to be caught; after hiding one body (let alone thirty-three) it seemed inevitable that his crimes would eventually reveal themselves through the walls and floors.

While police were busy protecting and shooing away White people from the supposed mistake of going to Black neighborhoods, the Chicago Police missed the serial killer in their midst—one who actually was preying upon White children. A racial veil allowed them to ignore a real threat, prompting the retrospective question that no one asked: *How much can a White person get away with before the Chicago Police and White neighbors even notice?*[29]

In total, John would be charged and convicted of murdering thirty-three boys and young men; some suspected that there were even more victims. People called him the Killer Clown, and he was a real-life Pennywise, sharing an eerie resemblance with the horror character introduced in the 1986 book *IT,* by Stephen King—a book published while Gacy was awaiting execution on death row. Gacy was one of the most murderous serial killers of that time—a literal superpredator. Not the fiction that was placed on Black boys, but a bona fide monster in human form. With this dubious title, the media would mark him by three names, John Wayne Gacy, just as they would do for an innocent

"Lee Arthur Hester," who encapsulated these racist fears about Englewood and the changing city. This form of moral panic and fear would allow White Chicago to ignore the likes of Gacy while believing that Lee was capable of murdering a beloved White teacher.

## A Crime in a "Difficult" School

Like many Black families living in Englewood in the 1960s, the Hester family was stuck somewhere between their own dreams and White fears. Emmett Hester, a city garbage truck worker, and his wife, Helen Hester, were raising eight children. Their son Lee was disabled: He was at least three grades behind his age-comparable peers.[30] The family lived in a modest five-room bungalow, where during the bracing Chicago winters, one of the children would stuff newspapers in a small potbellied stove to heat the dining room.[31]

Their home was across the street from a campus of three schools that served the majority Black community: Englewood High School, the Princeton Annex (a school for those who had dropped out of high school), and the Lewis-Champlin Elementary School for kids in kindergarten through the 8th grade.[32] The president of the Chicago Teachers Union, James Fewkes, referred to this cluster of schools as "difficult," a veiled code for the way teachers viewed educating predominantly Black children in Black schools.[33] A growing number of White teachers were requesting transfers out of districts like Englewood. It was educational White flight.

Mrs. Josephine Keane was one of the few exceptions to this rule. Beloved by the elementary school, she endeared herself to Lee, an academically struggling boy. Mrs. Keane was a masterful teacher, one who mentored less experienced educators and tutored children with learning and behavioral disabilities.[34] These were kids who struggled to read or maybe sit still. She supervised five classrooms with 620 students.[35]

On April 20, 1961, she went missing.

At around 9:30 a.m., the assistant principal at Lewis-Champlin saw

Mrs. Keane, still wearing her spring coat, go into the bookroom. It was the last time she was seen alive.

With so many kids, so many teachers, and so much noise in the school, it was not until around 3:30 p.m., when the day finally quieted, that fellow faculty suspected that something was wrong. The principal, assistant principal, school carpenter, and engineer became an unlikely search party, navigating the hallways and colorful classrooms, opening doors and closets, but repeatedly passing the locked bookroom, which at first glance appeared secured—and to which few people had the key.

After forty-five minutes, as the search became more desperate, Mr. Grant, the school engineer, finally opened the door of the bookroom. Mrs. Keane was on the floor, only three feet from them. Her coat was still on but lifted over her head. Her keys were missing, but her purse was next to her. Her clothes were disarranged in a possible sign of a struggle. The bookroom, now called the "death room" by reporters and police alike, was near a first-floor door where a would-be killer could easily escape. The first police at the scene attempted to seal off the school in their search for a suspect.

Across Chicago, a single headline in the *Chicago Daily Tribune* gripped the city: TEACHER MURDERED IN SCHOOL: FIND MOTHER OF 6 STABBED ON SOUTH SIDE.[36] To White Chicagoans, the South Side had begun to signify the "Black" part of town; the location of Englewood only served to confirm this casual suspicion.

In reports, Mrs. Keane was a teacher and mother but, most important, a relative by marriage to Police Captain James Riordan, deputy chief of patrol.[37] Her death, aside from a personal loss to many, was seen as an affront to law and order and a cautionary tale: Do-gooders like Mrs. Keane who ventured into Black neighborhoods could end up dead. The combination of these elements transformed her murder into the ultimate "heater" case creating intense political pressure for police to solve the crime by any means necessary.

The newspaper described Mrs. Keane being stabbed seven times, with wounds to her chest, underarms, and back, and left in a pool of blood. A bolded sub-headline stated that her clothing had been disarranged and that police believed she had resisted a sexual assault. Below these details was a map of the area, with an arrow pointing to Englewood Avenue near Halsted, Wentworth, and State—demarcating the school, the neighborhood, and the criminal accusations as they would soon be intimately fused in the minds of the media and the public.

To police and White Chicagoans, the death of a vulnerable White victim implied the race of the suspect. Who else could the killer be but a Black person? A murder, a possible sexual assault, in a Black school in a Black neighborhood. The facts spoke for themselves—seemingly. This case ignited a moral panic in the city and signified the danger of neighborhoods "turning Black"—specifically for White women. The article included a gruesome image of Mrs. Keane's body, draped by a cloth in the bookroom next to a wooden ladder with a White officer kneeling at her side.

Police and media swarmed the school. Fingerprints and a palm print were recovered from the scene, and a grease smudge was found on Mrs. Keane's undergarments—leading them to initially suspect that the killer might have a job as a mechanic or in a machine shop or garage. Detectives also found microscopic particles of wood, fiber, and metal in the victim's underwear. An unfinished note in Mrs. Keane's handwriting was found under her body, and there was a stamped heel print of an adult male's shoe on a piece of paper lying on the floor.[38] Police searched in vain for both a murder weapon and the keys used to get in the locked door of the bookroom.

The police had given the media near total access to the crime scene, and the news stories were coming faster than clues. The case made the front page of the city's top newspapers. Reporters came and went, taking pictures near the pool of blood, near the hallways that a potential suspect might have used to enter or exit, and near where officers were dusting for prints.[39] With few leads, a sloppy crime scene, and the anxiety of a city breathing down their necks, police narrowed their field of view and began questioning the faculty and staff at the school.

Englewood's Lewis-Champlin offered up any number of possible

Black suspects. Among the nearly 2,600 students attending the school (in shifts, to compensate for overcrowding), there were few, if any, White students. The police were not enticed by the clues found at the crime scene, like the grease, the fingerprints, or the adult-sized shoe print. Instead, the police followed what they saw as the most compelling evidence in the case: Mrs. Keane was an innocent White teacher killed in a Black school. The police were looking at a crime that implied a type of monster as their suspect.

Two of the White officers—Anton Prunckle and Sheldon Teller—decided to stop wasting time at the crime scene.[40] They headed to the front office and asked the teachers and secretaries whether they had any kids in mind as possible suspects—a problem child who disrupted class frequently or who had a history of sexually inappropriate behavior. On its surface, this seemed to be a standard investigative question: *Were there any bad seeds worth unearthing within their midst?* But the question signaled an important shift in the case. The police were disregarding the physical evidence, such as the grown man's shoe print, and instead were choosing to zero in on the students in the school.

When the police asked for names of misbehaving students, it appeared that they had decided that the suspect was Black and, therefore, suspicious *in spite of* their age. It implied that all the children in the school were not really *children;* they were "suspects," subsumed into the same imagined category of potential criminal monsters. A person with enough strength to overpower an adult woman. And that suspect was in their midst, right there, in one of the classrooms.

Ultimately, it was a White gym teacher who first mentioned Lee Hester to the police. Lee was a special education student that Mrs. Keane had once tutored. He was behind academically. He was fourteen years old.

With the suggestion in hand, the police were allowed to go into Lee's classroom and begin the interrogation on school grounds. Ms. Jean Webster, a young Black teacher, was aware of Lee's intellectual and behavioral challenges in class, but she felt she could reach him and help him control his disruptive behavior. By the time the police entered her classroom, there was little help she could offer Lee, but it was not for any lack of trying. She was a crucial witness in this case; Lee was in her class and under her supervision at the time of the murder. She was Lee's alibi. Yet the police still insisted on taking Lee in for questioning.

In a Black community, such an "ask" by White officers is always a command. Once Lee was taken away by the police, any alibi Ms. Webster could have offered for Lee would be ignored—one of the many, *many* Black witnesses who would be cast aside in favor of police fictions.

## Interrogating a Boy

The kids and teachers in the school knew Lee Hester. He had trouble listening to directions; when he spoke, he had a stubborn stutter, which made his intellectual disability more obvious. To Lee's peers, stuttering was the sound of being behind in school, which opened him up to being teased and laughed at. He had a slight frame, was five feet tall, and weighed less than 100 pounds. Those who teased Lee knew that he was no threat.

But Lee was a likable child. He shined shoes outside a real estate office on 63rd Street in Englewood to make a little money to help his parents. There, he met prominent men, White men, who appreciated his industriousness and who tipped him for shining their shoes and running errands for them. It was through this work that Lee met a mentor, a young lawyer named Jerry Feldman who so believed in the young boy that he decided to help him with his homework. For two years, they met three times a week for tutoring—sometimes more often—and Jerry understood that Lee was young for his age, even something of a mama's boy.[41] If he stayed late, he called his mom for permission. Jerry often talked to Mrs. Keane about Lee and to Lee about Mrs. Keane and was a witness to the mutual respect they shared in their student-teacher relationship.[42] But after Mrs. Keane's murder, Lee wasn't just Mrs. Keane's special education student. He quickly became the lone suspect.

Officers Prunckle and Teller began by taking Lee to the third floor of the school. There was a balcony that was perfect for questioning a suspect, a tight space where the boy could be cornered: nowhere to escape except over the railing.[43]

After fifteen minutes, the police moved Lee to the school auditorium, where the sun acted like the beam of an interrogation light. There they could more closely examine the stains and spots on the boy's clothing.[44]

But this was the day after the murder. In that span of time, Lee would have gone home and could have played outside, roughhoused, bathed or showered, and come to school in entirely different clothes. There was no investigative logic to such an inspection; it was pure gaslighting and an assertion of power, with the officers fully capitalizing on Lee's many social deficits.[45] The police got close to him, stared at small markings on his shirt and pants that they believed could have been blood, a scrape or scratch, fibers, lint, or hair too small to notice except in the sunlit auditorium. They stared at Lee and inspected his body and may have even moved his limbs like a puppet.

Anyone looking on would see the police performatively doing everything they could to solve the mystery of Mrs. Keane's death; the officers could dramatize good old-fashioned policing. Getting in Lee's space, demanding answers, roughing him up: This was the type of drama that laypeople expect from the police and that police are all too happy to perform.

No matter where they brought him in the school or how many times they asked him, Lee stood firm in his innocence, displaying the type of childlike confidence that comes from knowing you did nothing wrong. After all, this was his teacher, *his* Mrs. Keane who helped him and was patient with him. As fast as they asked the questions, he gave back answers, defiantly.[46] But for such defiance—according to Lee—Officer Prunckle had to send him a clear message. He gave a jolting kick to Lee's left shin, letting Lee know that they could kick Lee down the street like a can if he didn't tell them what they wanted to hear.[47]

The police moved Lee into the principal's office and left him there to wait, alone, with Sergeant Frank Follis as his guard.[48] The principal's office was the kid-equivalent of being in custody, a punitive limbo. Like any child, he thought about what his teachers and his mom would say. He likely thought about his beloved Mrs. Keane as the officer had described her to him. He sat with the fact that Officer Teller said they saw blood on his clothing and a strand of long hair on his sweater, and that was enough to take him into police custody.[49]

Then Lee saw a beacon of hope. Two Black officers, Officers Robert Perkins and Harold Thomas. Two Black men dressed in blue with skin as dark as that of his dad, uncles, cousins, and neighbors would escort him to the police station.[50]

Lee was allowed one indulgence: to go back and retrieve his jacket in Ms. Webster's class. Of course, the class was abuzz. Mrs. Keane was dead, and now Lee was missing from class and had been seen with White uniformed officers. No teacher could have restored order. Kids were moving around with fear, excitement, and curiosity, asking what had happened. Lee bluntly told the class: "They think I killed Mrs. Keane." The entire class burst out laughing.[51]

As he grabbed his jacket, Lee had no way of knowing that those sounds of laughter, perhaps mocking his small size and disability, were the last thing he'd ever hear from his classmates or anyone else at the school, for a long time.

Officers Perkins and Thomas drove Lee to a police station in the neighborhood—a place a few blocks from his home. But it was a bait and switch. His mom was not going to be there waiting at the local station; she would not be notified that Lee was missing and in police custody until rumors of Lee's arrest echoed through the playgrounds, homes, and streets of Englewood.

In fact, Lee was actually headed to the Arthur J. Audy Home. It was several miles from the neighborhood Lee knew and farther away from his mother.[52]

## The Black Boy in the White Gown

Chicago is often credited as the "epicenter" of the progressive child-saving movement, which was aimed at improving the lives and welfare of impoverished and immigrant children. In 1899, the opening of the Cook County Juvenile Court signaled the triumph of a new ideological belief in rehabilitating children, who were viewed by these reformers as inherently innocent.

What often goes unspoken, however, is that this ideology was never extended to Black children. For them, the juvenile justice system consistently came with a brutal, punitive bite. Seen as lacking that primal childhood innocence, Black children were viewed, by the system and its stakeholders, as irredeemable. This created an entire class of children (mostly Black) that seemed "disposable" to police and the criminal justice system at large.[53] Attorneys often talk about these kids as "defuturized," youth for whom prison is predetermined.[54] Those who believe Black children are going to inevitably end up in prison are the same people who have the power to make that destiny come true.

Poor native White children and immigrant children from Europe were the imagined consumers of child-saving. Black children, in contrast, encountered a functionally separate juvenile system that marked and criminalized their vulnerability—even decades prior to the era of hypercriminalization or the so-called school-to-prison pipeline.[55] Black children, orphaned by death or abandonment, were labeled by the juvenile court as "delinquent," unlike White children, who were labeled as "dependent" or worthy of care.[56] Black children, regardless of age, academic standing, or temperament, were labeled as "criminal" even when no crime had been committed. Their very expression of need was recorded as a type of offense to be settled by jail time.

From the beginning, the juvenile justice system, often heralded for its humanity and rehabilitative ideal, was simultaneously a racialized state process resulting in the criminalization of Black children.[57] Unsurprisingly, Black children were disproportionately represented in the juvenile justice system, and this created a vicious cycle. The overrepresentation was the result of a prejudicial system, but it also became a rationale for their blameworthiness. This created a pernicious lie that Black children were something *other than* innocent; they were a threat or problem to be contained.

The juvenile justice system was a racial management system, a way to herd and contain Black children into juvenile detention preemptively. By the mid-1930s, Black sociologist Earl Moses noted that the rate of Black children criminalized as juvenile "delinquents" (sevenfold increase in criminalization) in Chicago had grown faster than the Black population (threefold increase in Black population).[58] Moses attributed the increased criminalization of Black juveniles to a lack of community resources in segregated Black communities, the stress and trauma of migration from the South and, importantly, the racial stigmas and stereotypes about the supposed "criminal nature" of Black people, including children.[59] Despite the migration away from the South, the stigmas so associated with Southern anti-Black racism followed migrants and their children to the North. More specifically, a "Confederate diaspora" after the Civil War moved White Confederates and their views into places assumed to be more racially equitable. This intergenerational transmission of Southern norms to the North would indoctrinate Northerners to systemic anti-Black racism.[60]

In addition, for decades, Hollywood sensationalized racism as a type of horror story to be consumed as nationwide entertainment. D. W. Griffith's *The Birth of a Nation* (1915) was the motion picture that imagined this racist mythology on the grandest scale.[61] In effect, the movie played a central role in igniting a consensus around the supposed threat of the "Black brute" and the vulnerability of White women.[62] The film promoted the idea that lynching was the only possible vindication against such threats. The Klan was portrayed as the police force in defense of White womanhood. And this savior role was neatly subsumed into the culture of policing. *The Birth of a Nation* is also perhaps the original "true crime" thriller.

Such a worldview impacted all facets of social life and became an explicit rationale for perpetuating inequality, affecting educational opportunity, policing, housing access, jobs, wealth creation, and healthcare.

Perhaps it was predictable that the juvenile justice system would become infected by such racist beliefs. By the 1960s, this system had ballooned, disproportionately targeting Black children.[63] And this tendency has not diminished over time, either nationwide or for Chicago more specifically: In 2018, 70 percent of all admissions to the Juvenile Temporary Detention Center (JTDC) in Cook County were Black children.[64]

By the time Lee was being driven to the Audy Home by two Black officers, the juvenile system had ratcheted up its capacity to criminalize children to unprecedented levels. The Audy Home was the belly of the beast, the stuff of playground lore; Lee was headed into a world he had heard plenty about.

In the Englewood side streets and alleyways where kids convened and played, there was a common refrain when someone stepped out of line: *Straighten up, or you're going to the Audy Home.* Tales of neighborhood boys being sent to the Audy Home were hair-raising, local campfire stories rooted in reality. This was a place that could vanish young Black boys—where kids could be taken for weeks or even months at a time. Lee likely knew that Audy Home was no "home"; it was a jail. It was a place for boys, but there was nothing "childlike" about it.

The ventilation was poor, and the air was stale. The lights were dark and dingy. The walls were stripped of color. By the end of the workday, the attached juvenile courthouse would be garbage-strewn—cigarette ashes and butts on the floor, cups of spilled coffee, and other visible remnants of the perpetual streams of people coming and going.[65]

Kids wore marked prison jumpers, some so oversized and ill-fitting that they tripped on their pants and their sleeves stretched well past their hands.[66] Kids marched, boot camp style, to nowhere—an audible echo of childhood punishment, foreboding to newcomers. Other punishments were more clandestine. Kids stood facing the walls (or even with their noses touching the wall). Any child—even those there for neglect and care rather than delinquency—could expect to be placed in isolation if they indulged in an emotional outburst. Something as simple as crying could lead to solitary confinement.[67]

Guards put children in isolation in the windowless "Blackstone cells." The origins of this name are uncertain, but the lore from staff and guards was that it was a reference to Blackstone law books and the sense of "having the book thrown at you."[68] The cells, smaller than a parking space, were intended for punishment.[69]

Since the juvenile court and its magistrates were adjacent to the Audy Home, police could have routed Lee to the juvenile justice system.[70] But that would have required seeing Lee as a boy (inherently innocent and therefore worthy of this system). And the cloud of suspicion placed upon him made only one option seem viable: interrogation.

An admission of guilt by their suspect would be the most compelling evidence to convict Lee, as they lacked evidence linking him to the crime. For police, this was the best bet, with a city and the media breathing down their backs. Interrogating Lee was the quick and easy way to get things done, just like pressuring suspects to plead guilty in court. It was efficient; it was a resolution; there was no need for further investigation. For the police, once they pointed a finger at Lee, their job was nearly done; the case was cleared. So the police were set on interrogating this boy.

On its surface, interrogation involves a nosy conversation, linguistic sleight of hand, empty promises, bright lights in cold windowless rooms, and often multiple officers playing the game of good cop/bad cop. But law enforcement professionals also know that timing is everything. Setting matters. Conditions create the environment where the delicate work of interrogation can be flawless and quick. And the game starts much earlier than one would think.

Lee was routed into the cavities of the Audy Home's infirmary for this specific ritual. Some of it was consistent with the "booked in" procedure, where children were processed, showered, and given a medical exam.[71] But Lee was being primed for a discussion with police officers. He had already met two Black officers, the only faces in a sea of White that gave him even a slight measure of hope. They were his chauffeurs, but their role upon entry to the Audy Home was unclear.

Being "booked in" required a descent into a world of bars and concrete; the process generated the perfect perverse conditions to wear away at Lee even before the formal interrogation began. It was a threefold punch to prep him for a confession, and it could only take place in a jail because jails are "where accusations are made true."[72] *Disintegration* and the removal from his peers and loved ones began from the moment Lee left his classroom. As the hours passed, the toll of isolation began to kick in. There was *disorientation* through sounds, lack of information, and uncertainty. There was the shock of Lee being plucked out of his everyday life and dropped into the Audy Home, a process made worse by his age and disability. Lee was told when to stand, sit, speak, or remain silent. All of this established the officer's absolute authority and control.[73]

Children are already primed to submit to authority—deferring to adults for permission to go to the bathroom or leave the dinner table—and jails exploit this compliance to the point of abuse. *Degradation* begins before arrest and continues in numerous forms as a suspect navigates the intake process. Bodily autonomy is denied; personal space is violated; threats and commands are barked. The joyride to the jail is purposefully rough. It is a type of social humiliation where those in authority deny the social worth and identity of the captive. And if the crime that the suspect is charged with is violent, the humiliation increases through practices rationalized as standard precautions for the sake of "safety." The removal of street clothes in particular converts a newcomer such as Lee into a manageable inmate.[74] The captured are literally costumed to play a part. Such a transformation produces a docile prisoner; for a child, it induces uncertainty and fear. There are no windows to escape through, no covers to hide under, no comfortable chairs where the body can sink and transfer its pain and trauma.

Regardless of one's guilt, confessing is an attractive out.[75] Children are already conditioned to believe in fantasy, imaginary play, superheroes, and Santa Claus. Children in jails are ushered across a psychological barrier, a point of no return. They are groomed for the possibility of saying—and believing—anything that might save them and are additionally gaslit into believing that the police may know something more about themselves than they do. A disabled boy like Lee, who may have often felt like he knew so little about the world—its logics, its speed—was far more susceptible to these lures and tactics than a child who was neurotypical.

Police act as if they are human lie detectors. Making it worse, interrogators often make an initial assessment of guilt based primarily on the nonverbal cues and body language of the suspect.[76] Fidgeting in a chair, talking incessantly, not making eye contact can all be signs of a disability, and yet police read them as indicators of guilt. Even saying "I don't know" as an admission of confusion or a need for help may be a common refrain for a learning-disabled child.[77] But when police interpret this phrase as a sign of guilt, such an admission of confusion or denial can serve as a signal to the investigators to come on stronger and harsher, to get in the face and space of the suspect.

Perhaps it's no surprise then that for all these reasons, Lee was targeted and marked, staying firm in his innocence but cognitively out of his league against professional law enforcement who were trained to treat this boy as though his guilt was a foregone conclusion.[78] Black, disabled, and adultified, Lee was an easy target for a police "win."[79]

In the first stages of the interrogation at the Audy Home, Lee surrendered his clothes, and the staff removed the marbles from his pockets. They gave him a white hospital gown—the kind of gown given out in psych wards and before surgeries. The kind that makes the body cold and vulnerable, ready for examination, and provides little dignity.[80] It signals shots, unfamiliar instruments, bitter medicines, and other indignities that can come from visiting a doctor. The surrender of his clothes and his toys was the first stage of his interrogation, the transformation of the child from the boy who left his home for school into the suspect who was being booked into the Audy Home, naked and draped only in a smock.[81]

The next stage was less dramatic for the police but essential to warming up the boy. They made Lee wait in a room he called the "dark dungeon room."[82] There, Lee remained in that white gown with his thoughts and only the ability to pace in a room the size of a walk-in closet—with a 12-foot ceiling. It was barren, covered in concrete. There was a hospital bed with an innerspring mattress, a hospital table, a stool, a light fixture, a radiator, a transom, and a 42-by-52-inch barred window. One can imagine Lee fixating on the wrinkled sheets on the bed, the patterns on the tiles, the chipped paint, and other insignificant facets that in any other place would fade out of consciousness.

The hospital setting mixed with the bars on the window allowed Lee to wonder whether his punishment would be doled out by a doctor. What other purpose could a hospital gown and a hospital bed have if he wasn't sick? In this tiny room, he had nearly six hours to ruminate on such puzzles.[83] Six hours to think about what to say about Mrs. Keane, whether the officers from the school would be outside the door waiting for him or whether the Black officers that drove him to Audy Home might be able to lend him some help.

Six hours is a long time for a fourteen-year-old boy, especially one who had trouble listening and sitting still in class. This was a 360-minute-by-minute lesson in subordination and conversely, the power of those who placed him in this condition.[84]

By 4 p.m., the officers determined that Lee was likely ready for a talk. He would be confronted by four officers. The two Black officers, Perkins and Thomas, would stay on the case. They would be joined by two White sergeants, John Killackey and William Keating. Race would be a weapon. The officers would engage in the tag-team questioning, with the Black officers playing the "good cops" and the White officers playing the "bad cops." Lee never saw an attorney, nor was he read his rights, but as any child would do, he asked at least three times while in custody for the most likely person who could save him: his mother. "I want to see my mama," he said.[85] He would repeat this plea, but no one responded to such requests. If anything, his interrogators likely interpreted the request as a potentially useful lure in an interrogation. A child's needs can be used as collateral, and Lee needed his mama.

Just as he had done at school, Lee continued to insist on his innocence. Even in the face of police authority, Lee stayed firm in this faith: "God knows I am innocent." Killackey replied to Lee, "God also knows what the results of the crime laboratory tests are and you know they show you are the murderer."[86] Killackey pointed a pen at Lee's face and got so close to him that Lee could feel the sergeant's breath. The sergeant also screamed at Lee and spat on him.[87]

One must imagine that opening the interrogation with such force would have triggered Lee's stutter. Yet, there was no pause in the interrogation.[88] One of the White officers lied and told Lee that they found his fingerprints on the icebox near where Mrs. Keane's body was found.[89]

When the White officers left, the Black officers remained in the room and reassured Lee. Seeing these Black officers with skin like his uncles, friends, and dad sent a message that he wasn't alone. But it also meant that he had to listen and then obey to be safe, especially in a world where a local boy like Emmett Till could go missing and end up dead at the hands of White folks. In Lee's view, the Black officers were likely the only people in the Audy Home who understood the rules of engagement and could help secure his freedom.

Thomas and Perkins told Lee that his blood was found on Mrs. Keane's clothes and that they had found her hair on his sweater.[90] All Lee knew was that they had taken his clothes; they had been tested, and now these officers were telling him that he had failed the test. Lee was used to failing, used to struggling, and when he did fail, there was no debating adults about it. It was so.

Out of earshot of the White officers, Perkins and Thomas offered to protect him. Officer Thomas assured him, "We ain't going to let them knock your head through the wall."[91] They promised that they could even get his clothes back and, most important, they could let him see his mama if he would just do one thing for them—confess. The exchange made sense to Lee. The officers explained the looming threat of violence, and they gave him a way out. They likely even could pronounce "mama" with Black affection.[92]

As the officers laid out their terms, they showed Lee the violent crime scene photos of Mrs. Keane lying in a pool of blood, her clothes bothered and lifted. In any other context, sharing such graphic images would have been seen as child abuse, especially after the trauma of his arrest.[93] But for the officers, such a ritual was standard. The police were going to show him the pictures of what they claimed he did; they were showing him a mirror and telling Lee who he really was. After twelve hours of being denied outside contact, Lee Hester broke. He signed the confession.

In the officers' account of the interrogation, Lee first denied killing Mrs. Keane, but when told by the officers that the crime lab found blood, hair, and lipstick on his clothes that matched the victim, he confessed to stabbing his teacher accidentally.[94] The problem was, the police didn't have the crime lab's findings until days later, but of course, Lee did not know that. When Lee provided more details to the officers, they claimed that they used the crime scene pictures to "clear up a few points," as though they were just trying to get the facts correct rather than terrifying the boy.[95]

Hester testified that the police showed him photographs of the crime scene before, not after, his confession. He stated that he fabricated his confession after viewing the pictures and that the police coached him in describing the details.[96] According to the confession the police wrote for Lee, he was returning milk cartons to the cafeteria with a classmate when he told his friend that he was going to see Mrs. Keane in the bookroom. He had a knife up his sleeve, secured by a rubber band that had been given to him by a classmate earlier in the day. As he walked into the bookroom, toward Mrs. Keane, he tripped on some books. He stumbled, and somehow the knife came out of his sleeve, and he accidentally plunged it into her back. Attempting to get up off the floor, Lee stumbled, stabbing Mrs. Keane in the back again. This series of falls and mishaps at first made the crime seem like the actions of a buffoon, but then the narrative took a turn, portraying a crime with intent, the work of a sexual predator.

The written confession stated that when Mrs. Keane turned toward Lee after her initial injury, he became excited and struck her twice in the breast. It claimed that he then pulled up her dress, cut her garter belt, unzipped his pants, and laid down on top of her, exposing himself.[97] These inflammatory details would have sounded to a jury like deflowering and denigration. And the mental image of a Black boy exposing himself to a White woman was the ultimate racist horror fantasy.

According to the police, Lee checked for Mrs. Keane's heartbeat—getting lipstick on his jacket—locked the door, dropped the key, and went back to class.[98] Even on the surface, this narrative didn't make much sense. Some aspects of the confession were clearly too vague. Like how a knife—with its blade exposed—could fall out of a boy's sleeve without injuring his wrists and hands or tearing his clothes. After stabbing someone numerous times, how could he have returned to class with no evidence of blood covering his clothes, shoes, or body? Then parts of it were overly precise, such as the timestamps of the crime written into the confession in language that reeked of police-speak. How could Lee have committed the crime in the window of time when he was returning from dropping off milk cartons? But these details allowed the police to fit the confession to the crime so that it would seem like the police found Mrs. Keane's murderer.

Indeed, the police's word *was* the evidence.

The police would argue that the interrogation took only five minutes.[99] That they could break the boy so quickly was an indication of his guilt. However, no one acknowledged the exhausting hours in which Lee was primed for that final, five-minute interrogation.[100] In all, it was over twelve hours from accusation to isolation and incarceration and then to confession. The officers rehearsed his script five or six times before the Assistant State's Attorney came in to capture the story for the record.[101] As they made corrections, they showed the confession to Lee. But Lee could barely read. If he was able to, he would have realized that the confession was pure fiction, built on tall tales and fantasies spun by the officers.

Lee was given false promises in exchange for his statement.[102] And yet, a judge denied the request to suppress his confession, finding it to be "voluntary."[103] Because the crime occurred in a neighborhood that had turned Black, and because the victim was a White woman surrounded by Black children, the many inconsistencies and improbable accidents seemed plausible.[104] Racism was beyond reason in this case and in the many cases to come.[105] Lee was charged in the murder of his teacher.

Despite their promises to Lee, the police did not allow him to see his mother until 10 a.m. the next morning. But it was not for the lack of her trying. When she headed to the Audy Home, she was unable to see him. When Lee was finally allowed to see his mother and an attorney, he recanted his confession. It had always been a means to an end.

## The Inquest and the Media Storm

When news of Lee's confession hit the media, it ignited a fury in a city that was already on edge. Large portions of the confession's transcript—including the details about Lee stabbing Mrs. Keane's breast and putting his head on her chest and the alleged sexual molestation—were reprinted for the public. The media described Lee as being "as strong as an ox" and a "bully" to the other Black children in his school.[106] He was described as an "unusually powerful boy" who intimidated his classmates[107]—the same ones who had erupted in laughter at the idea that Lee could have overpowered and killed his teacher.

The crime itself was referred to as a "sex slaying," which led the police and media to cast a motive upon Lee.[108] With a White victim who had ties to law enforcement, this was a racially explosive term that cast Lee as a "slayer"—a coded word for a "brute" driven by the supposed desire for White women and an inherent tendency toward superhuman violence.

Jerry Feldman, the attorney who had helped Lee with his homework, agreed to represent Lee alongside two other lawyers, and he prepared a plea of not guilty on Lee's behalf. He told the media that Lee had recanted the confession, denied all of it, and maintained that the police had roughed him up to get it.

On the day of the inquest hearing, prior to the grand jury's indictment, 150 people jammed into the inquest room for a chance to see Lee.[109] By the time the doors closed, an overflow crowd was crammed in the hallways. One reporter described Lee as lacking "bravado" and "remorse," as though it were a feature of his character rather than an indication of possible innocence—or confusion.[110]

Lee was overwhelmed by the crowds, the noise, the crush of reporters. He struggled in a scrum at the entrance until he was led by the wrists to sit between his mother and a Black social worker named Mary Adams.[111] He cried; the ends of his mouth stretched back toward his ears as if he were wincing in pain. Mrs. Adams gently pressed on his chest as though she could lay hands on him and slow his terrified heart. Cameras flashed in his face, and he cried, "They're going to shoot me. Get 'em out of here, Jerry; get 'em out of here."[112] As he yelled to his attorney, he buried his head in his mother's arms. During part of the hearing, Lee sat on the knee of an unnamed Black man, presumed to be his father but more likely part of the social work team.

When the court went into recess, his mother tried to reassure him that no one would harm him again. But Lee, still terrified, begged for his Bible. He hid his face behind the small book, clutching it to himself like a shield. When the recess ended and the police came to take him into the hearing room, he cried out to his mother a last promise and a request, "I ain't going to leave you, don't ever leave me."[113] Then Lee sobbed and clung to her as the police pried him away. He fought back, kicking, screaming, and swinging as they took him away. His father, Emmett, emerged from the back of the room as the hearing ended and the drama unfolded.[114]

To his parents, the attorneys, and the social workers, Lee's behavior would have been a clear symptom of the intense terror Lee must have felt after his interrogation, isolation, and incarceration. As the news reported on such courtroom outbursts, White Chicagoans were prone to interpret this same behavior as further evidence of Lee's supposedly uncontrollable nature.[115]

Lee would eventually be convicted by a jury made up of eleven White jurors and one Black juror. During Lee's trial, he took the stand in his own defense, but he was not alone. Classmates, an assistant principal, and a crime lab analyst all testified on his behalf.[116] In addition, Lee's mother testified that she did not learn that Lee was in police custody until after he had confessed to a crime that he did not commit.[117]

Ms. Jean Webster, Lee's teacher who supplied his solid alibi, still believed in the integrity of the criminal justice system and the idea that there was such a thing as truth and justice. She took the stand in Lee's defense, and that was particularly brave because to testify *for* Lee meant that you were testifying *against* the Chicago Police.[118] As a Black woman, there was an inherent danger in doing so, but she believed that her status as an honorably discharged serviceperson and as an educator with a master's degree would give her credibility in the eyes of the jury. Ms. Webster testified under oath that Lee was with her, in her class, during the time of the murder. The Chicago Police's timeline for the crime was wrong and did not match the basic details of the school day.[119]

For the jury, none of that mattered, and neither did the holes in the evidence. The blood found on Mrs. Keane's clothing was not Lee's, and the hair found on Lee's sweater could not be matched conclusively to Mrs. Keane. Lee's fingerprints were never found in the murder room. All the physical evidence was junk science and lies. And Ms. Webster's word was no match for that of the Chicago Police. Like many other Black witnesses, she would be dismissed in favor of the police's lies.

The false confession proved decisive.[120] Lee was convicted of murder on October 9, 1961, and sentenced to fifty-five years in prison. He reported to the prison immediately and began to serve his time.

## Goodness and Grace

In 1961, the *Chicago Daily News* published a profile about Lee.[121] Lee was still young and fresh-faced and able to reflect on what he had been through. He was quartered in the jail's infirmary, where he tended to patients' needs and was protected from the general, adult population. His nights were left to dream about his future and freedom. He would dream about going home, and he felt certain that his dream would come true.

As a child who dreamed that freedom would come through faith, Lee tried to pray his way out of the jail. He told reporters, "All I got to do is pray and read my Bible every night and God will take care of the rest." He also maintained his innocence and offered a prescient warning: "The boy who killed the teacher is out there now and I'm in here. . . . He could do it again. They think they got it solved, but they ain't got it solved."[122]

Lee was right; there was another suspect that the media would barely mention. The details connected to that suspect fit the physical evidence—it was a White suspect who at every turn had been protected, transferred, and shielded from public scrutiny while an innocent Black boy remained in prison, a scapegoat for the racist fears of a city.

Attorneys and investigators would reveal that Mrs. Keane's killer was almost certainly a White engineer at the school, a man named Cooley with a long history of violence and mental illness.[123] He was a World War II veteran and had suffered from mental health issues. But his brother was a police captain. As one of Lee's attorneys, Steven Drizin, described,

> He was given a pass because he came from a good White Catholic family with strong ties to the church. He was also

> likely given a pass because his brother was a well-respected police captain. He was protected throughout his life, given break after break, released even with the knowledge that he would likely harm others . . . while Lee Arthur Hester's life was deemed to be disposable.[124]

In the weeks after the teacher's death, Cooley jumped into the Chicago River, where he may have been attempting to kill himself. The details were spotty, and it was treated as a drunk and disorderly conduct charge. He was sent to the Psychiatric Institute for testing while awaiting trial with a bond set at $10,000, an astoundingly high price for 1961; what remained a dirty secret was that the engineer, while detained, had confessed to killing Mrs. Keane to someone at the Psychiatric Institute.[125] Lee's lawyer, Jerry Feldman, received a tip from someone in the Psychiatric Institute that the real killer was in custody,[126] but it still wasn't enough to stop the wrongful conviction machine that was aimed at his young client.

Before Jerry could interview Cooley, the engineer was transferred out of Chicago to a veterans' hospital, where he was held under lock and key. Alarmingly, after Lee's conviction, the engineer was released and returned to his civil service job working for the Chicago Public Schools while Lee struggled under the weight of his prison time. The engineer would die alone in a booth at a bar, his body unclaimed at the county morgue for over two weeks.[127]

## The Blank Check

As Lee began his seventh year in prison, his case was appealed to the Illinois Supreme Court. Though a skeptical Justice questioned why a boy so young and so disabled had been prevented from seeing his mom, or even a magistrate, in the Audy Home before the police began to question him, the Illinois Supreme Court affirmed the conviction and sided with police.[128]

In 1969, the case was appealed to the United States Supreme Court. Lee's attorneys filed a writ of certiorari, asking that the court review Lee's murder conviction and the confession that led to it. Some held out the hope that this case could be *the* case that would provide greater protections to children during police interrogations.[129] At issue was whether a boy as young as Lee without an attorney or a parent present should have their confession taken and included in their case. Lee's attorneys vehemently argued for a *per se* rule "excluding all confessions taken from juveniles who are unrepresented by counsel."[130] They asked a provocative question that summarized all the liabilities that Lee faced:

> Can the petitioner's [Lee Hester's] conviction stand whether the petitioner conviction is based in whole or in part on the secret incommunicado taking, during a period of unlawful detention, or the oral and written confessions of a 14 year old Negro boy in the fifth grade of grammar school, with severely limited intelligence, without counsel, a parent or anyone else standing in loco parentis [in place of the parent] to him, without adherence to any of his constitutional rights . . . ?[131]

The Court initially granted certiorari, agreeing to reconsider the Illinois Supreme Court's decision to affirm Lee's conviction.The case was fully briefed, and oral arguments took place on November 18, 1969.[132] Several months later, the Supreme Court clerk sent a Western Union telegram to Lee's attorneys that the Justices had dismissed the writ of certiorari as "improvidently granted."[133] In other words, the Supreme Court believed its decision to hear the case to be in error.[134] There was no explanation for the dismissal except that Lee's claim did not "merit the plenary review" the Justices thought it might deserve. The Supreme Court's refusal to rule all but guaranteed that innocent children like Lee would continue to be targeted by the police.[135]

This haunted Jerry Feldman, Lee's attorney, for decades. He thought the Court would only take the case if it were prepared to reverse the conviction.[136] But it was the twilight of the liberal Warren Court's Due

Process Revolution, the end of the era when the Supreme Court ruled on extending protections like the right to counsel for indigent or impoverished defendants (*Gideon v. Wainwright*) or requiring police to provide warnings (colloquially called Miranda warnings) to protect people from self-incrimination (*Miranda v. Arizona*).[137] The country's political tides had changed, embracing President Nixon's law-and-order agenda, which sought to curb the civil rights gains of the 1960s. This shift was reflected in the changing composition of the Court itself.

During this period, the Supreme Court's inaction enabled police and prosecutors to double down on their win-at-all-costs approach. Without a new rule in place, police could deceive anyone: children, and even children with disabilities. They could, with impunity, take them from their parents for long stretches of time, isolate them, make promises to lure them into admitting to something that wasn't true, feed them details of violent crimes, and even convince them that nothing bad would happen to them if they just told the "truth"—as if the confession was the only way to alleviate the pressure of an interrogation. And for those interrogated children who begged for their parents, the Court would rule that it was not the equivalent of asking for an attorney and that such requests did not have to be honored.

After Lee's case, several cases made their way to the Supreme Court that tested whether police had exercised the "greatest care" to ensure the confession was truly voluntary.[138] Often, Justice Thurgood Marshall, the first Black Justice on the Supreme Court, dissented on denials of certiorari and substantive decisions that didn't protect the interests of children in the hands of police. Perhaps, as the lone Black Justice, he knew that the children most likely to be targeted and alone with police (and therefore the most likely to be in need of such protections) would be Black children.

It's possible that, even at the highest court in America, some of the White Justices decided the existing protections were adequate because they could only see a Black child as guilty.[139] The White Justices often ignored Black children's request to see their parents, bypassing Black parents' right to protect and advocate for their children.

What remained after these legal challenges was a "totality of the circumstances test, while theoretically giving judges flexibility to take into account the unique vulnerability of children on a 'case-by-case' basis."[140] By the early 1980s, discretion went to lower court judges, most of them White and many of them former prosecutors themselves, to challenge police on behalf of children. In practice, this "offered little protection to juveniles," and courts had a "near-unfettered and unreviewable discretion to admit juvenile confessions into evidence."[141]

For generations, defense attorneys would hear police and prosecutors cite Lee Hester's case as a justification for the importance of allowing a confession from a child—even a disabled one—to be admissible in court. Lee's case became a precedent—a blueprint—that would be weaponized against another generation of innocent Black children.[142] By refusing to review Lee's case, the Supreme Court, in effect, allowed law enforcement to continue its exploitation and persecution of Black boys.

In the period after the 1961 wrongful conviction of Lee Hester, an entire industrial complex of targeting, surveilling, and directing Black boys into interrogation rooms and into false confessions emerged. Law enforcement in Chicago's Black neighborhoods increasingly targeted these boys, creating a secondary "shadow system" of wrongful conviction.

While Lee's conviction was fought in the courts, Martin Luther King Jr. would march in nearby Marquette Park to protest poverty and deprivation in Black Chicago. King would be met by angry White mobs that patrolled segregation in the city. Northern mobs shouted slurs and threw rocks, bottles, and bricks at Dr. King; they were a force greater than the crowds that King faced in the South. He would reflect: "I've been in many demonstrations all across the South, but I can say that I have never seen, even in Mississippi and Alabama, mobs as hostile and as hate-filled as I'm seeing in Chicago."[143]

Perhaps it is no surprise, then, that the racist mythologies about boys like Lee spread. This urban legend grew so fierce that it was used as a rationale for continued segregation and the restriction of the movement of Black people in the city.[144]

## The School-to-Conviction Pipeline

Even before Lee was convicted, the president of the Chicago Teachers Union, John Fewkes, declared that there is "no place where a policeman can do more to preserve, promote, and maintain respect for law enforcement than in a school."[145] Fewkes met with Mayor Richard J. Daley and Police Superintendent Orlando W. Wilson. Fewkes demanded increased police protection in schools, but not specifically for the children. The Teachers Union wanted at least forty officers in "troublesome areas," code for where Black people lived and teachers needed protection. Wilson was called upon to reform existing police practices.[146] But such reforms were used to protect White interests at the expense of Black freedom.

For many educators, school in these neighborhoods wasn't about math, reading, and writing; it was about conditioning the "troublesome element" (coded language for Black children) to respect law and order.[147] White political leadership sold the presence of law enforcement in Black schools as a type of social good, a lesson for Black children as well as a preemptive measure to stop crime before it started. "Had a policeman been stationed at the Lewis-Champlin school," Fewkes intoned in defense of this logic, "Mrs. Keane might not have been murdered."[148]

Within a few weeks, schools for Black children in the city changed. Youth division policemen searched lockers in six elementary schools and three high schools as part of a new system of spot-check investigation. Robert E. Lewis, a Harvard-educated Black principal, saw through the new tactics, telling the media that all police found in these searches "were some nice clean lockers."[149] But that ship had sailed; a new era of school surveillance had begun, and, with it, increased police access to Black children.

But a school-to-prison pipeline needs a destination. Within years of Lee's conviction, the city would create a showpiece. The Chicago police station at 51st and Wentworth opened in 1970 with all the fanfare one might expect from a new five-million-dollar police headquarters. Built to project law enforcement's manpower needs for the next twenty years, the two-story building could house approximately 1,300 patrolmen tasked with covering thirteen square miles.[150]

The new police station, featuring an auditorium built to seat 150 people, was designed in the shape of the police's five-point star; it also had a pistol range, holding cells, and interrogation rooms.[151] Taking a cue from California, the police station also had a heliport (22,000 square feet), a modern addition that signaled the increasing professionalization of the police and their embrace of the newest technology in crime fighting.[152] The helicopters would allow police to "expand the service" of the Chicago Police and aid in "traffic control, crime prevention, searching for lost persons and emergency services to area hospitals."[153] This was a shorthand for patrolling the area that stretched from the Dan Ryan Expressway to Lake Michigan and from 31st Street to 60th; this was Black Chicago.

Police Superintendent James B. Conlisk Jr. touted the many benefits of such a state-of-the-art facility to reporters. The new location would allow for police efficiency and better, faster services to the community.[154] For the people of Englewood, this was *their* neighborhood and for them, this police station was long overdue.

In March 1970, dignitaries including Mayor Richard J. Daley. came for the dedication of the ambitious project. Local papers published images of smiles and handshakes, and Commander Robert M. Harness assumed a symbolic role in the opening of a state-of-the-art district in the heart of Englewood.[155] He was Chicago's second Black police commander—replacing pioneer Commander Kinzie Blueitt, who was known for his leadership in establishing a Narcotics Court to control drugs in the city. This was the 1950s version of the "war on drugs," and

Commander Blueitt demonstrated to politicians, educators, and community leaders that Black officers were not just important for walking Black beats in Black neighborhoods but could lead and change policy and practice.

Commander Harness, Blueitt's eventual successor, quickly became a local legend on the South Side. After watching the Chicago Police continue to racially integrate, some in the Black community marveled that a Black officer such as Harness could enter the police force in the 1930s and soar through the ranks of a mostly White department.[156] By 1961, he was a lieutenant; by 1962, he was a captain; by 1963, he was a commander. But what most on the South Side remembered about him was that as a beat cop on what was considered a South Side ghetto, Harness walked the neighborhoods commanding the friendship, trust, and respect of the people, especially the kids he would meet. He embodied a belief that police must have close contact with the people they served. "Sometimes I think that we do more complaining about today's youth and spend too little time in helping and developing programs for young people," he said in 1969.[157] As commander, he prioritized human relations activities that built trust between officers and the community and developed the nation's first "Junior Police" program.[158]

Seeing Harness's image next to dignitaries and Mayor Richard J. Daley meant something to the folks in Englewood and indeed, all around the South Side: It meant that Black people were getting a police station that was for them and led by them. It meant that they would be getting the type of policing they knew White Chicagoans were getting in their neighborhoods.

But it was all an illusion.

While Harness's intentions were good, the Chicago Police establishment used integration for their own purposes. The police saw the usefulness of Black officers walking the beat. They were first responders, patrolling Black neighborhoods on behalf of the Chicago Police, building bonds that could seduce targets, creating the possibility of preemptive strikes against more innocent boys. Black officers could be deployed in the interrogation room and in police leadership. They could legitimize places like 51st and Wentworth, making it seem as though the station was in service of the Black community, where it was located.

What the Black community would discover was that 51st and Wentworth became a place where children like Lee, even children as young as Romarr and Elijah, would eventually be held and interrogated. Where Black families would have their children taken from their arms and into police custody through threats of custodial termination and fear of arrest.[159] It would be a place where exculpatory evidence would be buried like discarded bodies in a boiler room basement. For the Chicago Police, 51st and Wentworth would be a place to manage the mythical superpredators in their midst despite their age and any potential disabilities.[160]

While I was researching Lee's case in 2023, I went to see the police station steeped in fear. I walked into 51st and Wentworth and was immediately surrounded by the ghosts of this history. There was a plaque honoring Robert Harness for his thirty-seven years of service to the community and his "fostering of better police-community relations." The official name of the building was now the Robert M. Harness District Station. But somewhere in time, a new narrative was created. The plaque rendered his likeness to look like an elder White man (somewhat resembling Jackie Gleason) and it made no mention of him being a first Black leader on the force. And in honoring him, it obscured another secret: The Chicago Police forced Harness to retire, and it would be a legend in the legal community named R. Eugene Pincham who would try to fight this injustice.[161] Mr. Pincham was a powerful Black attorney with more flash and grandeur than Johnnie Cochran, and he would eventually end up representing Elijah Henderson—one of the most vulnerable Black boys interrogated in the station now emblazoned with Harness's name. This was nearly forty years after Lee was interrogated and only steps away from where I was standing.

When I asked the officer on duty working the desk about this "Robert M. Harness" after whom the station was now named, he snapped at me, "This is 51st and Wentworth."

He didn't know who "that guy" was.

## The Quiet Admission

In 1972, Lee was quietly released from prison on parole. Given the length of his initial sentence, it was remarkable that he would be freed after just over ten years of time in prison. For the attorneys who worked on this case, finding the parole files was difficult, even as they began to think about reinvestigating the case to clear Lee's name and reputation. In fact, for some, those files appeared to be missing or buried within the bureaucracy.[162]

For one of Lee's attorneys, his early release was a quiet admission that many in the prosecutor's office, the police, and corrections department knew that Lee was innocent. Enough of them knew about Cooley, the real killer. Such news traveled in hushed tones, through the hallways and corridors of the prison.[163]

Incarceration could not contain Lee's dreams. Even in the days after he was convicted, he had big plans about his freedom and future. Plans to be like his "best friend," Jerry Feldman. Feldman was his attorney, but more than that, he was the only person who would be allowed to still call him "Lee Arthur Hester" after the wrongful conviction.[164] "I promised myself I wanted to be a lawyer because my best friend is a lawyer, and I'm going to be a Jew just like him."[165] Lee had been through so much. And even in those dark days, he was still hopeful, young, and idealistic. In childhood, and eventually in adulthood, Lee wasn't the type to complain.

# 3

# Building the Case

*Our criminal justice system works like a meat grinder. You are supposed to proceed, in orderly fashion, from arrest to guilty plea to sentencing. More than 90 percent of criminal cases are resolved just that way.*

—**Paul Butler**[1]

## Black and Blue

I met George Jones through one of his civil rights attorneys, and frankly, I was too exhausted and too overwhelmed to receive the introduction. I was convinced that I was writing a book about false confessions and wrongful conviction. George Jones did not fit those patterns.

I had worked for a year to assemble a sample of the one hundred false confessions in Chicago alone. These confessions, spanning decades of time, were scattered across the city: In dingy law firm file cabinets; in the hard drives and data clouds of law clinics and private attorneys; and in the files of civil lawsuits, where the false confession was evidence of harm against the wrongfully convicted.

Even with a team of four students, it was arduous work to get these confessions—getting on the phone, chatting up law clerks and legal secretaries in order to assemble the documents. I was looking for patterns amid the chaos; in the end, we found nearly fifty of the one hundred confessions. Given how hard they were to secure, it was a significant victory. But finding patterns across the cases, decades, and precincts took time and effort.

It was at this stage in my research that I interviewed Flint Taylor, the legendary civil rights attorney. Taylor doggedly sued the City of Chicago when the police brutalized Black suspects with physical violence, but I knew him best for his work representing the family of Fred Hampton, the Black Panther chairman who was executed by the Chicago Police while sleeping next to his pregnant fiancée.

It was in this interview that Flint first introduced me to George Jones, his former client.[2] I had never heard of George Jones, and I knew that he wasn't in my sample of false confession cases, even though he had been wrongfully accused of a crime. My inflection, at the suggestion of this case, was one of resignation; I trailed off, in politeness, as though waiting for Flint to get back to the confession cases. Flint made a barely perceptible "hmmm" sound, followed by a pregnant pause; I could only hear his subtle judgment after listening repeatedly to the audio recording of our interview after the fact.

George Jones didn't fit the pattern of my theory. George was a middle-class child. An honor student. A track star. A conservative-looking young man who wore collared shirts and thick Clark Kent glasses. He was even "blue"; his dad was a Black police officer. And most importantly, George Jones, when accused of a heinous crime, never gave a confession, and the police never created one for him.

Jones was a Black boy who lived in a Black neighborhood and went to a Black school, but those were the only things he shared with the other false confession cases.

This was strange to me. It seemed to challenge the blueprint of wrongful conviction cases that I had studied up to that point. What I had learned from my research was that false confessions are like a virus: They are contagious and potent. They are the most convincing evidence that can be presented in front of a jury or judge to convict a defendant. Just look at what happened to Lee Hester.[3] Like most jurors, I could not imagine anyone (anyone but the truly guilty) incriminating themselves, nor that police have ways of making the innocent do it.

Without a false confession, George Jones was an *inconvenient* case. Surely, he was a Black boy wrongfully accused and harmed, but he was an outlier nonetheless. But it was precisely because he was an outlier that I was able to understand that false confessions were merely one of many tools police had at their disposal to ensure a suspect's conviction. I started heading down the rabbit hole, following the George Jones case through Flint's memory, legal documents, old news clippings, and the assemblage of documents that was never intended for public view.[4]

What I found was a shadow system, a set of patterns and practices that allowed police to bury evidence like the dead and create guilt through omission and lies. This shadow system functioned just outside the gaze of researchers and the public, an institutionalized infrastructure that tampered with the investigatory stage of cases before they ever made it to court. And that system, that double system of justice, was built for Black people in America.

Even the son of a Chicago Police officer wasn't immune.

## A Pointer Family Nightmare

A Black couple on the South Side, Mr. and Mrs. Pointer, went to the emergency room during the early-morning hours of May 4, 1981, leaving their three children—ages four, ten, and twelve—alone. In that window of time, there was a break-in, and their children were attacked. When they returned, Mr. Pointer found their daughter dead, partially unclothed with her limp legs dangling from the edge of the bed.[5]

Sheila Pointer, the victim, was a student at West Pullman Elementary School. She sustained a massive blunt trauma injury to her head, along with multiple contusions and abrasions to her face and forehead.[6] Sheila was pronounced dead at the scene by Chief Medical Examiner Robert J. Stein. Later, the case's microanalyst, Mary Ann Furlong, would confirm evidence of sexual assault. The other victim,

Sheila's younger brother, Purvy Jr., was not killed but suffered deep lacerations on his head and sustained a fractured skull that put him in critical condition. The youngest child, Tiaa—the baby of the family—was thankfully left unharmed. Police noted that this case also involved home invasion and burglary. The Pointers' Sears black-and-white 19-inch television was recovered inside a nearby rear yard, discarded in a green plastic trash bag; after being processed, it was returned to its owner, Purvy Pointer Sr.

A parade of people stood vigil around ten-year-old Purvy's hospital bedside as he lay unconscious. For four days, the small boy was in a coma. Doctors thought he might have permanent brain damage. His skull was fractured from bludgeoning by a pipe, the same pipe that killed his sister.

Purvy floated in and out of consciousness while officers, including Detectives James Houtsma and Victor Tosello, floated in and out of the hospital room, waiting for Purvy to wake up and talk to them, even when nurses said that it was way too soon.

A lot was riding on young Purvy. The littlest sibling, Tiaa, was only four years old and in the house during the break-in. When police approached her with questions, she kept falling asleep.[7] Purvy was their only witness to a horrendous crime, and the officers did not have any other leads. The medical staff warned the police about possible brain damage and the significant likelihood that he would not be able to remember what happened. Purvy's testimony would be unreliable at best.

Such warnings didn't dissuade the police. The stakes were too high.

A case like this is hard on the police. A crime that featured breaking and entering, murder, and rape was undoubtedly going to get significant coverage in the media; the public would demand a resolution. They were detectives working in the Black part of Chicago, and in the police's view, it was a Black-on-Black crime. But what was to prevent such break-ins in other places—White places? Such sensational crimes brought expectations, pressure, press conferences, and the like. So they had an agenda: Get the boy to name a suspect before it was too late.

Seven days after the murder, when the doctors were finally able to gently remove the breathing tube, the officers were there waiting.[8] It was painful for Purvy to talk. For a while, he was only moving his mouth, and there was a suggestion that police should bring in a professional lip-reader to decode the contorted shapes his mouth was making.[9] Purvy was weak and ended up communicating by squeezing Detective Houtsma's hand to answer their questions. Once for "yes"; twice for "no."[10]

*Was it someone in your family?* No.

*Was it someone you knew?* Yes.

It was like talking to a Ouija board. The police posed the questions and waited for a disoriented boy to give them answers they needed.

Purvy whispered the name "George."[11] Purvy said he was a kid from the neighborhood, a gang member with a lighter complexion than his.

This lead gave the police a hunting license to find a neighborhood kid named George, and they came up with "George Jones." But George Jones was a high school senior who was known as "Bookworm" to all the kids in his neighborhood because he was smart, a do-gooder, a sensitive and hopeful boy with big dreams.[12] He was also the son of a Chicago Police officer. So when the Chicago Police detectives asked George's dad, their fellow brother in blue, for a picture of young George, Officer Jones likely complied without worry. There was a brotherhood that protected him, and that code extended to family. This was one of the benefits of being a Black officer in a still-integrating police department.

Officer Jones gave them a picture of George in a suit, ready for his upcoming graduation from Fenger High School. In it, George was dark-complected, nothing like Purvy had described. Police brought the picture to Purvy's hospital bed. He recognized him but did not respond when asked if George was the attacker. During the interview he said a last name that sounded like "Anderson."[13] Definitely not "Jones."

Cursory efforts were made to find another George to fit the crime. Police went canvassing the area and found a teen who knew a George

Brockman who was described as a "bad dude" who hung around the elementary school that the Pointer children attended.[14] Still groggy, Purvy didn't think he was the kid, so they took Brockman's pictures and prints and let him go. They found a few Anderson families who lived in the neighborhood, but none had sons named George.[15] The police encountered a twelve-year-old girl who had told some people that her cousin, Ricky Shaw, mentioned that he had killed the girl but the police noted that she was "slow," so they didn't bother to interview him.[16] An anonymous call claiming that the killer was Antonio Coleman went nowhere—the tipster sent them to a location that was a vacant lot, a literal dead end.[17]

So they stayed focused on the George who lived next to the Pointers: George Jones. Police figured that Purvy just needed another chance to see his picture. The next day the police came back to Purvy's bedside to show him George's picture again. At some point during the second interview, Purvy said: "Yep, yep, that's the one who did it to me," but when the officers asked whether they called the kid "Bookworm," Purvy apparently gave no response.[18] Other accounts suggest that Purvy started crying when he saw the photo.[19] He was no doubt flooded with emotions from memories of the attack and was unable to regulate them for any number of reasons. It was nonetheless on the weight of this uncertain statement—from a child recently injured with possible brain damage—that police decided that they had the right George for their crime. As they had in the Lee Hester case, they immediately went to George's school, Fenger High, to grab him.

George was interrogated at the police station. As he would later explain, he was threatened with the electric chair as part of the police's regular dance to gain a confession.[20] Despite the police's claim that Purvy had identified him as the killer, George maintained his innocence, saying he "didn't care" what they said or what Purvy thought.[21] Later, someone removed the context from the officer's investigative notes, making it seem as if George was "not caring" about the person who was murdered.[22]

Despite all this pressure, the boy never broke. He told them that he was at home sleeping in his bed during the time of the murder. His parents were his alibi, and their stories matched. But, as in other cases of wrongful conviction, Black people's alibis were negligible at best. In the Lee Hester case, his Black teacher, Ms. Webster, had known that Lee was in class during the murder, but police relied on the White gym teacher for answers.[23] And now this alibi, from George's parents, was treated as an unreliable piece of evidence even though the real killer was still on the loose. It wasn't because they were found to be lying; it wasn't because they were found to be untrustworthy or inconsistent in their stories. What mattered was that Officer Jones, a father who was blue, was also Black, and that superseded all other factors and even common sense. So an alibi from a Black person, especially one contradicting their narrative, was rendered negligible by the Chicago Police—a type of crucial evidence unseen.

With neither a confession nor physical evidence, a prosecutor suggested to the police that they bring George to the hospital for a "show up" at Purvy's bedside—a one-on-one identification usually conducted in a police station at some distance from the victim. George was ordered to stand a few feet from the traumatized boy. Though Purvy had been a witness to his sister's gruesome murder and was a victim himself, there was little acknowledgment that bringing a stream of strangers to his bedside might be terrifying. Having the supposed killer at the child's bedside while he barely could move or speak—this was the stuff of horror movies. Nonetheless, Purvy was calm as the nerdy George stood by his bed. George was wearing his signature thick glasses. He had that "Alex P. Keaton" look; he was a boy who wore a collared shirt like a Ronald Reagan Republican while his peers wore tracksuits and Chuck Taylors. Even if the police were trying to profile someone as the murderer, George didn't look the part, except for the fact that he was Black and lived in a Black neighborhood. He had the formality of a more mature soul, someone wise and sensitive. And maybe that was what initially calmed Purvy. He looked at George and said, "No, that's not the man, that's not the man, no, no, no."[24]

Two nurses, a prosecutor named Bryan Schultz, George's defense attorney, and Detective Houtsma all heard Purvy's statement. But Houtsma was not done; he ordered George to take off his glasses and step closer, which made Purvy waver, with a string of "yes" and "no" on whether this was the suspect.[25]

With the fluctuating answers from the only eyewitness, the police would have to "fix" certain details and omit others to support a guilty narrative. And because Black boys were viewed as blameworthy and interchangeable, it really didn't matter which one was accused. In their view, "one black person is the same as another black person," even a nerdy do-gooder like George.[26]

## Fabrication and Omission: Shading

Building a case requires policing skills. There is a process. Norms. Practices. Training. Know-how. Unlike creating confessions, case building is not just about creating a narrative with dramatic tension and visual imagery. Building a case requires "editing," omissions, and even lies. But neither the police nor the attorneys working the cases ever use that word. Neither do the attorneys working in the courts who receive these cases. Instead, they use the word *shading*.[27] "Shading" denotes the many grades of truth telling that are normalized for police to get their "bad guys." It's an artful technique used to construct a picture, brightening some of its aspects and obscuring others into the distant background.

Shading cases is an exercise in persuasion in which the officer frames information in reports or testimony to make a case more convincing for conviction. Sometimes it means altering the weight of a defendant to "match" the build of their suspect. Sometimes it means downplaying how long a defendant was handcuffed to a radiator while waiting for interrogation. And sometimes it means increasing the volume of drugs seized on a particular case so that it lands just above the felony limit. The tiny differences involved in shading can make a big difference, such as whether a person is charged with a felony or a misdemeanor, but it is always used to stack a case toward conviction.

Shading is also used to deal with "negative evidence," the type of contradictory evidence that can kill a case and cause a suspect to go free.[28] In such situations, shading means making sure that some memos, reports, and details go missing from the "official report," a name that gives legitimacy to the police's version of facts in a case. It sounds complicated, but in practice, omission is easy: Take fewer notes, bury exonerating details, keep certain details out of memos, and keep the case under police control. If it's not written down, then really, *it never happened.*

Nobody needed to know about the hesitancy and confusion Purvy showed during the identification. So those details were better left out of their files, notes, and memos. Some of the evidence enshrined on paper needed to be routed away from their "official reports."

But more on that later.

This process takes surgical precision, careful consideration of which facts *could* and *would* work to build an official account for the court that will, in the end, ensure a conviction.

The police rarely consider the ethics of the practice, nor whether any of the suspects are in fact innocent. The assumption is that the bad guys are nearly always Black, and blameworthy from the beginning. If the suspect is viewed as blameworthy—and a danger to society—then shading seems just and logical and is valorized among officers. So, when the police set their sights on George Jones, they immediately began the shading process. Their assumptions were written into the arrest report, which would influence whether George stayed in jail during his trial.

For this system to work, the police need to work in tandem with prosecutors to help anoint their version of truth. They are the prosecuting crew from "felony review"—a group of prosecutors whose sole role is to create charges based on their police work. The word *review* implies that these attorneys were exerting some type of oversight. But the reality of this shadow system is that prosecutors and police work hand in glove to create convictions.

Bryan Schultz, the prosecutor working felony review in George's case, had the power to file charges. Despite being in the hospital room and watching the inconclusive results of the show-up, Schultz said, "There's my murderer."[29] Regardless of what George wore, the fact that he was darker skinned than the suspect Purvy described, or the fact that he was not a "gang banger," as the police claimed, George was Black in Black Chicago.[30] And despite the doubt in the room, Schultz saw a criminal, not a bookworm, not a track star, and not the son of a cop. And to make matters worse, the police had created a report that was full of lies that incriminated George and left him without an alibi while excluding details that should have exonerated him.

A day later, on May 13, 1981, without any physical evidence linking George to the crime or a confession, a grand jury indicted him for six felonies: murder, rape, attempted murder, armed violence, burglary, and home invasion.[31]

During the bond hearing, prosecutors urged the judge to hold George in the Cook County Jail while he awaited trial. Freedom came with a cost, and a Black middle-class family, like the Joneses, would be at the mercy of the judge's bond determination. The bond was set at $250,000. To get their teenage son out of the Cook County Jail, George's parents would have to pay a portion of the total bond—$25,000—which they couldn't afford. George would have to remain in the adult jail as he awaited his trial.

When news of the case hit the media, they had their collective spin on George. Reporters called him the student who "had it all."[32] He was a senior, the child of a police officer, a junior deacon in his church. He ran track, was editor of the school paper, and was college bound. He was the neighborhood "Bookworm." However, very soon, the accusations from the police report that were read into the court record and circulated in the press turned George into a cautionary tale.[33] Even a Black student who "had it all" by day could transform into a dark suspect charged with a "rape slaying" by night.[34]

## Felony Review

On its surface, the process that transformed the police accusations against George into an indictment seems like a black box. Police were the authors of the accusations and were responsible for building their case against the suspect. But for George to go from his school to awaiting trial in a jail cell required an entire web of actors—from prosecutors to judges.

One crucial piece in all of this was the prosecutors who worked in felony review. Prosecutors evaluate the evidence collected by police to determine whether felony charges should be brought. They don't just have the formal power to charge; they have the informal power to protect the police and make their police work appear legitimate. These prosecutors in felony review were not conducting oversight, as the name implied; they were enablers.

Felony review can be seen as grunt work. It requires long, sleepless nights and being on call. If any duty is close to pop culture's portrayal of *CSI* or *Law & Order: Special Victims Unit,* it is this. There are ride alongs to a crime scene, reporters to keep away, and possibly a dead victim. All of it seems out of a movie, and nothing from law school can prepare you for it. In many offices, prosecutors working in felony review are often young, inexperienced, and enamored by the drama.

On the surface, the name "felony review" implies legal review of cases in real time, making sure that the actions of law enforcement are constitutional.[35] But the name is a façade, obscuring the way in which prosecutors work, hand in glove, with police. Prosecutors are yes-men with the credentials and the formal power to help sanction police's cases. Alongside the officers, prosecutors prepare the necessary paperwork for the cases created by police. The police interrogate and engineer a confession from a suspect, and the prosecutors memorialize the confession.

The police become mentors, teaching young prosecutors the protocols of investigations. If police are the creators, then prosecutors are the "finishers," and in that capacity are expected to play by the cultural rules of engagement. The most important of these is deference to police as the keepers and creators of the case.

As I learned from my research, there is an unspoken rule that questioning an officer's testimony or investigation is a breach of trust and respect, and it is considered a serious infraction.[36] But there are other, more subtle ways that a prosecutor can fall out of favor. Interviewing a police officer separately from their partner to ensure their stories are consistent with each other is perceived as a sign of disrespect rather that a simple cross-check on a case. For police, a cross-check on ethics implies an accusation and casts the prosecutor as disloyal or worse, an outsider unworthy of their support and trust. This can tarnish a career before it starts.[37]

When I worked in the prosecutor's office, I was taught to fear the police. I learned that these officers could ruin not just your cases but also your career and your future in the office. Police can ignore a prosecutor's subpoenas and can ghost prosecutors prior to trials. They can also shun, humiliate, and tarnish the reputations of prosecutors who don't fall in line. (They are also armed, and it was unclear how far they would go to stop those who dared to whistleblow on this informal system with so much institutional weight.) The remedy to this was to act with deference and obedience.

What is clear from my years of research is that police saw the creation of cases as "their" work.[38] In an interview, one prosecutor told me that their job became much "easier" once they had built up some trust with police. As they said, "It's so much easier, once they [the police] trust you with their case, because it is their case first."[39] When police handed those cases over to prosecutors and then to the courts for processing, they maintained a sense of territorial ownership and prosecutors were left proving their allegiance.

This partnership created a shared cultural understanding between prosecutors and police as well as a unified vantage point on the suspects they profile. Often, they referred to suspects as "monsters," "scum," or "bad guys."[40] This lens is racialized because the primary targets are Black kids. Proving the so-called moral failures and blameworthiness of the defendants is a shared project between police and prosecutors.

Prosecutors need the police to win trials, and winning trials is the only way to advance and get promoted in the office. Because the police are their star witnesses, they live within a toxic codependency: Prosecutors' careers are quite literally in the hands of police.[41]

As a result, many prosecutors would go to any lengths to back up a police officer's narrative, even if it meant lying. Indeed, to be a prosecutor, one had to become comfortable with the many shades of truth telling they could expect from officers. Prosecutors often let police officers confer with their partners before questioning them so that the officers could "refresh" their memories on police reports while the prosecutors left the room to get coffee.[42] These rituals allowed prosecutors to perform their loyalty to the officers—proving they were on the same team. The cancerous undercurrent of all of this was that lying (and covering up lying) was an integral component to police work.

Certainly, the U.S. decision *Frazier v. Cupp* (1969) essentially made it permissible, under certain circumstances, to lie to suspects during interrogation, but it was naïve to think that it would stop in the interrogation room.[43] Even in 1982, political scientist Jerome Skolnick showed how police perjury in New York was an accepted cultural norm. According to Skolnick, police lying was "a routine way . . . to compensate for [what officers view as] limitations the courts have placed on [their] capacity to deal with criminals."[44] In Myron Orfield's 1992 study of Cook County–Chicago judges, prosecutors, and public defenders, 92 percent of respondents said that police lie at least some of the time under oath at suppression hearings—a central stage of due process where judges can theoretically cross-check police practices.[45] The study also revealed that prosecutors admitted to coaching police on what to say on the witness stand. Perhaps unsurprisingly, perjury is called a dirty "open secret."[46]

Alarmingly, high-stakes heater cases, like murder and sexual assault, were often the ones where police were more likely to lie. Overwhelmingly, respondents admitted that judges were less likely to find police testimony unbelievable.[47] As the norms went, the hotter a case was, the *less* likely the judge would protect the defendant's rights and more likely to broadly accept the police's version of truth.

Clearance rates are used to gauge the effectiveness of police.[48] It is a measure of what percentage of their investigations result in a criminal charge (not necessarily conviction). In a very real sense, police "win" if they find a suspect, any suspect, to blame a crime upon. And yet, embarrassingly, police still struggle to clear cases. The United States has one of the lowest clearance rates in the world.[49] That is, for most major crimes, police don't even make an arrest or identify a suspect. The national rate for clearing a homicide—wiping it away from investigative responsibility—is approximately 50 percent.[50] For 2020, in Boston and New Orleans, for example, the figure was 30 percent; in Los Angeles, the clearance rate was around 55 percent.[51] Flip a coin; there is a heads-or-tails chance that you could kill your worst enemy and get away with it.

As for Chicago, despite its enormous $1.7 billion policing budget, the Chicago Police Department has some of the lowest clearance rates in the country.[52] Less than 50 percent of homicides and 85–90 percent of nonfatal shootings go unsolved.[53] And there is a racial disparity in these clearance rates. Clearance rates in Black and Brown neighborhoods are less than half of the clearance rates in predominantly White communities. By pinning crimes on innocent people, the police are able to inflate their performance as competent crime fighters.

In heater cases, the pressure to clear a case is adjudicated in the media and by the public. When a terrible crime is committed, the public wants resolution and reassurance that the police are serving their mission of crime control and public safety.[54] With their reputations on the line, police are incentivized to charge a suspect and wipe clear their investigative responsibility. They can then push it onto the prosecutors and judges to sort it out in the courts.[55] These norms have implied that in the most serious cases, there could be a groundswell of wrongful convictions hidden all throughout the system.

Orfield's study was conducted nearly ten years after the George Jones case, but it is still reflective of the trend.[56] In 2008, I conducted a study that found that judges and prosecutors willingly admitted that police perjury was part of their rules of engagement with officers.[57] For the minority of respondents who did not admit to the practice or chose not to respond, one had to wonder whether the denial was due to a fear of speaking the truth.

One prosecutor reflected that only when the lying was most apparent would they consider dropping a case. Otherwise, they just went along with the police's version of it. As the prosecutor described:

> Sometimes the Chicago police detective doesn't like to hear a negative response. . . . And there's the whole culture thing that I was telling you about [police regularly bending the truth]. A couple of times, I dismissed cases when it was clear that they were lying, but I was also younger, I didn't have perspective, and I was working on their side, so I'd let them look at their police reports for ten minutes before [questioning them about a case].[58]

Prosecutors often protected police lies with litigating skills. As former federal prosecutor Paul Butler has noted, "A very good prosecutor has the skills to convict some innocent people."[59] Once police had picked out a suspect, other police and prosecutors alike would often vehemently believe in their guilt, and this entrenched belief in the accused's guilt made even the most nefarious tactics seem just, serving a greater mission.[60]

In Chicago, both officers and prosecutors see defendants as "mopes"—the word they used to describe Black defendants when using the word *nigger* began to seem unsavory.[61] "Mope" is spat out with the same venom as the slur and signifies that defendants are unworthy social burdens. In their shared mission to keep the streets safe from "mopes" and their more violent corollary *monsters,* police and prosecutors are willing to cast aside any rights that might get in the way of winning a conviction.

Prosecutors and police saw Black children as already destined for prison, even a bookish, middle-class kid like George Jones. In order to rack up convictions, prosecutors pinned guilt on these kids in small, nonviolent cases, streamlining their convictions by stripping down due process to the minimum of legal compliance.[62] This strategy laid the groundwork for more punitive sentencing in the event that they were ever named in a violent case.

I saw many of these norms firsthand. The court call or daily docket was riddled with "cookie cutter" cases in which police would reproduce the exact same police report for a parade of different defendants. Drugs would "fall out" of defendants' pockets as they "fled on foot."[63] Most prosecutors and judges could spot these cases and the police officers they belonged to. But there was little reflection on the part of lawyers and judges on whether the police were violating lawful search and seizure protocols or implicating innocent people. The only time I ever saw anyone in the system pause this machine was when a judge took me aside in their chambers to teach me about these practices in order to bring me in on their "inside joke." The judge taught me that a certain neighborhood had an epidemic of "holy" pockets. Of course, the defendant (and neighborhood) was Black. The judge laughed at the "fabrication of police reports like it was a novelty rather than an abuse of power."[64]

Despite these due process violations, in order to reduce friction and keep the assembly line of cases moving, defendants were urged to plea-bargain—essentially, to admit guilt and forgo a trial. Plea bargaining was treated as a sport in which adjacent courtrooms competed to get the most "pleas" or "dispos" in a day. *Dispo* was lingo for a resolved case, but the term also implied that the case (and the defendant) was literally "disposed" from the court call or docket.[65] One prosecutor in this machine-like system was an assistant prosecutor named Dan Locallo, who would eventually lead the trial of George Jones. Locallo was the son of a police officer, August Locallo. His dad warned him to not always trust police. . . . Sometimes informants were lying and the police would put words in their mouths. Sometimes the informant didn't exist at all. And sometimes, like I had learned in the court, when police testify that they saw a suspect walking down the street and drop a package of drugs, it's usually "bullshit" but effective at catching guys "seven days a week."[66] He also warned his son about police's expectations for prosecutors; he knew police who regularly lied on the stand in the 1950s and 1960s.[67] He wasn't one of them, but he knew how it all worked. In his telling of this history, Locallo was shaped by these "open secrets" passed from his father, a police officer, to him, as a lawyer.[68]

Dan Locallo came of age as a prosecutor in the 1970s and 1980s. His superiors, other veteran prosecutors who worked in the felony division, at one time engaged in a game Locallo called harmless "gallows humor."[69] This game has two names. Sometimes they called it the "Two-Ton Contest." Other times, prosecutors more blatantly referred to it as "Niggers by the Pound."[70]

At the heart of the game was a preoccupation with quickly disposing of cases and people. Prosecutors would look at the weight of the defendant on the case file and compete to be the first prosecutor to convict four thousand pounds of Black defendants over the course of a week or month. Prosecutors were incentivized to convict fat defendants because doing so would put them closer to victory. While these experienced prosecutors played this game, the heavy defendants, regardless of what they had done, would get the best deals. Locallo reflected on these courtroom antics, even though he never played the game himself: "A lot of fat guys . . . were getting great deals. . . . Let's say a prosecutor's got a guy who's 350 pounds. Where the guy normally would have gotten ten years, the prosecutor might offer him a year. . . . Skinny guys wouldn't get offered anything."[71]

The game had no regard for the actual guilt or innocence of the defendant. No regard for due process. No regard for the quality of evidence in a case. No regard for the impact on public safety. No regard for individual lives and dignity. It was just another mechanism to incentivize conviction during basic court call and to have fun treating due process like a game. There was no room for innocence: Every Black defendant, regardless of size or weight, was destined to be convicted, pawns in a White man's game. And what was most appalling was that these ideas and practices had cultural endurance because Locallo's stories matched my observations decades later.

Locallo would eventually get a promotion; he was elected to the bench and served as judge until 2009. What is curious about Locallo's career is that despite his dad's warnings about the police, his firsthand knowledge about the George Jones case, and his awareness of the prosecution's dark, insider culture, on the bench he exhibited a consistent pattern that one may not predict: Locallo ruled with prosecutors in over a hundred cases where defendants sought to suppress coerced confessions. By Locallo's own admission, he was "asked at least a hundred times to suppress a confession by a defendant [who] alleged coercion."[72] He would listen to the predictable denials of detectives and also the felony review prosecutor who memorialized the confession for police. In every single case, Locallo sided with the police's version of truth: that the defendant confessed voluntarily.

As a prosecutor and on the bench, he achieved professional success in this system despite police duplicity.

To get a conviction in a big "heater" case like the Jones case took more technique; it involved strategies in the investigatory stage that I did not see in the courts. I just accepted fat files, filled with reports, pictures, lab results, and the like, never questioning how the police assembled them. Once evidence was in the file, it seemed fixed, factual, undebatable.

The events of the Jones case, the complicity of felony review, and the strength of the bond between police and prosecutors may seem too outrageous to be anything more than a feature or even an idiosyncrasy of Chicago, but this is not the case. On the national level, prosecutors expend significant effort fighting on behalf of police power. They ask judges to "adopt pinched interpretations of the Constitution and individual rights."[73] They are the blunt force behind the Supreme Court's approval of "racial profiling, pretextual stops, widespread drug testing, camera surveillance, and police lying to suspects."[74] When the police say that a defendant consented to a search and the defendant says they did not consent, it is the prosecutor's job to prove the defendant is not just lying but *is* a liar.[75]

So, at the bedside show-up, when there was doubt in the room about Purvy's uncertain identification of young George, it was felony review prosecutor Bryan Schultz who expressed his unwavering support of police and their story. After the show-up, Schultz would later testify that he said, "There's my murderer."[76] He wasn't just commenting on the case; he was commenting on his allegiance. Schultz was a loyal prosecutor, and he would be there to facilitate the police's vision. With the right spin and the acquiescence of the prosecutor, even an honors student like George could be cast as a "mope" and made into a "monster."[77]

## Tunnel Vision

Many legal scholars refer to the fixation on a potential suspect as "tunnel vision."[78] Once the police and prosecutors decided George Jones was guilty, they were more likely to elevate evidence that supported their conclusion—even as they ignored and suppressed evidence that could exonerate him. Legal scholars outline this predictable pathway of error but absolve the actors who do it, saying that tunnel vision is a product of the human condition rather than maliciousness or indifference. But Schultz's confidence that George was "his murderer" belies this theory. Schultz was putting into motion a familiar protocol.

Dismissing such tunnel vision as human nature fails to interrogate how these processes constitute a system, an underground bureaucracy of cherry-picking facts and letting other facts vanish as a matter of police protocol.

Once police lie, their lie becomes a nearly indisputable truth. False evidence provided by the police in the early stages of criminal cases infects all the later stages of due process and even appeals. Courts will generally not revisit factual issues on appeal, only matters of law and procedural rights. Facts, it is assumed, are for juries and judges to assess during trials. In plea bargains, defendants waive this fact-finding process entirely. But when the police control the creation of the facts—and thus shape the narratives presented in court—those wrongfully accused and convicted have little recourse once a verdict is delivered.[79]

Even though scholars acknowledge that wrongful conviction disproportionately impacts Black people, tunnel vision is often presented as a race-neutral concept. What many legal scholars will not acknowledge is that it is especially likely to disadvantage Black people, even an honors student like George. Black men and even young boys are imagined to be inherently more likely to commit crimes like murder and sexual assault. This racial imagination guides tunnel vision and acts as a type of "evidence of things not seen" that is inherently persuasive to police, prosecutors, and juries.[80]

## The Show

Dan Locallo was one of the prosecutors tasked with running the George Jones trial. To him, Purvy was the perfect witness for a jury. He was young, traumatized, and full of dramatic potential, the type of witness a prosecutor could really get behind.

They had a horrific crime on their hands. Vivid pictures. A dead victim and a brother writhing in grief. Locallo's team could simply show the jury the violent scene and point at the defendant, a technique used to heighten drama and pave the way for a conviction. But they also had Purvy. True, Purvy was shaky on the stand and during cross-examination; after all, he had sustained a serious injury to the frontal lobe of his brain. He would "perseverate" on the stand, answering appropriately in one context and then fixating and repeating the answer when the context was no longer relevant.[81]

But Purvy was useful nonetheless. At one point during the trial, Locallo pointed at George after a gruesome description of the crime. Then, under the guise of showing evidence to the jury, a member of Locallo's team pulled out the bloodstained shirt of Purvy's dead sister and asked Purvy if he could identify the clothes. Purvy let out a heart-wrenching wail and burst into tears. It was a cry so raw that Judge William Cousins Jr. called a recess and ushered the jury out of the courtroom. Jones's defense team requested a mistrial, and Purvy was guided out of the court, still hysterical. Later, Locallo admitted that he was both surprised and elated by the reaction. Purvy had amped up the drama enough to make the case front-page material. The next day's *Chicago Tribune* would read: WITNESS, 11, HYSTERICAL AT MURDER TRIAL.[82]

# 4

# Burying the Evidence

*If they come for me in the morning,*
*they will come for you in the night.*

—attributed to Angela Davis

Like other Chicagoans, Detective Frank Laverty woke to the headlines of Purvy's trauma on the stand.[1] It was a busy morning because Laverty was getting ready to leave for vacation. He was a fourteen-year veteran in the Chicago Police Department, and of those fourteen years, he had spent nine working as a detective in Violent Crimes—in Area 2, to be specific. Prior to that, he had been assigned to Area 1. For Chicago cops, Area 1 and Area 2 signaled more than just a location or district. These were the detectives policing the heart of Black Chicago. The original thin blue line between White Chicago and Black Chicago.

Laverty was not just a veteran of the Chicago Police; he was also experienced at policing Black neighborhoods and building cases for violent crimes like shootings, rapes, and homicides. He was seen as a good cop, one who kept his nose down and did his work, and he had received nearly sixty commendations.

Laverty had worked on the Jones case and found overwhelming evidence that Jones was innocent. New hair samples, new statements by a confused Purvy, and on Laverty's watch, a similar killer struck again, attacking another local woman while George was in jail. Laverty sent his memos with evidence to clear George to his superiors and was told by his Area 2 colleagues that the charges would be dropped—in part because Purvy was an unsuitable witness given his medical condition.

So, when Laverty read that Purvy was on the stand and that the defendant was George, he was astonished. Immediately, he called the main courthouse at West 26th Street and South California Avenue and asked to be transferred to Judge Cousins's court in the hopes of talking with someone to stop the trial. It was a lunch break, so the clerk handed the phone to the attorney closest to them, defense attorney Jeffrey Haas. "They got the wrong guy," Laverty said. Haas responded, "I think so, too, but who are you?"[2]

The fact that the defense attorney did not know Frank Laverty—a key detective working the case—was part of the problem. Laverty's work should have been in the discovery packet of evidence passed on to Haas and his team. But it was missing.

Haas should have known Laverty's name, and he should have seen all of his memos. But Laverty's work did not fit the incriminating narrative in the official report, so it had been removed. Police could "double-file" cases. They could route memos favorable to incrimination to the courts and bury memos and evidence exonerating suspects in file cabinets that were never meant to be seen again.[3] In policing vernacular, the files that would never see the light of day were called the "street files."[4]

## The Street Files and the "Official" Report

The Chicago Police have a tradition of vanishing people they want to interrogate. In fact, Homan Square was the industrial-sized, secret detention center where they interrogated people for days without booking them. Torture is always on the menu. Between 2004 and 2015, the Chicago Police vanished over seven thousand people without attorneys or even a phone call; nearly six thousand of them were Black.[5] People at Homan Square did not have access to a phone. Some were vanished for hours, others for days.[6]

Compared to being sent to Homan Square, vanishing files and memos may, on its face, seem like a lesser form of abuse. But the lasting consequences were that some unknown number of innocent people were routed to prison. George Jones was one of many on this assembly line.

*Brady v. Maryland,* described earlier, required prosecutors to give defense attorneys access to the full evidence against their clients.[7] The case represented a significant leveling of the playing field, giving the defendant a chance to fight their case with the same information held by the state. However, in practice, police have vast discretion to decide what *they* think is "relevant" to the case.

In any criminal case, especially big ones involving rape and murder, there are bound to be pesky details that distract from the overall goal of building a case against a suspect: fingerprints and hair samples that don't match, alibis and witnesses that place the defendants far from the murder scene, and the like. Those are the details and notes, often scribbled on file folders and written up in memos, that are consigned to the oblivion of the street files and never make it to the defense. Like hiding a body in a murky lake and disposing of the murder weapon in another location. It isn't just about hiding the items; it's also about dispersion and confusion. This is a type of slow violence that is enacted upon innocent Black suspects like a form of torture, a suffocation that lasts for decades.

According to law enforcement guidelines, police officers have a duty to make sure that case files and the official report are "complete and accurate."[8] This criterion places vast discretion in the hands of the officers because they (and they alone) are the arbiters of what is "complete" and "accurate." In practice, most commanders allowed individual detectives to decide what was relevant to any particular case. As a result, each "official report" was a perfectly crafted narrative[9] with cherry-picked evidence that carefully scaffolded a suspect's guilt. What resulted was a sanitized version of the case, with officers erasing what prosecutors called "negative evidence" that might weaken their case.

Frank Laverty would eventually take to the stand in civil trials that put the street file system under a microscope and he would admit under oath that there were no additional guidelines for what should be contained in official reports. Officers put in what they "felt belonged," which was usually less information, rather than more, omitting many exonerating pieces of evidence.[10]

Police had near absolute power to define facts in cases and then use these facts to paint a guilty narrative. They defined the standards, and they determined this fake cross-check.

This double-filing system was one of many dirty open secrets of policing, and it inevitably bled into the court system. Judges and prosecutors often looked the other way as police tampered with the cases that queued in the court docket. As one police officer said of the double-filing system that was used throughout the city:

> I would question them [judges and prosecutors]—"Do you think it's right?" They'd say, "Well, yeah, it's an accepted thing—you don't want to put a lotto shit in [an official] report, the less you put in the better." Well, the "lotta shit" can be something that shows the guy is innocent. But I was alone in my thinking.[11]

Everyone in the courts and the police knew these rules of engagement. And there was a blind faith in this double system and the street files. As they saw it, it served their mission to protect the city. By their logic, the "right" evidence would move forward, the courts would sort it out, and the "mopes" would be routed to prison where they belonged.

George's street file was thick with information that was never meant to be seen. Some of the memos were gathered by Laverty but not all of them. The memos revealed snapshots of the police culture that sustained the street file system and its reach. The logic of cherry-picking extended into so-called crime science.

In the Jones case, lab technician Mary Ann Furlong discovered that George had different semen and blood types than the victim. Even without Laverty's additional investigation findings, this scientific finding alone could have eliminated and exonerated George. But, of course, this information, like so much other evidence, did not even make the official report because it didn't fit the narrative of the police's case. Unlike academic settings, crime lab technicians typically work without independent oversight or peer review to hold them accountable to ethical norms.

Furlong was part of this untethered and unaccountable system. So when the lab findings disproved George as the killer, they were placed in the file of a related murder case but not in the Pointer file.[12] Furlong would later claim this was an accident, which a civil jury would choose not to believe. Using the street file system, police controlled all possible cross-checks on wrongful conviction.

Dan Locallo, one of the prosecutors working the case, left the task of sorting it out to the jury. But the jury didn't have access to all of the facts. It could only work from the official report that the police had rigged and crafted around George's guilt.

That George was the son of a police officer should have given him protection. Normally, there is a brotherhood in policing, unspoken rules that "brothers in blue" protect each other. Keep each other out of trouble. Get the stories straight when the worst happens, when scrutiny from the media or the judicial system inevitably comes for the police or their families.

But George's father, a Black officer, did not receive this consideration. The street files didn't just reveal George's innocence, they showed how White officers viewed Black officers and how easily they could turn on them and betray them. Memos buried in the street file revealed that they began investigating their fellow brother in blue, a breach of the brotherhood's code of silence; they disparaged him and mocked him by calling him "Daddy."[13]

The street files also showed how the police mocked the Black victims. There were memos showing that the Pointers were being investigated like criminals. They made fun of Mrs. Pointer with the term "mama," an affectionate term in Black English vernacular but one that I often heard used in court when referring to Black women. Police interviewed a neighbor who claimed that "Mama" was cheating on Mr. Pointer with a boyfriend who had a "pretty blue van," bought marijuana, and mixed with some "shady dudes."[14] It cast a Black family—the victimized family—as one defined by moral failings like a common "mope."[15]

In these street files, beyond the exonerating evidence that could have protected George was a window into how the police saw Black people and families. Even this term, *street* files, denoted a whole system of meaning. On its surface, it seemed race-neutral; these were notes taken while patrolling the "streets." But in my research studying lawyers and police working in the courts, *street* was also code for "Black." In their view, Black people were assumed to be raised on the "streets"; Black children were not considered children because they were "street-smart." "Street people," people who did not have housing, deserved their fate because of their moral failings.[16]

Buried in the street files were the true facts: Many Black people were innocent; *they* were the ones who were victimized by police. Victims were disparaged as criminal, Black officers received few favors. They were investigated, mocked, and dismissed as "Daddy" for the offense of insisting on advocating for their son's actual innocence.

## The Shadow System in the Light

Laverty refused to let George Jones's file stay buried. After he spoke to Haas, he drove to police headquarters, grabbed the street file, and headed to the court to try to stop George's trial, putting the files and the shadow system—indeed, the entire police institution—under an interrogation light.

Laverty would eventually pay for breaching the code of silence that governed all officers and prosecutors. Indeed, it was the expectation that police protected police practices and the brothers that upheld the institution. It was a code, a bond, a line that no one could cross. Whistleblowing officers—the troublemakers—were as good as dead on the street. As Laverty began investigating the case and reported that the wrong person had been charged, Officers Houtsma and Tosello confronted him for "messing up their case," with Tosello even threatening to "blow him away."[17] But Laverty did it anyway.

With Laverty's evidence in hand, Judge Cousins Jr. declared a mistrial. Four days later the charges against George Jones were dropped. Soon after, a supervising prosecutor, Michael J. Angarola, would have a message for Laverty. He was a career prosecutor whose legal talents and easygoing, affable nature had helped him rise up the ranks in the Cook County State's Attorney's Office.[18] He reported directly to then Cook County Prosecutor Richard M. Daley's first assistant, Richard A. Devine. But he was also part of the establishment and understood how the system worked as well as his role within it. Over the phone, Angarola would chastise Laverty for his actions and accuse him of being in collusion with the defense, a claim that Laverty would vehemently deny, even going as far as offering to take a polygraph to show he was telling the truth.

At one point, Laverty asked if Angarola intended to pursue some kind of criminal charges and waited to see if he would read him his rights. Instead, Angarola would give a prescient warning as a prosecutor and as an extension of the Chicago Police. "I'm not talking about any [criminal] charges against you, but you're in trouble at work."[19] When Angarola said "trouble at work," it could have meant any number of things. It might involve isolation or being ostracized in the office, removal from high-status cases, or any number of other professional costs as punishment for doing the right thing. But it could have a darker meaning, because Angarola, like other high-ranking individuals, was known for rolling with police officers who were interrogating with a side of torture.

There was nothing Laverty could do about any of this swift retribution or the looming threat of the consequences he could face. Laverty was a good cop, and within a tight community of defense attorneys, he was hailed as the "Serpico of Chicago."[20] But by freeing George and exposing the street file system to the entire city, he was now a marked man.

## Kissing the Ring

While George was still sitting in jail awaiting trial, two White officers were killed at a routine traffic stop, shortly after attending the funeral of another officer who had been killed only days before. The alleged suspects were Black, and they fled the scene. And the threat of three dead officers meant that the thin blue line had been crossed. It was a racial line, a line that represented order, and it required constant watch by the officers on patrol and the detectives who engaged in George Jones–style investigations.

This police murder became the ultimate heater case for White Chicago. The death of these officers ignited a hot fury among the Chicago Police. There was a racial animus in their fury, as though Blackness itself were to blame. It wasn't a time for words and the likes of officers like James Cassidy and his manipulative approach to interrogation; it was a time for war. To remedy the moral panic that was spreading from the police to the public, what commenced was the "most massive manhunt" in Chicago history.[21] Frank Laverty was on duty and would be forced to decide whether he was part of the policing establishment or against it.

Superintendent Richard J. Brzeczek assigned Lieutenant Jon Burge to direct the manhunt. Burge symbolized a style of policing rooted in heroism and duty, one that emphasized the burdens taken on behalf of the city. Designating Burge as the leader was a signal to all the Chicago police officers in the area that they had carte blanche to do whatever was necessary to put order back in its place. They would look for the suspects, but they would also teach the Black residents to *know* their place.

Burge was a legend among Chicago police officers, a Chicagoan from the South Side who had watched his own neighborhood "turn" Black. At the time, he was the supervisor of detectives assigned to the Area 2 Violent Crimes Unit, and he would later be promoted to the rank of commander.[22] He was also a military veteran. During the height of the Vietnam War, Burge was one of the military police assigned to a prisoner of war camp in South Vietnam's Mekong Delta. There, he interrogated enemy soldiers. Investigations conducted after the war revealed that U.S. interrogations included murder and torture such as the use of electric shock.[23] Burge, who was in proximity to these practices, "claimed to have killed an unknown number of the enemy."[24]

As a police leader, he was known for being "hands-on" in his training and his leadership.[25] He was creative, able to repurpose even the most mundane objects for pain. A phone book. A plastic bag. Alligator clips. A black box that cranked like a child's music box. Then there was the "dry submarino," an international technique imported into Chicago, but with Burge's own particular twist.[26] A plastic bag would be placed over the suspect's head; one benefit to Burge and his boys was that this technique would create no detectable marks. Burge would be next to the suspect calling them "nigger" and warning them not to bite through the bag.[27] His approach had an insidious intimacy.

The announcement of Burge's position of oversight over the manhunt was a signal to the rank-and-file officers that it was open season. Police interrogation tactics could spill out of the hallways and rooms of police headquarters and into the street. Indeed, Mayor Jane Byrne even stopped by headquarters for a pep talk and announced a bounty of $50,000 (this was on top of the $10,000 bounty offered by the Fraternal Order of Police). Byrne told the men to do whatever it took to get the suspect. Burge and his troops had been waiting for just such an order, so their work didn't have to be relegated to the shadows of the police precinct.

All around the Black Chicago, homes went into lockdown. Police officers under Burge's command kicked down doors, ransacked homes, and wrangled objects and people from their beds. The violence drew people to their windows to see the terror. The violence was a warning to all Black residents. Accusations against one Black person meant retribution for everyone.

The ransacking was more than destructive. It was a political project, a reinstatement of the power and segregation in the city. It was a signal that the only way Black people could live in this city was to keep to their assigned place or risk wholesale retribution. As one South Side resident commented, "When white people kill blacks, no one cares. It's just like an animal being slaughtered. It's no big deal. But let a White policeman get killed, regardless of how rotten or dirty he might be, and it's a city-wide catastrophe."[28] Upward of two hundred complaints over police abuse were filed with the Chicago Police from community members that included a fireman, a taxi driver, alleged street gang members, and of course many Black mothers.[29]

The manhunt went on for several days before the police zeroed in on six young Black men. A crew of Area 2 detectives, including Frank Laverty, headed to take the men into custody. Laverty was about to transport the men when Burge told Laverty to relinquish custody so that Burge could take them to headquarters, where he could conduct the interrogation *his* way. Laverty, an experienced officer, knew full well what that could mean for the six suspects, so he was direct with Burge, and tried to persuade him otherwise. In response, Burge scowled at Laverty. As Burge saw it, *he* was handling the case "right"; he *was* the law. From that point forward, Burge relied on an inner circle of trusted officers for what needed to be done. Laverty later said that Burge cared more about retribution and a "punch in the head" than the case being done "right" or by the law.[30]

What would happen next was, to Burge, both business and pleasure. It was everything that Laverty knowingly refused to do. The police would take turns on each of the men. One suspect would get a bag over his head—the dry submarino—and when he would maintain his innocence, the police would add a beating. In other interrogations, they used a cattle prod–like shocking device. They tied people to radiators and left them for hours; suffocated others with typewriter covers and plastic bags. They used assault as a weapon of war. Like the officers who terrified Lee Hester on the balcony of his school, they brought suspects to the police station roof to threaten them, with one suspect having his hand placed in a bolt cutter for added effect. Burge had trained his force so they could be efficient and professional at what they did, leaving as few marks as possible.

Normally, police did this in secluded areas, so suspects could scream where no one would be able to hear them. But on this occasion, the suspects were placed in various rooms in the police station, and the screams reverberated and bounced across the hallways, with officers matching the brutality of other rooms and escalating the terror. At one point, Burge entered the room where one of the suspects, Anthony Williams, was being interrogated. Burge cuffed Anthony to a chair and used a phone book as his weapon. It was an interesting choice—thick, heavy, over a thousand pages long. Burge literally beat Anthony with the names and addresses of Chicagoans, the weight of the entire city. He held it and swung it repeatedly. And then he finished it off with the signature submarino—a plastic bag on the head.

"Let's take the cuffs off him, take him to the staircase, shoot him and say he was trying to escape," Burge said. He then went away and came back with a showy, silver-barreled gun. Placing it next to Anthony's head, he announced that he was "going to shoot this nigger."[31]

What saved Anthony was a Black officer. He entered the room at an opportune moment, intentionally or not.[32] The torture paused for a moment, but there was an expectation that this officer would continue doing his job, a Black ambassador of policing, a sadistic twist that abused both Anthony and the Black officer who was now required to finish what Burge and his boys had started. After Burge left, the Black officer told Anthony to continue screaming to pretend that he was still beating him. Burge might be listening, so their safety depended on a good show.

Similar scenes were playing out in every room. Many of the officers believed that one of the suspects, Andrew Wilson, was the so-called cop killer.[33] Andrew was brought to a small interrogation room after being slapped, kicked in the face, and stepped on the neck. The tiny room had a radiator; Andrew, twenty-nine years old, having only a first-grade education, called it a "heaterator." He would be cuffed to handcuff rings on either side of the window. There, the "heaterator" would burn him, subtly, making it look accidental, as though the handcuff loops just happened to be located in an unfortunate place. An officer then brought in a brown shopping bag and took out what Andrew later called "little gizmos."[34] The electrical device was known among officers as the "nigger box."[35] It was a black box with a crank and wires. Another device looked like a hair dryer and had a plug. The box with wires had alligator clamps that could be affixed to parts of the body. The machine delivered rounds of electric shocks that caused Andrew to scream in terror.[36]

Laverty picked a side. He opted out of this night, and the act spoke volumes to his colleagues, especially Burge. On a night when so many of his colleagues were coming to see the big show, Laverty's absence seemed to be a silent protest—one that he was conducting alone. Saying no to Burge was an affront to the establishment, an establishment built through compliance, fear, and silence. A "no," especially to a direct order, was an affront to this entire system and could leave an officer "dead on the street."[37]

There were two kinds of "dead on the street." Both were meant to punish people who refused to be team players. One was where the other officers don't have your back if something happens. The other consisted of merciless harassment with the direct threat of violence, like a mafia hit that could come at any time, from anyone, and from any direction. And Laverty knew that Burge and those he had trained could stage accidents, hide bruises, whisper in your ear so only the target knew what was coming. He knew that people could get "disappeared." They could be taken to places in the city where no one could hear you beg for forgiveness or mercy. The police knew how to make murder look like an accident.

Laverty knew this but he still never saw it coming when it was his turn. Laverty was working a Sunday morning shift.[38] His assigned squad car had just come out of Area 2 Maintenance. He was driving down the street and was merging onto the Dan Ryan Expressway when his brakes failed. He pushed on the pedal, and it went right to the floor. Fortunately for Laverty, Sunday morning traffic was light, and he was able to ease the car off the side of the road in order to get it to stop. If there was any doubt in his mind as to his status with the Chicago Police, he didn't have doubts anymore. He knew that he was dead on the street because his colleagues were trying to kill him.

By the time Laverty came forward about the street files, officers had threatened his life by promising to "blow him away." Michael J. Angarola had already foretold that he was in "trouble" at work. As a marked man, Laverty had little choice but to kiss the ring and beg for forgiveness from the de facto leader of the police establishment: Jon Burge.

Laverty would try to make the Jones case seem like an "outlier," a "screwed-up case" that was out of the ordinary.[39] Burge didn't buy any of Laverty's explanations: "You're working afternoons and . . . nobody's going to work with you and the state's attorneys aren't going to approve your charges on your cases, and you're going to be dumped as a detective."[40] Burge also shared his outrage with other officers. As Laverty walked through the main detectives' room in Area 2 where anyone could see, Burge pulled out his gun, pointed it at Laverty's back, and said, "Bang."[41] The moment was right out of his time in the prisoner of war camp. If Laverty loved saving Black suspects, then Burge would treat Laverty the way they were treated—a gun, threats, and all.

Burge and his fellow officers would make a spectacle out of Laverty, transform him into a cautionary tale that all officers could understand: Stay in line and know your place. If the loyalty of a police officer came under suspicion, other officers could now say: "Do you want to turn out like Laverty?" and there was a shared understanding of what that would mean for one's career[42]—as well as their safety and peace of mind.[43]

Laverty was brought up on administrative charges because he testified without clearance from his supervisors.[44] Basically, he was punished not for violating any laws but for betraying the Chicago Police Department. Such internal rules made whistleblowing a type of criminal offense within the police department and its chain of command.[45] Although the administrative charges were eventually dropped, Burge made good on his promise to Laverty: He would never work homicides again.[46] They transferred him out of the Detective Division and ended his career as he knew it. They would anoint Laverty with the hero's assignment he deserved: He would oversee the new recruits as they gave urine samples.[47] No other officers involved were ever disciplined for what they did to George Jones.[48]

For those outside the police department, however, Laverty would have a significant impact on how detectives did their jobs. In 1982, a federal judge ordered an end to the street file system, reaffirming the expectation that police had to abide by the law.[49] Alarmingly, the order was later effectively reversed on procedural grounds in a related case (*Palmer v. Chicago*).[50] But the light that Laverty placed on the shadow system helped force the Chicago Police to issue a new general order in 1986 that eliminated the street file system in favor of general progress reports.[51]

In a sense, Laverty was the sacrificial lamb, trading in his career prospects for the greater good. There were many like George, and Laverty's sacrifice gave the city hope that the shadow system might be destroyed in the light. But the pressure to reform also spurred the police to preemptively try to fix the situation so the change could come from "within" their inner circle. A police commander issued a memo to the Detective Division of Area 2 with the subject line "Recommendations."

"The term 'Street File' should be immediately removed from the vocabulary of the Division. A term should be standardized to emphasize <u>the personal property</u> of the Detective. . . . at no time will detective personal investigative files be stored in Unit Administrative office filing cabinets."[52]

On its surface, it seemed as if the police were eradicating the street file system. Detectives could no longer refer to the street files, but even without these words, the street file system was still alive and well, in a new and insidious form.[53] Now, facts were more covert and harder to uncover, with more discretion in the hands of individual officers. What would once have been considered street files were now the "personal property" of the officers and therefore not subject to *Brady v. Maryland*.[54] Detectives could still conceal files and keep them from defense attorneys, and it would all seem legal if they just called them their "personal property." In a sense, this change in vocabulary was rooted in the age-old expectation, one even upheld by prosecutors, that police were the true owners of the cases in the criminal justice system.[55]

By comparison to the physical violence the street file system that operated in the shadows may seem benign, but the system was the workhorse of the Chicago Police Department. A side of policing that didn't require touching to get a false confession; these rigged cases could literally vanish innocent people off to prison for decades of their life. It was a slow violence that stole life from Black children and teenagers because once these young people went into prison, they could be expected to come out—if at all—as old men.[56] This system was so insidious that it would eventually be used as a threat while interrogating suspects. Physical violence and slow violence were companion techniques with the same goal.

## "Fuck *People v. Jones*"

Mainstream culture has little language to express both the innocence and victimization of Black children, but in the George Jones case, at the heart of the suffering were two Black boys. Purvy's pain was manipulated on the stand, used to implicate another Black teen. One trauma was weaponized against another. Purvy was another Black victim experiencing justice denied—a consequence of the police's failure to investigate and close a case without lies, distortions, and rigging the system. Purvy would reflect on all that he suffered: "Have you ever had a nightmare that's repeated itself over and over? Mine has been doing that for thirty-five years. . . . That boogeyman will never go away."[57] For Purvy, the boogeyman were those repetitive memories that circled in his thoughts and seemed to never die.

In 1987, George's family received compensation, with a jury awarding them $801,000 plus legal fees. The verdict included "punitive damages against the city, the Commander of Area 2, and ten police detectives and supervisory personnel."[58] In a grainy photograph, Flint Taylor and his legal team, the Jones family, and Frank Laverty wore celebratory T-shirts with the sum emblazoned across their chests.[59] A headline in the *Chicago Lawyer* read, GEORGE JONES GETS EVEN.[60] True, it was a victory lap amid the trauma, but despite George's smiles for the camera, he was now a different boy from the kid who earned the name "Bookworm." He had the classic symptoms of PTSD: nightmares, chronic depression, and anxiety attacks. While awaiting trial and unable to make his bail, he had fended off an attempted rape. He no longer was the sensitive, "hopeful" boy; he was deeply wounded.[61]

Dan Locallo, the prosecutor who led the criminal trial against George, called this outcome and the damages awarded "bullshit" and always maintained George's guilt, even after he was elected judge.[62] Locallo said his deepest regret about Laverty coming forward was that it ruined his death penalty case, because he believed in George's guilt.[63] However, Locallo gave little regard to the fact that his work, on behalf of the state, could have killed an innocent person.

For Burge, the "torture ring" had done wonders for his career.[64] It secured a high clearance rate for his cases, and it led to him being promoted to sergeant and then to lieutenant.[65] Accuracy was never in the formula nor in the Chicago Police's reward structure, but the clearing of a case was more important than accuracy, abiding by the law, or even the truth.[66] As the police saw it, the possibility of wrongful conviction was irrelevant because defuturized boys of this type were likely guilty of *something.* This racist idea made such preemptive strikes necessary and just.

There were career rewards for the boys' club that practiced this brand of justice. Prosecutors who won cases and looked the other way when police lied, vanished evidence, or physically abused suspects were promoted; many were even elected to the bench. Perhaps it's not surprising that from the late 1970s through 2007, no judge ever found a single act of torture to have occurred despite the hundreds of torture allegations made during suppression hearings, trials, and post-conviction proceedings in the Criminal Division of the Cook County Circuit Court.[67] There was an entire insular culture in which all of the players were part of the shadow system of justice, be it the police or the attorneys or the judges. Indeed, the same prosecutors who "sent police torture victims to prison" were now the judges who had the power to keep them there.[68] As the 2007 "Report on the Failure of Special Prosecutors Edward J. Egan and Robert D. Boyle to Fairly Investigate Police Torture in Chicago" asserted, "Eleven felony review ASAs [Assistant State's Attorneys] who took statements from suspects who claimed to have been tortured by Burge and his men have become judges, as have several other ASAs who defended against torture allegations."[69]

I spent many years researching and embedded in the criminal court system in Cook County—the same system that got Lee Hester and George Jones. I interviewed a sample of one hundred prosecutors, judges, and defense attorneys as they reflected on the practices that prevailed in the court culture. Judges admitted to knowing that police lied; some judges joked with me that they knew that police were framing Black boys in the same predictable neighborhoods—Black neighborhoods—and rather than doing anything to stop the practice, they were merely bringing me in on the joke. The shadow system was indeed everywhere in Cook County. But it took me over a decade to learn about the Jones case and its significance to the players that perpetuated this system.

In my interviews, a story from one defense attorney was particularly revealing. He described how judges loathed attorneys who were so "wet behind the ears" that they cited case law because there was the general sentiment that defendants, who were mostly Black, were undeserving of such rights and certainly were wasting the court's time.[70] He described an instance when he made the mistake of practicing law as he had learned in law school, only to be rebuffed and humiliated by the judge:

> One of my first introductions to the system was in front of Judge D'Angelo [not his real name]. I'm arguing back in chambers, and the judge says, "What's this motion about?" and I said, "It's based on *People v. Jones,*" and Judge D' says, "Fuck *People v. Jones.*" I was a young lawyer then. . . . It just struck me as a system that was not doing what it was supposed to do and that every participant in it was complicit in its failures.[71]

For years, I thought the attorney had made up a generic court case in his example. But then it occurred to me—this defense attorney was not only yelled at for his formality but for the loathsome case that he had the audacity to cite. The Jones case became a flash point for those working in the system. George was a Black boy who not only went free, but he was vindicated and now, in a power reversal, *they* were the subjects of scrutiny. One Black boy getting vindicated and freed was, clearly, one too many. And what made matters worse was that his case transformed, in their view, an undeserving Black boy into some kind of precedent that they were now obliged to obey. Instead of this being a moment of reflection or a call for reform, the Jones case was seen as an affront to the very system that these White attorneys managed in order to control and contain the supposed Black threats to their city.

This was a level of contempt for the law and Black boys that I found devastating because in this worldview, they still saw George's guilt as a foregone conclusion. For prosecutors in this culture, their failure was in not winning the prize of his execution. If attorneys held such contempt and disdain for one Black boy who was proven innocent under the law, what hope was there for any Black person who came before court?

When I asked seasoned defense attorneys who practiced law in these courts if they knew which judge could have been so hostile to the decision, most lamented that it could have been one of many.[72] Also, so many judges were former prosecutors who likely agreed with *how* the Jones case was investigated—minus Laverty's intervention.[73]

With the case having gone to court, I assumed that the street file system was also dead on the streets. How could something so publicly exposed for its own racist intent continue to survive? What I didn't realize, like so many in the city of Chicago, was that the police would find ways to sustain the street file system from its own ashes, like a phoenix primed to harm a new generation of Black boys.

## The Lost and Found

In November 2022, I was guest lecturing on false confessions and wrongful convictions for a Northwestern University class. I was Zooming in over a grainy feed to the "inside" of an Illinois prison, where incarcerated students were my audience of learners.

There I met Abdul Malik Muhammad. Malik, who was in his early forties, had a youthful face and energy to match.[74] He had to go to prison before finally getting the education he deserved. The more he learned and the better he could express himself through writing, the more he could speak the truth about his condition of being innocent and behind bars.

The prison system was killing him slowly. It was "Death by Incarceration" and he was one of many who were forced to suffer through the slow violence.[75] Because he was serving a life sentence, the prevailing assumption was, like so many men before him, that the prison would ultimately be his demise. All around him were young people dying before their time without warning, young men who, if on the outside, were meant to grow old.[76] And to be innocent under these conditions was even more sobering. As he put it,

> What this does for me, a person who is wrongfully convicted and serving death by incarceration with a de facto life sentence, is put reality into its proper perspective. A lot of prisoners will never see the outside world ever again and life in prison can end at any given time. . . . I am sitting here in this cage wondering what can I do to make an effort to shed some light on this subject.[77]

Malik was a star student. His lived experience gave him expertise on wrongful conviction, and he felt comfortable challenging me on my new research. "You're writing a book about wrongful conviction, and you don't know about 'street files'?"

Malik's voice rang out in the class with a hint of judgment, but I could sense that he was trying to save me before I humiliated myself. There also was an air of disappointment: like he trusted me to know more and to do better. I immediately began dancing around the question with a series of rebuttals that sounded more like excuses. I told him my book was about present-day practices and not the past. The street files—that was old terrain. There were policies in place to protect against them. My research was on police lying and the interrogations at the heart of false confessions. Yet, despite my monologue, Malik was unconvinced. He shocked me into silence with a one-sentence response. "You know . . . I have a street file."

It wasn't just a statement of fact. It was Malik's rebuttal to the myth that police were capable of reforming themselves or, at least, of complying with policies and safeguards as required by law. Malik's statement carried weight. The street files weren't dead. On the contrary—Malik was urging me to consider that they were alive and well, alive enough to put him behind bars for nearly twenty-five years even though he had resisted a false confession and had been tortured by police.[78] With his words, I was sent down the rabbit hole to chase a shadow system that had remained intact—a system that could imprison an innocent man like Malik and others, over forty years after George Jones was falsely accused.

Malik was one of many young people who could have been charged with the 1999 murder of a known gang member from his neighborhood. He was not in town on the night of the murder, but it didn't matter, because Malik's name reportedly matched a name given to police. So, like George Jones—who happened to be the closest "George" to the scene—Malik was taken into custody. For four long days, he was interrogated at Area 2.

The ordeal was hard on Malik; he was nineteen years old and could barely read or write. His cell did not have a bed, food, water, or a toilet. He had to urinate on the floor and defecate in his shirt in the interrogation room where he was being held. In this way they could humiliate him without touching his body.[79] But still, they struck him repeatedly and paused the beatings with threats. Repeatedly, he asked for an attorney, but to no avail. The police told him that they had two White witnesses who identified him as the killer, and *who would believe a kid like him?*[80]

The street files were tools of incrimination, a place where narratives were born and exonerating information, alibis and the like, could get lost. And the police controlled these files, buried them in file cabinets, and could use them to condemn Malik and others. But they also could take their act to the stage, so to speak. Detective Michael McDermott never got a confession from Malik, but would testify that Malik told him that he was the killer.[81] Malik claimed that McDermott pointed to a file cabinet labeled "Lost and Found"[82] and said, laughing, "See that? . . . Things get lost in there and things get found in there."[83]

Three other witnesses were tortured and therefore coerced into implicating Malik in the murder. One of them was Malik's cousin, Jermaine Bates. Jermaine was experienced in these issues. In a motion filed as part of an effort to appeal his conviction, Malik would allege that Jermaine had already been tortured by McDermott, and McDermott was trained under Jon Burge, and so many Black men in the neighborhood knew of the violence of the Chicago Police. For boys being interrogated by the police, if it wasn't lies and deception, it was a phone book to the head; if it wasn't a beating or a plastic bag tightened around the neck, it was a file cabinet of vanishing alibis and evidence. So Jermaine did what many other Black boys did to survive—he stopped his own interrogation by pointing to another kid. He had done this nearly seven years earlier in another case when he pointed the finger at a fifteen-year-old boy, Keith Mitchell, in a murder case despite Keith's factual innocence. For Jermaine, there was safety in doing this. It stopped the possibility of physical abuse but also prevented the cops from pinning the case on him. And at fifteen years old, Keith couldn't be eligible for the death penalty, so it was better to name a younger boy than an older one.

McDermott knew Jermaine and Jermaine knew McDermott; when Jermaine was back in the interrogation room, facing a similar situation he faced seven years earlier, in order to make it all stop, he knew someone else would have to pay the price. And that someone would be Malik. It was the only way to get out of the interrogation room. And Jermaine knew that no one would listen nor believe his word because in Keith's case, an entire jury could not fathom a world in which a respectable officer like McDermott would be capable of a lie of such magnitude, let alone torture. According to the National Registry of Exonerations, in the trial, the prosecutor stood in front of the jury and asked the jury to consider the absurdity of police framing a boy and mockingly asserted that McDermott "would have been in prison a long time ago" if he was able to lie.[84] In the end, Jermaine's statement was one of the many lies thrown at Malik to cover him in a cloud of guilt.

So many elements of this case cast doubt on the veracity of Malik's conviction. According to Malik, all of the techniques would be deployed: Documents, many documents, would go missing. Additionally, physical abuse, deception, interrogation, and the street file system would all be at work. It took four days to break Malik, but ultimately, the police created their narrative without him. In fact, according to

Malik, Detective McDermott would tell Malik how it would all end: "A jury would be more likely to believe White witnesses than a Black defendant."[85]

Malik would do real time; he faced a sentence of fifty years. He would go into prison as a boy and come out an old man. Prison, like the file cabinet, was a lost and found for discarded people.

Journalists had been writing about the street files in the past tense, and the blind ignorance of it all allowed me to believe that the lies told by the police were contained to manageable places like interrogation rooms and possibly the witness stand. The enormity of Malik's tip weighed on me. I fumbled because it defied the conventional wisdom and perhaps even my own theories about the extent to which police were culpable in creating wrongful convictions.

Malik told me to talk to his attorney, H. Candace Gorman.

Candace was known for her persistence. She was a local Chicago lawyer, a South Sider, who went from John Marshall Law School in Atlanta to arguing a case before the U.S. Supreme Court. She built her career in civil rights cases, where the stakes were high. But no case was more important than when she represented Nathson Fields, who was wrongfully convicted of a double murder and sentenced to death in 1986, five years after George Jones's arrest. In Nate's case, a death row case involving murder, there were fewer than ten pages of investigatory notes, all from the same day, the day of the crime. Nate was arrested over a year after the double murder took place.[86] It was as if Nate's arrest was a spontaneous event, an eruption of guilt striking him like a bolt of lightning from the sky. Police made Nate into a villain without an origin story.

Then Nate read about Frank Laverty and his whistleblowing in the George Jones case. Nate was convinced that there were street files in his case, and as Candace would later describe, it was like a "drumbeat" for Nate as he fought for his freedom while being wrongfully convicted.[87] Even his first defense attorney had a hunch about a street file. From the court transcripts, one could see that Nate's trial attorney protested to the judge about the sheer absurdity of such a "lean" case.

The judge asked, "Where's the rest of it?" And the state said, "That's all there was." And the judge said, "That's all there is."[88] No introspection. No questioning the word of the state. Only blind faith in police.

As he sat on death row, Nate filed numerous subpoenas, both with and without the help of an attorney, to get the missing evidence in the street file. They all came up empty. Some responses to his requests came with a tinge of mockery from the police as they gaslit the courts into thinking there were no additional notes. Ultimately, Nate would be granted a retrial—but not because of the missing street files. Attorneys like Candace considered them long gone. Instead, it was revealed that the judge in his case had accepted a bribe from a co-defendant. After being granted the new trial, the co-defendant was reconvicted in 1998 before being cleared in a third trial in 2009.[89] It would be another wrongfully convicted exoneree, Aaron Patterson, who would pay Nate's bail while Nate awaited retrial, making good on a promise that the two had made while they spent time in prison as innocent men.

Once freed, Nate would seek damages, in the civil courts, against the police who framed him and took so many years of his life. In the civil system, he would be the plaintiff, and the City of Chicago and its cops would be on the defense. Nate would even try to do this alone, pro se, without an attorney. That's when Candace stepped in to help him get damages.

Nate wanted closure, not just compensation. And to achieve that, he needed his street file. He wanted to be vindicated. From a legal perspective, the street file would allow Candace to show a jury just how much damage had been done to her client. But she warned Nate that she had little hope that they would find it. It was likely lost and never to be found.

Candace was a unique breed of hard-nosed attorney. She relished in the discovery process, in which the two sides of a case formally gather information and evidence prior to a civil trial. She could dig in and get her hands dirty in the details. Nate's evidence came in a box, and as Candace and her clerks thumbed through it, she saw xeroxed copies of what looked like a street file. Two hundred pages of notes that floated on the duplicated paper—notes that had never been seen by the original defense attorney.[90] Notes on business cards and scraps of paper with officers' handwriting on them. Information that was shockingly new on a case that was over twenty-five years old. She petitioned the court to see the original file because in her experience, there was value in seeing all the scrawled notes that could be etched on the manila folder itself or give context and clues as to the key facts of the police investigation that had been weeded out of the official narrative.

An attorney for the city said the original files were in a locked drawer in a lieutenant's office at 51st and Wentworth. The judge allowed Candace access to the drawer while the lieutenant kept watch. But accessing the file was not enough. She wanted to know more, but the officer was tight-lipped and unhelpful. He had no clue where the file had been discovered. He didn't know how long the file had been locked away, only that the attorneys had told him to provide access. He made sure that his answers were short and vague and routed Candace back to the court for what she said were the "games that were about to start."[91]

Attorney Dan Norland represented the City of Chicago and, by extension, the officers who framed Nate. Candace was a formidable advocate and undeterred by the back-and-forth that was about to begin. She was ready to play. She said to her opposing counsel, "Dan, I want to know where that file was."[92]

"Well, Candace, we don't really know."

It was clear to Candace that a file was missing for over twenty years and then was found. Someone in the city knew where the file was, knew to xerox it, and knew to lock it in a cabinet away from where it was originally unearthed. And now, there was a collective amnesia on the part of the Chicago Police. She doubled down on her demands for the missing files.

It would take another trip to the judge before Dan would come forward and concede that there was a file cabinet that had once housed Nate's street file. The judge would grant Candace access to see this cabinet.[93] She would go back to 51st and Wentworth and be brought to a room in the Detective Division that housed rows of similar file cabinets labeled by year . . . 2007, 2008, 2009, 2010, 2011. And then, there was an outlier: a file cabinet more worn and different from the others. It was labeled with dates that stretched from 1945 up to 1985. This file cabinet was right in the middle of the room. And the detective managing this room admitted that the file cabinet had been there for a while, but the rest of his answers to Candace's questions were a succession of terse responses like "I don't know" and "I don't remember."[94] Candace was in the game, and she knew it. She asked to look inside the file cabinet, but she was reminded that she had only asked to look *at* the cabinet, not *in* the cabinet. That would route her back to the judge for the next round.

Round two began. The judge granted her request to look inside the cabinet, but this time when Candace went back to the detective's room, it was missing, and a more recent file cabinet had been put in its place. This time, Dan looked shocked—almost visibly shaken. This may not have been his plan, but it was clearly the plan of the Chicago Police. To lift a file cabinet of this size, stuffed with forty years of cases, took a significant amount of planning and strength and could not just be some accident.

Dan would be forced to account to the judge. According to Dan, they told him they had moved the file cabinet to the basement because they needed the space. In round three, Candace would word her final request very precisely: She wanted to go to the basement, see the cabinet, and look through its contents. And the judge granted the request. This time, before anything vanished, Candace would bring two law clerks, and one of them would bring a camera.

She was routed to the basement level of 51st and Wentworth. After being led through the bowels and dark arteries of the old station, they would enter the police exercise room, littered with barbells and benches. There, in the back of the workout room, was an unremarkable door with a padlock on it. Her officer tour guide completed the combination and opened the door to the hot boiler room.

Behind the door, there was not just the missing file cabinet they sought; there were twenty-three file cabinets of the lost and the found, street files from cases in Chicago stretching over decades and eras of time. Candace was shocked. "Start taking pictures" was all she could think to say. Taking pictures was the only way that Candace had some guarantee that the twenty-three cabinets wouldn't vanish again. She wasn't sure anyone would believe that the street file system was still in effect.

Candace was advocating for the interests of her client, Nate. But this discovery meant that there was an epidemic of wrongful convictions, impacting generations of cases and countless lives. Vanished and discarded people who were languishing in prison while exonerating evidence was hidden in the depths of the 51st and Wentworth station. The thought she couldn't shake was that some of the cases in those file cabinets likely resulted in executions of innocent people.[95]

Candace unearthed a painful truth. The street files were alive and well. The reforms promised by the Chicago Police were only smoke and mirrors. The reforms were a sham that merely covered up that Chicago had a shadow system of justice that was systematically creating wrongful convictions.

Candace took a sample of sixty cases and was able to show "that more than 90 percent have information in the street file that was not in the defense file."[96] Put another way, the criminal defendants and their lawyers were fighting their cases with only 10 percent of the available information. And this uneven playing field was being fixed before the case saw a courtroom. The police had figured a way around *Brady* disclosure; by the time Candace was finished with the totality of her investigation, she would discover that about five hundred cases were impacted by the street files in these drawers. Many of the defendants were still serving time.

Candace got approval from a judge to contact the incarcerated people who might be innocent. But the news was mixed. She was only allowed to tell them of the file's existence, and they could only access their file if they had an attorney. Candace got as many volunteer attorneys as she could, but the work was ongoing, and most alarmingly, no new reforms were in place to stop the street file practice. So as she tried to fix the harm, it was very likely more cases were coming in and more street files were being generated.

But even if there were reforms, history predicted that the police would find new ways to do the same thing: construct a creative narrative around guilt through editing, omission, and lies. Candace had clearly "won" the game, but her success revealed a profusion of tragedy created by the Chicago Police—decades of mass wrongful convictions on a scale that could never truly be counted. And police and lawyers used layers of confusion, bureaucracy, processes, retrials, and other legal maneuvers to sustain this shadow system. There were denials and even the heavy lifting of file cabinets to obscure the patterns and practices of the Chicago Police.

One could dismiss the disorder of police's files as a type of outdated or unprofessional practice. But really, the mess and confusion worked in their favor. The more of a mess it was, the less likely that people like Nate and their attorneys could untangle it. Candace was forced to play this charade for months in order to save even one soul like Nate, and I felt the heaviness of that reality as I spoke with her.

There was only one question left to ask Candace after she described how she found the street files that were supposed to remain lost.

*How can this be reformed? Are there any positive paths forward?*

"I think all of the police stations should be raided and the files confiscated," she said.[97]

# 5

# Making Wolf Packs Real

*You think your pain and your heartbreak are unprecedented in the history of the world, but then you read.*

—**James Baldwin,** ***Life Magazine***

I met Omar Muhammad through his memoir and then took a leap of faith to email him about his story.[1] Omar is a writer and a truth teller. That is his passion. He likely could have written fiction, but the story he lived and the lies told about him showed that there was an abundance of fiction in the world. And some fictions are so perverse and painful that they can kill.

Growing up in the 1970s and 1980s, Omar was a typical Chicago kid. He was poor, but he lived in a neighborhood filled with family and friends. The summer brought carnivals, which would set up between the complex of buildings colloquially called the ABLA Homes.[2] To outsiders, it was the projects, but to him and his friends, it was just home. Omar remembers the older men of the community, folks with nicknames like "Chuckle-Luck" or "Chico" or "Page," singing those old doo-wop songs in the hallways of the buildings. There may have been crime, but Omar remembered that the kids of ABLA mostly felt free and delighted in the close community around them.

In school, Omar moved up two grades, skipping both 4th grade and

6th grade; the accomplishment was called a "double," which made it seem like a hopscotch trick or winning a game of jacks. Really, Omar was just a smart kid with plenty of potential. His most memorable teacher was a man named Mr. Cole. He was a Black minister, a tough disciplinarian. Mr. Cole pushed Omar, held him accountable, and cared for him. But what Omar loved most about Mr. Cole was that he taught him a lesson that no other adult had the decency to do.

Mr. Cole thought that he saw Omar cheat on a test. He brought Omar up to the front of the room and accused him of lying. Out came a paddle; in those days, Mr. Cole was permitted to swat at Omar's hands. Omar knew that he was innocent, and he also knew that Mr. Cole had told him that if he ever made a mistake, he should own up to it. Omar sat back down and reminded Mr. Cole of this lesson that he had espoused time and time again. Omar said that he could prove that he was innocent and only talking out of turn rather than cheating off his friend. He asked to take the test again. Omar got all the questions right. Perfect.

So, Mr. Cole called him to the front of the room, apologized, and handed the paddle to Omar. Mr. Cole told him to swing and then extended his hand. Mr. Cole was teaching a powerful lesson to Omar. Here was an adult capable of apologizing, owning mistakes, and repairing harm, an adult who understood that those with great authority and power should be held to a higher standard.

In Omar's life, only Mr. Cole ever lived up to those standards. Perhaps this is the origin story of how Omar was called to be a truth teller, regardless of the punishment or penalty. He resolved never to remain silent in the face of injustice. Omar was a witness, a conscience, and growing up poor, Black, and in the projects meant that, despite his noble traits, he was facing many liabilities.

Mr. Cole saw him for who he was, but what Omar would learn was that he could easily be seen as a threat.

Omar admitted that as a teen, he sometimes strayed from what he knew was best. He and his friends sometimes caused trouble, but none of them would ever harm, let alone murder, another human. But his knowing and the police believing were not the same thing. This was how Omar, like many boys before him, ended up in a holding cell as a teen, awaiting trial for a horrendous crime that he never committed.

The holding cells were adjacent to courtrooms where defendants awaited their fate in front of a jury or judge.

In that wait, Omar fell asleep. It was a deep sleep, from exhaustion or perhaps to temporarily disassociate from the trauma of it all. For Omar, many of his dreams were nightmares. In one, he would see everyone he knew, but the pupils of their eyes were missing.[3] It was as though everyone he loved had lost the power of sight, the ability to see what he saw or to know the truth. But this time, as he slept, he had a new dream and vision. It was a figure, a woman, sitting next to him, and a sense of calm and peace enveloped him. Her name was Lori. She had a soft glow of light around her, and she was smiling. Before Omar could speak, she said: "I am sorry for what has happened to you and your friends." She looked back at an old clock that hung on the wall and then looked at her watch. "Everything is going to be all right."[4]

It would be all right—but not for fourteen more years. And in that wait for justice, Omar would anoint himself with a new name of his choosing, one that reflected his power and survival, one that honored God.

He changed his boyhood name, which was Omar Saunders, and became Omar Muhammad, the man called to be a truth teller for himself and his friends. Omar honed his truth-telling skills by first exposing the truth in his case, and he did it against all the odds. The police tried to make him small and disposable. They tried to reduce Omar Saunders into just another boy who was part of the "Roscetti Four" wolf pack.

Time would tell that Omar would not accept becoming a scapegoat for a crime that police could not solve. From the ashes, the teenager, Omar Saunders, would rise into the adult, Omar Muhammad, and free himself and others.

## The Crimes Against Omar

Omar was eighteen years old when he and three of his younger childhood friends were charged in a high-stakes "heater" case.[5] When Lori Roscetti, a White student at Chicago's Rush University Medical College, was sexually assaulted and murdered, an army of police officers were assigned to guard the school—a border between White Chicago and Black Chicago. It was 1986, and Black people from the ABLA projects couldn't cross over into the affluent school neighborhood without harassment by police. Like the frenzy started by Mrs. Keane's murder in the 1960s, images of the beautiful, young Lori ignited a familiar moral panic. Omar remembers seeing images of Lori everywhere; perhaps they inspired the vision of her in his dream.

Media coverage of Lori's virtue spread through the news: a hard-working girl with big dreams of being a doctor, a girl walked to her car by a responsible friend.

Lori was also a "Roscetti," and thus an extension of all "ethnic" White Chicagoans with Italian-sounding surnames. News of a Roscetti being murdered was a reminder that one of their daughters could be next. In fact, her body was found only two miles from Chicago's Bridgeport neighborhood, a White enclave known for being a "policing" neighborhood. Some residents were actual police, and some were just White people acting as racial vigilantes, assaulting Black people if they came through their neighborhood. This murder was considered close enough to Bridgeport to signal a threat to its inhabitants.[6]

These heater cases catalyzed fear around urban centers, especially when the victims were White women. They put pressure on police to solve these crimes before danger could strike again. Such pressure usually came from the media headlines, but this case was so inflammatory that it drew protesters to the police station itself. Soon after Lori's murder, a group of about twenty angry residents descended on the local police headquarters to protest the violence in the area and demand that police solve her case quickly.[7]

But the police couldn't solve it. Months went by; the case went cold. In January 1987, the Chicago Police turned to an FBI profiler named Robert Ressler. Ressler consulted on the case and reviewed all the police reports and crime scene photos. He concluded that Lori had pulled up to a stoplight and "some people had blocked the car, and one had pulled a door, which happened to be open, even though she had thought it was locked. These people then forced her to drive to the somewhat isolated location, where they had raped, killed and robbed her."[8]

In saying "these people," Ressler was edging close to his real intent. In the vernacular of court culture and policing, using phrases like "them" or "these people" to refer to defendants was a way to talk about them as a second and lesser class of people. Such terms were mostly used to talk about Black people.[9] Ressler told the Chicago Police that the incident was gang-related and instructed them explicitly to look for "black youths, somewhere between three and six males, ranging in age from fifteen to twenty, who would have previously been in jail and who lived close by the scene of the abduction and the railroad trestle where Roscetti had been killed."[10] He would eventually write a book titled *Whoever Fights Monsters.* In his book, he would reflect that if he had known the term *wilding,* which was popularized during the Central Park Five case three years later, he would have used it to describe the profile of those who had likely killed Lori Roscetti.[11]

It would be easy to cast Ressler and the Chicago Police as creating the "wolf pack" profile itself, a trope that seemingly has its origins in the "superpredator era." However, the truth is that Ressler was merely mobilizing a tactic that transcends generations.

## Imagining the Wolf Pack

Starting in the 1980s and extending well into the 1990s, there was a renewed media frenzy built upon the myth that Black children were growing up to be more monstrous than those of previous generations. Influential criminologists of the 1990s played with numbers and got it terribly wrong. They issued predictions of a vast crime wave that was going to rip through American cities like an epidemic. They developed their own racially infused vocabulary to describe who was to blame: "superpredators," "radically impulsive," "brutally remorseless," "elementary school youngsters who pack guns instead of lunches" and who "have absolutely no respect for human life."[12]

Two of the academic ringleaders, John Dilulio and James Fox, gained fame and regard within the field of criminology for these bogus claims that the criminology establishment never challenged nor questioned. Their predictions were wrong: "In fact, violent juvenile crime rates started to fall in the mid-1990s. By 2000, the juvenile homicide rate stabilized below the 1985 level."[13] However, even with misleading data and analysis, politicians articulated an explicit goal of "heeling" their collective threat through the 1993 Crime Bill.[14]

> Just as in a previous generation, we had an organized effort against the mob. We need to take these people on. They are often connected to big drug cartels; they are not just gangs of kids anymore. They are often the kinds of kids that are called super predators. No conscience, no empathy. We can talk about why they ended up that way, but first we have to bring them to heel.[15]
>
> —Hillary Clinton

I am old enough to remember the rallying cry by Hillary Clinton and other prominent Democrats as well as Republicans because these boys in question were in my age cohort. This was not "coded language"; it was not racism with veiled niceties.[16] It was explicit. Poor Black and Brown children were described in the metaphors of animals and contaminants and mutations of a virus. A new threat for the era and a politically potent enemy for both sides of the political aisle.[17]

And given how racially segregated the United States is, this depiction of Black children as predators might be the only lens through which most White people will ever understand Black people.

The media of the 1980s and 1990s focused on these types of "predators" working in tandem—in wolf packs—like coordinated animals on a hunt in cities like Chicago. And it wasn't just the news media that turned groups of boys into packs of predators. Hollywood too had a love affair with this drama.

*Lean on Me* was an award-winning movie released in 1989, the height of the superpredator era.[18] It was based on a true story, so any creative license taken by a White filmmaker, such as screenwriter Michael Schiffer, was interpreted as truth. The whole thing was made worse by one key casting move: Morgan Freeman, the voice of God, was cast as the Black, bat-wielding principal who resorted to violence in order to keep Black teens in line. This was not Omar's Mr. Cole; Freeman's character was a Black educator who ran his school with fear and an iron fist.

When I was in middle school, our teacher rolled in a TV on a stand for "movie day," and the kids all begged for *Lean on Me.* The movie begins with a flashback to Eastside High in 1967, showing mostly White teens dressed in neatly pressed shirts, skirts, and sweaters. The halls are portrayed with White nostalgia somewhat like the set of *Happy Days* until you see the dark and slow transformation of time and racial integration. The hallways clear, the music changes, and mobs of teens seem to invade the graffitied hallways of the school, a "troublesome" school "turned" Black, much in the way that Englewood was.

"Welcome to the Jungle" by Guns N' Roses becomes the soundtrack of the violent mob scene—the music not so subtly equating these kids and their school as a place *of* animals *for* animals. A light-skinned girl gets bullied in the bathroom by darker-skinned Black girls, only to get sexually assaulted in the hallway while her terrified teacher tries to clothe her. Sinks are ripped from the walls and fly through the windows as Black boys laugh at the destruction. A teacher, beaten, leaves bloodied on a stretcher.

This film touts a message of racial uplift, a Bill Cosby–style pull-up-your-pants politics of "personal responsibility" that inevitably blamed poverty and violence on the victims. The movie was about education, tough (when not violent) "love" by Black educators, and the prospect of redemption through respectability. In one climactic scene, a huge group of primarily Black teens is rounded up by the principal, Joe Clark (Freeman), and brought to the auditorium stage. More obedient students sit in the audience as Clark commences a monologue that devolves into a "racial degradation ceremony" with the superpredator talking points of the time. Clark's words transform the teens into an immoral spectacle for White audiences to see:

> These people have been here up to five years and done absolutely nothing. These people are drug dealers and drug users. They have taken up space. They have disrupted this school. They have harassed your teachers. And, they have intimidated you. Well, times are about to change. You will not be bothered in Joe Clark's school. These people are incorrigible. And, since none of them could graduate anyway, you are all expurgated. You are dismissed. You are out of here forever.

Sociologically, such ceremonies are meant to express profound "moral indignation"; the "ritual destruction of a person being denounced . . . is intended literally."[19] And more important, these ceremonies are a trial of sorts, a morality court in which the people being denounced are convicted of being profane—all the while an audience watches and issues their implicit judgment.

With Freeman, a Black actor, as the mouthpiece of this doctrine, it buffered the racist intent and the political climate in which this movie could be a hit. In fact, Schiffer, the screenwriter, even gives Freeman the phrase "these people," as if to distinguish, for the benefit of White viewers, between "blameworthy" and "respectable" Black people. The Black boys are portrayed as nothing more than dealers and users, unconcerned about education, determined to do nothing rather than work—incorrigible, unredeemable, and not able to be reformed. The claim that the boys wouldn't have been able to "graduate anyway" is tinged with the eugenicist ideology about the "low IQ" or supposedly low cognitive ability of Black people. According to Clark, these boys were just taking up space.

The solution to the problem of Black boys was expurgation—a literal removal of that which is unsuitable and profane. Clark tells them they are dismissed: "You are out of here forever." A Black "dean of security" plays the henchman, Clark's avenging angel. He taunts the boys with a "kiss" and a wave, pushing them out of the school with gusto. But make no mistake, audiences imagined these types of boys being routed to incarceration *forever.*

White Americans living in segregated spaces saw movies like *Lean on Me* as a profound warning. Hollywood's portrayal of a Black school affirmed their racist fears for a new generation: Black kids were a problem to be solved. Ghettos were incubators, and solutions like containment, heeling, and expurgation were a necessary burden that society must bear.[20] And having separate and unequal criminal justice systems (and, indeed, school systems) was made to seem natural and proper.[21]

In the same year that *Lean on Me* was released, the Central Park Five case ignited in the news, as a monumental heater case that garnered national attention. A twenty-eight-year-old investment banker named Trisha Meili was raped, beaten, and left for dead in New York City's Central Park. Within hours, the case was pinned on five innocent boys.[22] Perhaps it is no surprise, given the cultural climate of the time, that what police said these innocent boys did seemed plausible to Americans across the political spectrum.

Cases like the Central Park Five dramatized the intricacies of how Black packs of kids supposedly worked when they had strength in numbers. It gave Americans a shared imagination of race—no different from how Americans saw *The Birth of a Nation* as a fiction born of reality.[23]

In the days after the attack of the Central Park jogger, a *New York Daily News* headline read: WOLF PACK'S PREY—sending a clear signal that predators work in the plural, hunting together after spotting their target.[24] In this case, the prey was a White woman, successful and wealthy. She was "repeatedly raped, viciously beaten, and left for dead by a wolf pack of more than a dozen young teenagers."[25] The reporting claimed there were more than five (maybe as many as thirty), and they were accused of sexual assault as the culmination of a crime spree. The six boys in custody, ages thirteen to seventeen, were described as "savages," and it was heavily implied that there were more savages still out on the loose.[26]

Police called it a "crime of opportunity."[27] As criminologists understand it, a crime of opportunity occurs when a perpetrator sees a chance to commit an unplanned act of deviance. The phrase implied that Black teens were always criminals waiting to attack White women, if given the opportunity. This served as a national warning: Unattended White women could end up victims of the same savagery if they were not protected. In decades past, the solution was the lynch mob. In our time, the solution was the police.

## The Wolf Pack Technique

Lawmakers passed new, draconian laws that made it easier for police to fulfill this mission. Promises to vanish these boys were made good with the introduction of harsh laws criminalizing youth. Three-strikes laws were ratcheted up around the nation, as was the war on drugs and other policies that fueled mass incarceration.[28] There was a movement to charge juveniles, particularly Black boys, as adults.[29] These types of policies codified racist beliefs into law, and they had a large impact. Between 1992 and 1999, forty-seven states and the District of Columbia revised their juvenile transfer laws and increased the number of children tried in adult courts and incarcerated in adult prisons.[30]

The "mob action" law in Illinois was one of the many examples of this trend.[31] "Mob action" implied large unruly masses of people, but legally, it could be deployed against as few as two people, and the police had total discretion as to what the offense would be. These laws were enforced almost exclusively in Black neighborhoods. The "mob" could be two boys standing on the sidewalk and blocking a walkway or playing music too loud, or being in possession of cannabis near each other, or drinking alcohol socially and in public, a staple of rebellion for many youth.

And if more than one Black kid did commit a petty crime together, like stealing or shoplifting, the police could now charge them with that crime as well as "mob action," which would give them two felonies in one effort.[32] Any next offense, no matter how small, would make them a "Class X" felon, and that meant they were not eligible for probation and must serve from six to thirty years in prison.[33]

Laws like this that layered on charges and marked certain boys as criminals set up a feeder system for another technique, wrongful conviction. Wrongful conviction was less an official policy than a tried-and-true practice, like the street file system or lying under oath. All of these allowed police to "fight crime" by implicating groups of innocent Black boys with little regard for accuracy.

Wrongful conviction could be weaponized—not just against one Black boy but many. In fact, creating a hair ball of accusations, twisting and tying unrelated boys to horrendous crimes, like they did to the Central Park Five, served an end: It allowed police to round up Black boys and eliminate them more efficiently, in one fell swoop. It was the corollary to what was happening in the criminal courts. While prosecutors were playing "Niggers by the Pound," a game that rewarded them for convicting the greatest sheer quantity of Black people without regard for guilt or innocence, police were scooping up suspects and letting the legal system sort it out. But the courts weren't sorting anything out.

Indeed, politicians like Hillary Clinton and Joe Biden gave the police a call to arms—not unlike the one given to Jon Burge. In a 1993 speech on the Senate floor before a scheduled vote on crime control, Senator Joe Biden said this:

> Unless we do something about that cadre of young people, tens of thousands of them, born out of wedlock, without parents, without supervision, without any structure, without any conscience developing. . . . A portion of them will become the predators 15 years from now and Madam President, we have predators on our streets. . . . They are beyond the pale, many of those people. . . . We have no choice but to take them out of society.[34]

Biden's message vindicated a long-standing criminal justice strategy with a very simple logic: Why charge one Black boy when you can charge many? Such convictions stuck because police had so many levers to implicate Black boys and because the public had so many narratives of fear and racism to draw on: fear of Black boys and their nature, fear of what grows in the "ghetto," and fear that such terror leak over into White places.[35]

Even when science, alibis, and DNA proved otherwise, the police would double down on the collective guilt of suspects by charging even more kids with the crime, an "anthill" strategy that insinuates a piling on of disorder and violence, like an infestation.[36] Police use a strategy of excess, adding more and more Black boys to the case. And with each new case built upon these narratives and lies, the cycle of belief is reaffirmed.

Imagine ants piled on top of each other as they swarm over a treat. Known for working together with brute strength disproportionate to their size, ants serve as an effective metaphor in projecting animalistic qualities on Black boys. Implied in the metaphor when used to describe cases involving rape was the idea that the "treat" to pile on was a White woman. Beyond this metaphor but parallel in meaning, it may be no surprise that many of the boys in wolf pack cases are portrayed as "gangbangers." This term has historically implied gang affiliation or the "bang bang" of shooting a gun. However, it also has another dark association, where *bang* could imply a group sexual assault of a White woman. These overlapping associations, applied to Black boys acting in "packs," triggered multiple racist tropes.

Many Americans have come to think of the Central Park Five as one misguided, racially biased mistake. A singular tragedy rather than a trend. However, history tells a different story, and that story is nationwide in scale.

Chicago and many other cities had similar cases that predated the Central Park Five. Indeed, depending on the time and place you grew up in, an iconic wolf pack case may come to mind. All of these cases mimic an iconic case from the South—the Scottsboro Boys of the 1930s. In 1931, nine Black teenagers were riding on a freight train in northern Alabama when a racially charged fight erupted after a White man allegedly stepped on the hand of one of the Black teens. As a result, the men were forced to get off the train. Removing the White men rather than the Black teens was an affront to the Jim Crow order and meant that there would be retribution.The White men devised a story about assault. One of two White women who might have been facing criminal charges of vagrancy and illegal sexual activity falsely accused the Scottsboro Boys of raping her and the other woman.[37]

The oldest Scottsboro boy was seventeen; the youngest Scottsboro boy was younger than Lee Hester, only twelve years old. Another was nearly blind. All but one were convicted by all-White juries and sentenced to death. The trial of twelve-year-old Roy Wright ended in a hung jury because the jurors were disappointed that the prosecutor was seeking only life in prison rather than the death penalty, due to his age. Any argument that Roy was too young to be put to death was inexcusable. Those jurors protested their opposition to leniency by holding out for the death penalty, which prevented a unanimous verdict.[38] While the Supreme Court demanded a retrial on the basis that the boys did not have proper legal representation, the retrials that followed in Alabama were marred by the same racial prejudice and hostility and were mostly pageantry.[39] All were convicted again despite recanted testimony and weak evidence; the group collectively served over one hundred years in prison, with the last one freed in 1950.

What I would learn was that the wolf pack concept wasn't just an idea or trope. It was a tried-and-true *technique* used to vanish Black children forever.[40] It allowed police to disappear those boys deemed "defuturized" and vanish them, preemptively, to serve the greater good. The superpredator myth of the 1980s and 1990s ignited the proliferation of such cases. It unleashed a new blood lust for this technique—a bloodlust driven by the public and its politicians and carried out by the police.

There were so many wolf pack cases in my sample of wrongful convictions that my research assistants and I spent weeks carefully vetting which cases would be included in the book and which falsely accused teens would have their story told. Among the eight wolf pack cases that we were considering, there were nearly fifty kids and young adults who deserved to have their stories told. We were drowning in cases. Our meetings were solemn. Each research assistant was a specialist in a case, and each made an impassioned argument for why *their* case should be included in the book. And yet, in these meetings, the real takeaway was how *similar* all of these cases were—repetitive, even. There were familiar characters and scenarios that police duplicated time and time again.

Inevitably, so much suffering was left on the cutting room floor, so to speak. There was a heavy guilt in not including every boy, teen, or young man that we could. However, in that process, we could see the magnitude and gravity of what the Chicago Police had done to so many Black boys across the generations.

In Ressler's assessment of the Roscetti case, he was calling on the Chicago Police to assemble a wolf pack in order to speed up the process of making an arrest.[41] Chicago Police had their hunting license, and no Black child in ABLA was safe. Ressler's stature as an FBI agent lent legitimacy and power to this call to arms. Police would have open access to questioning all the Black boys of ABLA, and it was all normalized as good, old-fashioned crime fighting.

## Hunting for Their Pack

The murder of Lori Roscetti brought tension to Omar's neighborhood.[42] The Chicago Police started bringing people in and pressuring them to talk about the Roscetti case. One of them was Larry Ollins, sixteen years old. In the neighborhood, he was affectionately known as "Lil Larry." Omar and Larry had had years of innocent fun together, playing tackle football or doing flips off the fences that surrounded their buildings.

When Larry was thirteen years old, he was implicated in the battery of an eleven-year-old boy. He was hanging around with the wrong kids and, by proximity, had been charged, along with the others, in a wolf pack case. He was interrogated, and in his bewilderment he signed a false confession. This resulted in a two-year sentence in juvenile detention. This trauma taught Larry what the Chicago Police were capable of doing. And he knew that resisting a false confession was the most important thing he could do to protect himself from getting pinned with Lori's murder.

But now, as an older teen, Larry would get the full Burge-style treatment. He was interrogated and threatened, and when that didn't work, the police escalated their tactics to physical abuse. And yet no matter how bad the beatings got, Larry knew, at all costs, not to confess.

Without a confession, police had no choice but to let Larry go free—at first. Larry's initial thought was to warn his friends that the Chicago Police were coming for them, coming for all the Black boys who lived in the projects.

The police's next target, Marcellius Bradford, had an even messier record that supplied the police with more pressure points they could use. Whereas Omar had been a star student, Marcellius would smart off to Mr. Cole, which would inevitably end with him getting kicked out of class; eventually he was transferred to another school. From there, his juvenile record was littered with petty offenses. The police felt that Marcellius was the kind of kid who could be persuaded to take a plea deal. They persuaded him through a fifteen-hour interrogation that started with them stripping Marcellius of his clothes, just as they had done to Lee Hester.[43] When they asked him questions like who was with him when he killed Lori, Marcellius maintained his innocence. That was when the beatings began. Police, wearing black gloves, kicked him and punched him until his nose bled. They threw dirty mop water on him to wash away the evidence. As the beatings proceeded, the police assured him that they would get a confession one way or another. And as the hours of humiliation and pain continued, Marcellius did, finally, relent to the abuse after police threatened to kill him. In his murder confession, he implicated Omar, Larry, and Larry's younger cousin, Calvin Ollins.[44]

Calvin was a gift to the police. When the police went to the ABLA projects to look for Larry, they met Calvin, an eager fourteen-year-old who looked up to the police.[45] Calvin ran out to meet them, introduced himself, and told them that he was from the Cabrini-Green housing development. And that introduction—and the fact that Calvin was disabled with severe cognitive delays—made him the perfect target.

Like George Jones, Calvin didn't fit the police's model profile. Calvin had no juvenile record and had never been arrested. But he had other factors that made him vulnerable to criminalization. He was Black, disabled, and from Cabrini-Green. Being Black and from Cabrini-Green was enough to bring him into the station; the disability made it easy to get him to talk.

Police brought in Calvin and interrogated him from 2 a.m. to 12 p.m. with no parent or attorney present.[46] They made him a promise that they'd made to young Black kids so many times before: All he had to do was confess, and he could go home.[47] And, to a boy as vulnerable and young as Calvin, in a room with White police officers, it sounded like a way out.

In the end, the police gave both Calvin and, ultimately, Marcellius, phony confessions and told both boys to study them so that they could repeat the story in the form of a court-reported statement.[48]

Calvin's false confession implicated Marcellius, Larry, and a character named "Daniel." This version of the confession was so compelling that police brought Marcellius back and had his confession dated two days after Calvin's in order to match Calvin's version of the narrative, naming the same group of boys, including this fabricated character named "Daniel." This boy was all fiction: his name, his presence, and his story. He was merely a placeholder for the police.

Daniel's name hangs there like an error in a novel. A character that walks in and out of a scene and never speaks. Police literally created a boy in these two confessions so that they could go find a "Daniel" that would fit the story they had concocted, even if his name turned out to be . . . Omar.

At first, police treated Omar as just a witness to the rape and murder. However, when Omar refused to read the statement handed to him on how he was a witness to the crime, the police made him the fourth defendant in the case.[49] Omar was now their "Daniel."

The Roscetti case was a quintessential wolf pack case, not just because of the number of boys charged but because of how the police had assembled the pack. In wolf pack cases, the police would pit friend against friend to deceive groups of kids and force confessions. For example, the officers would tell one child that their close friend had named them as being involved in the case. To this child, it would register as both a lie and a betrayal. The police would even go as far as to bring one child into another's cell to imply that they already knew of the boys' connection. Though they were in proximity, the children were not allowed to communicate with one another; the police knew that if they conversed, the children would likely discover that the police were lying to them and the entire hoax would fall apart.[50] Until 2021, when Illinois passed a law banning the police from lying to children, there was nothing that prevented this interrogation tactic from being used against not only one kid but many, as police created witnesses and suspects.[51] And these tactics worked against people like Calvin, who were more vulnerable because of their disabilities. This also worked against a teen like Marcellius, who both was terrified as a result of police torture and had a juvenile record that police could exploit.

In addition, police would entangle many boys in one case, using some as witnesses and some as suspects. Each kid would play a role in the narrative, and the line between witnesses and suspects was precarious. Witnesses were coached to say what the police needed them to say in order to implicate the main suspects. If the witnesses refused to help, police would give them the third degree, using physical violence to coerce a false identification.[52] If the violence wasn't enough, they always had the option of turning a witness into a defendant—which is what happened to Omar.

In 1978, a decade prior to the Roscetti case, the police used these tactics on the Ford Heights Four. In the Ford Heights case, the city was incensed by a couple that had been murdered execution style after they were abducted from a White neighborhood and brought to a Black one.[53] There was also an additional claim that the four boys raped the White woman seven times, which animated the crime fictions that made the rounds in the media.[54]

Not only was there no physical evidence linking the four boys charged to the crime, but the police withheld evidence, as they had in the George Jones case. There was an informant who was enticed with a deal from police to avoid being charged himself. There was also a disabled Black girl who was interrogated by the police for two days. In the end, she was coerced into saying that she had seen the four boys commit the rape and murder.[55] When she recanted, the police punished her by adding her to the wolf pack, convicting her for perjury and first-degree murder. She was sentenced to fifty years.

The Ford Heights Four were found guilty. One of the young men was sentenced to seventy-five years and one to life in prison; the other two were sentenced to death. Ultimately, all four served nearly two decades in prison before being exonerated in 1996.

In both the Ford Heights Four and the Roscetti Four cases, the strategy was the same. Police would amend their narrative to include more suspects, portraying Black teens and young adults as piling onto victims like ants on an anthill.

Flint Taylor was the attorney who worked on the George Jones case. He also represented one of the Ford Heights Four. He explained that police advanced an "anthill theory" to explain away the inconvenient details as to why his client's DNA did not match what was found at the scene.[56] The answer was a fiction born of fear.

For the police, the racializing anthill theory served another purpose that was more practical in nature. Police could continue adding new defendants to a case even if their DNA didn't match any sample taken at the crime scene.[57] Because the police had a monopoly on the truth, their word, their witnesses, and their science would always be enough to condemn the boys and send them to prison.

With so many false narratives from multiple co-defendants and even coerced witnesses, it made it more difficult for appeals courts to unravel the case and discern the truth—which kept defendants in prison for long periods of time. Among murder exonerations where the wrongful conviction is caused by official misconduct, the average time to exoneration is 17.7 years. But Black defendants have it worse: Their time to exoneration is an average of 19.1 years, while White exonerees are, on average, freed after 16.6 years.[58] It took fourteen years to get the innocent Ford Heights Four freed.[59] An unknown number of innocent people are never exonerated and are still entangled in the false narratives that police create.

These tactics were weaponized against the boys in the Roscetti case. That's how Omar ended up as part of the police's wolf pack, linked by proximity to boys he once knew as well as Calvin, whom he had never met. Two other Black boys played the role of witnesses in order to fabricate statements that pointed to Omar's guilt.[60] One so-called witness was incentivized by the reward money, and the other was promised leniency on another charge.

All the boys were charged as adults—even fourteen-year-old Calvin. For resisting the police's interrogation and torture, the police painted

Larry as the ringleader of the crew in both Marcellius's and Calvin's false confessions—the pack leader of the so-called Roscetti Four, who was too cunning to confess.[61]

These tactics would live on after Omar, of course. In later cases, like the Dixmoor Five (1991), police would follow the Roscetti template. The Dixmoor case involved the sexual assault and murder of a young Black girl named Cateresa Matthews. Like targeting Calvin in the Roscetti case, police went after a fourteen-year-old disabled boy named Robert Veal, a child with an IQ of 56.[62] Interrogated first, he agreed to the ready-made statement invented by police. He parroted it and was made to sign the written version even though he could not read.[63] Robert V. signed the statement in the belief that it contained his fervent denials of involvement in the murder.[64]

Another co-defendant was named Robert Taylor, whose name was the same as one of Chicago's notorious housing projects; he believed he was being questioned as a witness in a drug investigation, much the way it started for Omar. The police physically abused Robert T. until he agreed to sign a short confession that did not match the facts of the case.

After pretrial DNA testing excluded all five boys—Robert Veal, Robert Taylor, James Harden, Jonathan Barr, and Shainne Sharp—as perpetrators of the crime, the prosecutors would not relent nor drop the case.[65] They relied on the "anthill theory," explaining to the jury that a rogue necrophiliac must have sexually tampered with Cateresa's dead body after the boys had committed the crimes. Police and prosecutors declined to change the narrative and instead amplified the outrageous story to include an unidentified sexual predator in order to explain away the contradictory physical evidence.[66]

In this "anthill" case, Robert Milan was a senior-level prosecutor whose role in felony review was to memorialize the confessions extracted by police. He was present when the handwritten confessions were signed by Robert V., Robert T., and Shainne.[67] Milan, his team of prosecutors, and police would get three boys in the pack to the confession. The two half brothers, James and Jonathan, refused to accept their guilt. Indeed, they had alibis just like Lee Hester, George Jones, and Malik Muhammad. But none of that mattered.[68] And like Lil Larry, the brothers who resisted confessing would be depicted as the ringleaders; eventually, they received the stiffest sentences of the group.

As in other wolf pack cases, the Dixmoor boys' exoneration was painfully slow. Eventually, DNA evidence would be made available in the case, and it did not match any of the five boys. But it took nearly a year and a half after DNA testing before the results identified a different suspect and the case was reopened. Anita Alvarez was the elected Cook County State's Attorney at the time, and despite knowing that the DNA evidence did not match the boys who were in prison for the crime, Cook County prosecutors under Alvarez doubled down on their guilt. In predictable form, she would not reopen the case nor admit that their innocence was a possibility. The narrative of "Black guilt" carried more weight in the justice system than hard science. The Dixmoor Five would eventually be declared innocent but would collectively serve ninety-five years for a crime they did not commit.[69]

The boys labeled the "Roscetti Four" by the media did not have the slightest idea that they were a part of an assembly line of false accusations and wrongful convictions. And they couldn't have known that what happened to them would happen to others as police perfected their "wolf pack" technique during this era.

In the criminal justice system, defendants are supposed to proceed, in an orderly and predictable fashion, from an arrest to a guilty plea to a sentence, no questions asked.[70] In a wrongful conviction system, boys who are thrown into wolf packs are expected to comply with the police's narrative, innocent or not. The boys should believe police promises in the interrogation rooms, fit the caricature of a "bestial boy," and parrot the statements that police give them. Police even had young boys sign their initials on parts of the false confessions, as if to demonstrate how "careful" the police were being about the accuracy of details—even correcting the police where it appeared that they had made errors. These initials are all over my sample of false confessions, making it look like the defendants were approving and co-signing the narrative in a complex manner when it was all a charade. Many boys were forced to be complicit in their own framing, initialing the lies that would eventually do them in.

## Confessions as Evidence

My research assistants and I knew that everything about these confessions was fake and authored by police. We knew that the initialing of the confessions was forced and was there to serve the purpose of making the confessions look more authentic. But the narratives that police created in those confessions were so vile that you could not unsee them.

Initially, I couldn't imagine how an innocent person could be persuaded to incriminate themselves. Everyone thinks that it could never happen to them. And certainly, our blind faith in the police enables the police's role in creating false confessions. More troubling is that judges and juries are extremely swayed by confessions, which often have an even more powerful impact than physical evidence. This is the reason that police go to so much trouble to generate false confessions.

My students and I had a taste of what it was like for a jury to read a confession as evidence. It was a terrible and unintentional experiment. We could feel the lasting effects of police fictions even though we knew they were all fake.

So many of these cases were created in Chicago, and reading the nearly fifty confessions created a troubling picture of how police narrated Black guilt, how they imagined Black children, how they envisioned them committing crimes in packs. There was a grotesque nature to the confessions. Aside from the story of the crime itself, each case has a drama born of persistent racist narratives so powerful that they become evidence more credible than science, a shared truth.

As my students and I started reading and coding patterns in the false confessions, we began to discern the method behind them. A playbook emerged of how to create a type of narrative contamination that was almost as destructive as the physical contamination of a crime scene. It wasn't just about associating the kids with a murder; it was the tiny details of how the police creatively authored their guilt into these confessions. They could contaminate the boys so that their very identity and morality were erased. Once the police narrated these details about the boys, it was virtually impossible to see them for who they really were.

In the case of the Englewood Four, another wolf pack case, the confessions had the boys standing around a Black woman's body after they forced her to have sex with them and beat her to death with a shovel.[71] The victim's name was Nina Glover; the media often referred to her as a "prostitute," and the phrase "a woman in Englewood" was also used frequently as a way of implying her race.[72] Quite often, the media omitted her name entirely. The confessions authored by police put dialogue in the boys' mouths, full of "gang banger" language and vulgarity. They had them doing the impossible. Carrying Nina's dead body down the street without anyone noticing and tossing her into a dumpster. As in the Dixmoor case and the Ryan Harris case, the DNA found inside the victim matched a serial sexual predator with no connection to the boys.

I walked the same city streets thirty years later, retracing the police's version of events. I brought a research assistant with me; he was a walking historian of Black Chicago. He remembered which landmarks had persisted over the thirty years and vividly described the ones that had vanished. The distance between where the crime was supposedly committed and where the victim's body was found was not a long distance, but the area was buzzing with people. Cars drove by the main boulevard; there were houses and businesses in all directions. People were out walking, waiting for buses and coming and going. The idea that the boys could carry a dead body through the streets without anyone witnessing it seemed impossible. Yet the narrative was crafted to include the boys callously going about the rest of their day after committing this gruesome crime and disposing of the body. They described one boy going home to smoke marijuana, while another visited his girlfriend. It was the mundane nature of these activities that heightened their monstrous qualities. The police imagined murder, rape, and then a collective joyride on the town, just kids having fun.

In the Dixmoor Five case, the police coerced three of the boys into confessing to gang rape and murder. As the narrative found in the confessions went, James Harden was driving a red car,[73] accompanied by Robert Taylor, Shainne Sharp, Jonathan Barr, and Robert Veal. Each boy was described as raping and then holding down Cateresa's arms and legs while another boy took a turn raping her.[74] The systematic turn-taking written into the confessions loomed in a way that was as gruesome as her final execution; no boy was left with any innocence. The narrative had the boys taking Cateresa's ring and jacket as souvenirs, with another boy heading to the candy store as though nothing had happened.

In the Roscetti case, the police did the same thing. The police made Larry the ringleader, and in Calvin's confession, Larry claimed "dibs" on Lori, raping her and not letting Calvin get his "turn." These details made the boys sound like carnivores fighting over a carcass with police putting vulgarities in their mouths . . . how they had "fucked her" and how each wanted to "have some." They depicted Calvin as keeping Lori's keys as a prize—much in the same way that White people saved lynching souvenirs of Black bodies.

After reading a number of these accounts, one of my research assistants backed out of the project, despite my trigger warnings as to the violent nature of the cases. Other research assistants apologized in their discomfort as they wrote vignettes that summarized the racist drama created by police in these confessions. It was as though the vile words and stories created by the police were dripping off the page and dirtying us all. Admittedly, I too felt symptoms of post-traumatic stress disorder (PTSD), reading the drama and feeling the nightmare even after the workday had ended.

If this horrified us as adults, I tried to imagine what it must have done to the young boys who were fed these details at the police station. These children were exposed to the horrors of rape and murder as police showed them graphic crime photos, supplied them with details of the crime, and put vulgar words in their mouths. If anyone other than the police had done this, it would be considered child predation. As I strategized over the structure of this book, I worried that sharing the confessions at the start of the book would make it almost impossible to see these boys for who they were and the system for what it was.

Astoundingly, some of the confessions indemnified police. In the Dixmoor Five case, each boy was forced to say they had been treated well and were well fed and had given their statements voluntarily. Their signatures are on the statement, but they seldom match the handwriting in the confession itself. In Robert V.'s false confession, the police made him say, "I have been treated good by the police and the state's attorney. I have been fed a Burger King and fries and have used the washroom." They had Robert T. say, "I have been treated good by the police and state's attorney. I have given this statement freely and voluntarily and it is the truth." For Shainne, they adultified him even as they indemnified themselves: "I have been treated nice by the police and state's attorney. They bought me food and pop and cigarettes." These affirmations absolved the police of wrongdoing, shifting all blame onto the boys as they signed the cooked statements and became complicit in a cover-up of police's actions.[75]

Larry and Omar stood firm and resisted confessing at all costs. Perhaps they were in a state of disbelief that this could happen to them. Or, maybe, they were in a state of indignation at what police were telling them they had done. This could have been why Omar's dreams, while awaiting trial, were so vivid and filled with hope. But Omar would discover that their trials were rigged and that the forensic science was crafted to create lies rather than truths.

## Junk Science and Regimes of Truth

Before there was DNA technology, the Illinois State Police crime lab would test semen to determine the possible blood type and character (secretor or nonsecretor) of the suspect. The swab tested on Lori's body did not match any of the Roscetti Four. This should have excluded all the boys as suspects, but in the wrongful conviction system, police doubled down on their case narrative. Police had written their incriminating narrative into two confessions and entangled all the boys. But they also had a crime lab analyst, Pamela Fish. She knew the findings didn't fit the narrative, but she was a crucial piece of the shadow system. Her performance of the science was a smoke-and-mirrors game for the jury. Fish could wear her credentials like a white lab coat costume, and the jury was her captive audience.

Science is supposed to be impartial and objective, a form of knowledge based on testing, confirming, and revising hypotheses to support evidence. When Fish took the stand at the trial, she gave credibility to the police's narrative, even though the science did not support it.

Police would never admit that Fish was lying on the stand—although to a layperson, she certainly was.[76] Remember, there are shades of truth telling in police work. For them, testifying is a persuasive technique that requires "shading," highlighting incriminating facts while downplaying exonerating ones. And Fish was artfully versed in the many shades of testifying under oath; this was a pattern of practice that extended from police to prosecutors and to the science that the jury believed was objective and unquestionable. It also was a practice that extended from the George Jones era of the street files to the Roscetti Four and many other cases to come.

Most of the research on so-called junk science and its link to wrongful convictions focuses on errors in the lab. And certainly, those errors are serious. Back in the 1980s, forensic science was mostly unregulated.[77] Clinical laboratories had higher standards to diagnose strep throat than a forensic lab, even though the latter had the power to put a person on death row. However, many of the problems of junk science were more than just unregulated errors in the lab. The problems were also linked to testimony and "testilying" about the science,[78] a pattern of practice that mimicked the street file system of ignoring and burying exonerating evidence while cherry-picking facts that sounded more convincing.[79]

Fish testified that the semen found on the body "could" have derived from Larry Ollins, but when her tests were examined, they revealed that her findings ruled all four boys out.[80] During the trials, she shaded out the exonerating evidence much in the same way that police hid exonerating details in the basement of the police precinct at 51st and Wentworth.

It would be easy to see Fish as a "bad apple." But in reality, Fish was an extension of the institution of policing. In this institution, science is neither regulated nor peer-reviewed by other scientists for accuracy. It is a forensic science born of cherry-picking facts and forcing scientific conclusions to build a case. Fish was a tool of the police and prosecutors, in this case and many more, because she was willing to do science their way, allowing the details that would have exonerated the boys accused in the Roscetti case to fall to the background as irrelevant.[81]

## The Field Trip

It is not often that a jury takes to the road during a trial, but in the Roscetti case, the prosecutors instinctively understood that the location of the crime would be an important piece of evidence for the jury. Jurors were driven the six-block route from the place where Lori Roscetti was abducted to the location where she was raped and ultimately killed. They stood solemnly among the dandelions stretching through the concrete and abandoned tires tossed near the rotting railroad platform, as Detective James Capesius recounted the crime. He let the desolate landscape animate the horror of the narrative. In fact, this little field trip would happen twice, once for the trial of Larry Ollins and then again for Omar's trial.

During Omar's trial, Capesius testified more like a tour guide than a police officer. He gestured as he spoke: "You are standing on the fire road of the Chicago and North Western Railway tracks. On October 18, 1986, at about 4:40 a.m., [railroad] agent David Sachs discovered the body of Lori Roscetti at approximately this location."[82] He pointed to the white evidence marker on the edge of the road. There was a pause, as if the next piece of information was most important to the case. Like Babe Ruth calling his shot, Capesius pointed north to 1510 West 13th Street, a building within Chicago's ABLA housing projects.

This was a part of the city so segregated that if a White Chicagoan happened to drive there, a police escort would swiftly shuttle them home. For White people, it was a site of voyeuristic macabre, a place well narrated by Hollywood and Chicago journalists alike—a supposed breeding ground for criminals and crime. It was here, Capesius told the jury, where the defendant Omar lived.

Such a tour did not signal merely a physical location. In the absence of a motive, this contaminating narrative was a compelling piece of evidence.[83] The young defendant and his three young co-defendants were portrayed in a powerful shorthand. Stigmas about the ghetto itself were projected onto them as though the social problems and violence associated with the projects defined the supposed immoral character of these particular boys.[84] In the prosecutor's view, the Roscetti case was a cautionary tale of a looming threat and of what can happen when such "ghetto" boys are "unleashed"[85] in the city.[86] In fact, the prosecutor would compare the suspects to a pack of "jackals" that were "pouncing" on Roscetti.[87] Indeed, they would use a similar script for the Dixmoor case, as though police and prosecutors were just recycling the same story for a new group of boys. In the closing statement, the prosecutor would narrate the "pack" as follows: "Their world is a world of savagery, ruthlessness and violence. . . . It was a world where so-called friends turn into a pack of jackals and hunt down their prey and then kill it when they're done with it just for sport."[88]

The image of a jackal carried meanings even more specific, and more damning, than a wolf. A jackal was also in the dog family and often traveled in packs but was primarily native to Africa. The verb "pounce" denoted a predator stalking, lurking, and then suddenly and unexpectedly attacking their prey.

## Street Smarts for Street People

It took the jury eleven hours to convict Calvin Ollins, who was the first to be found guilty.[89] When Calvin heard the verdict, he remained still, likely because he did not understand what had just happened. Likewise, when the police took his mug shot after his arrest at age fourteen, he was smiling. Perhaps it was because he had been told he could go home and see his mom if he just agreed and signed the confession that the police had prepared.

The media would portray Calvin as "emotionless," as though the signs of his disability and confusion about the case constituted evidence of the empty soul of a monster rather than a sign of profound developmental delays.[90]

One of the prosecutors on the Roscetti case told the media that Calvin was smiling because "this street-smart kid thought he had just talked his way out of a murder case."[91] Later, Officer James Maurer would say something similar when Calvin told the story of how he was lied to, coerced, and intimidated into giving a confession. Maurer denied that Calvin could be disabled because the neighborhood he lived in gave him an adult-like "sharp" edge that is bred into kids from places like Cabrini-Green.[92]

During my time working in the courts, I often heard people give voice to this logic.[93] In this same way, the term *ghetto* is used by White people to demean the cultural practices of Black and Latino people, the word *street* had a similar connotation among attorneys and police. While White people have intelligence and education, Black defendants were assumed to be shaped by their exposure to "street culture" and "street life." Instead of attending schools, Black kids were assumed to learn from criminal elements that were native to the ghetto; as a result, they were seen as less intelligent and less educated.

This viewpoint extended to how attorneys treated Black defendants in court. White attorneys mocked Black people and even occasionally changed their voices into a bastardized version of Ebonics or Black English vernacular. When Black defendants tried to represent themselves pro se, White attorneys would come to the courts to watch the performance as if it were a minstrel show, treating the defendant as merely "an actor dramatizing racialized stereotypes." In this view, the Black defendant was not a man with rights, but a "racial caricature of a coon or an inarticulate buffoon."[94]

Attorneys even developed a common language to socialize with each other, and I was around to learn it—even as a law clerk in the prosecutor's office. "Street" was an important qualifier and could be used in front of many nouns in order for White attorneys to clarify supposed Black inferiority.[95] You could make reference to "street smarts," "street people," "street cred," "street law"; all of these terms were integrated in how lawyers saw Black defendants and, often, how they saw Black people as having less intelligence. Think of President Trump's habitual characterization of politicians of color as having "low IQ." The many meanings of *street* demeaned Black people in much the same way.

When Maurer offered a rebuttal to the accusations that Calvin was both disabled and coerced by the police officers under him, he relied on these tried-and-true logics and used a vocabulary to match. In Maurer's words, Calvin was "sharp enough to give us the story or to remember a story that we planted on him in such detail that he's able to give this, but he thinks that he's going to—if he confesses to a murder, we're going to let him go home? That's ridiculous. . . . I don't care if he was fourteen years old or if he was ten years old. These aren't people that grew up under some mushroom plant someplace. They live in some of the toughest neighborhoods in this city. When you're fourteen years old in Cabrini, you're an adult."[96]

Maurer never said anything about "intelligence." Instead, he used the term "sharp," which is portrayed as a cunning and dangerous form of knowledge shaped by "the streets" and inherently a type of socialization that cuts like a knife. In the view of the police and the attorneys, *street smarts* is a type of socialized and dangerous knowledge that transforms Black kids into monsters by their supposed crude education in the ghetto.[97]

During the sentencing, Judge Christy Berkos refused any suggestion that Calvin might be vulnerable due to his age or disabilities. He told Calvin, "By all appearances you're not what we'd typify as a retarded young man. . . . You're street-smart, you're sharp, you're devious. . . . It wasn't just a murder. . . . It was a bestial, barbaric, horrifying, senseless massacre of another human being. . . . She was a medical student, bright, promising."[98]

Calvin's mother processed the guilty verdict in her own way. She huddled against one of the courtroom walls and wailed over the loss of her boy. Calvin's aunt, Carolyn Ollins, was indignant: "I just don't understand it. . . . They didn't have any evidence. No fingerprints, no blood, no nothing. All they had was a forced confession from a retarded boy."[99] She pounded her fists on a door outside the courtroom as she spoke. Carolyn Ollins wasn't an attorney or anyone with influence. She was a Black aunt who knew better. She knew her nephew beyond the lies that the police had created. But no one, not the media, nor the prosecutors or judge, would listen to her.

## Omar's Fate

By the time Omar got his day in court, he understood that the trial was going to be a charade. Again, there was no physical evidence nor science to back up his guilt. There were just the false confessions and the police's crime fictions. In Omar's trial, the jury would take the field trip to the murder site by the abandoned tracks with the crushed dandelions and the discarded tires. They did it for Larry and now they were going to re-enact the whole charade a second time to secure a guilty verdict for Omar. The ghetto would be painted as an inextricable part of Omar's character.

In exhaustion, Omar would fall asleep in the holding cell while the jury deliberated. Omar dreamt that his future would be okay; seeing the visions of Lori reassured him. After only two hours of deliberation, the jury declared Omar guilty. But Omar would never lose sight of who he was, no matter what the court ruled or what the police said. He was a truth teller—the same boy who stood up to Mr. Cole when he made a false accusation.

Omar would ultimately learn that freedom is fragile. He had believed that innocence would set you free. But that was a myth. Omar would enter the police station as an innocent person and exit the courts in shackles.

As an innocent teenager in a grown-up prison, Omar would find himself terrified and alone, imprisoned with real killers—even mass murderers—like John Wayne Gacy and Richard Speck. Terrified by his circumstances and appalled by the lies and vulgarity of the doctored confessions, Omar worked relentlessly to reveal the truth and free himself.

What Omar didn't realize at the time was that his case would reveal the truth about the whole shadow system. And that's the thing about personal troubles; it is hard to imagine that one's personal circumstances can be bigger than them.

# 6

# The Danger in the Mirror

*It never sleeps—that terror, which is not the terror of death (which cannot be imagined) but the terror of being destroyed.*

—**James Baldwin, *The Evidence of Things Not Seen***

Daniel Taylor was a poor Black kid going in and out of foster care. I heard about him at the time through the local media coverage of his case, which would reveal so much about the fictions that narrate Black guilt and how effectively police could impose them on the public. Daniel was a boy who moved around a lot. Like a lot of foster care kids, much of his life was moving from home to home, school to school, and having to rebuild each time. It was hard to meet and bond with friends and mentors, only to lose them in the end. Mostly, this cycle was one of love and then loss, replayed over and over throughout his boyhood. In fact, he estimated that he had lived in twelve different foster homes and facilities.[1]

For Daniel, everything was fleeting. And that was the most predictable part of his life. Maybe it was inevitable that he would join a gang along with some of his friends. That is when Daniel started accumulating charges: twice for theft and three times for "mob action."[2]

And then, on November 16, 1992, he got into a fight.

If that fight had taken place after school, in a park, in a White North Side neighborhood, the incident would likely have ended with police calling the parents or the school. But on Daniel's side of the city, it ended with his arrest for disorderly conduct—a common charge that gives police vast discretion to hold suspects in lockup. It means you did "something," not necessarily violent, but "something," and that something is better dealt with in lockup.[3]

Daniel was thrown into the police car, patted down, and placed into a cell for over three hours.[4] He was eventually able to leave custody and ended up at an emergency shelter, where he knew they had to take him in as a ward of the state. Then, in a stroke of luck, they were able to place him with his brother—they shared a room.

But Daniel's luck was about to run out.

Two weeks after his arrest for fighting, Daniel, who was seventeen years old at the time, was woken up by White people, and he knew that meant trouble. He was told to get dressed and go with them. He asked repeatedly what was wrong but didn't get any answers until he reached the police car waiting out front. "You know what you did," he was told.[5] When he replied that he hadn't done anything, the officer punched Daniel in the chest. That was how it all began.

Daniel was mostly calm, but he was also confused because he knew that he hadn't done anything wrong. He figured that he would soon be back at the shelter with his brother, even if the police were taking him to the station for some kind of questioning.

By this time Burge's legacy was cemented in the culture of the Chicago Police. They cuffed Daniel to the wall of the interrogation room and left him there. The tenor of it all was polite but serious; the police wanted to know what Daniel knew about a murder. They *told* Daniel that he was involved in it, that another guy had identified him in the crime.

According to police, a couple of weeks earlier, on November 16, 1992, Jeffrey Lassiter and Sharon Haugabook were shot and killed in Chicago's Uptown neighborhood, which was predominantly White.[6] According to police, Daniel was one of four killers at the scene. Four other Black teens and young men acted as lookouts, they said, so it eventually became clear that the police were implicating eight boys in all.[7] This was an ambitious wolf pack project for the Chicago Police, almost on a par with the Scottsboro boys.

Daniel was shocked by the mention of murder. It was true that he was a gang member, and perhaps the police saw him as a gang banger. But for a kid like Daniel, being in a gang was about finding a place to stay, being near his brother, and just keeping his head above water. Murder wasn't part of the equation.

When Daniel denied being involved in the crime, the police began to rough him up, beating his lower back with an old-school flashlight with a long black handle.[8] One of the officers told Daniel that he would enjoy beating him because he had dark skin and none of the bruises would show.

Daniel had been in fights before where he didn't hit back. He had been in fights where he had to run. But the fear invoked by the Chicago Police was like nothing that he had ever experienced in his life.

It was the same terror that Lee Hester felt on the balcony of his school, the same terror that Jermaine felt as he implicated his own family member, Malik, as a way out of torture. It was the same terror that Andrew Wilson, one of the Chicago Police's many torture victims, experienced as he was plugged into a homemade device and electrocuted by one of Burge's officers in order to force him to confess. And such true tales of terror were retold as lore and traveled through the networks of boys, from father to son, from friend to acquaintance.

For Daniel, this past, present, and future was embodied in the form of the police officer beating him. They were ambassadors of the torture machine that Burge and his crew of ass-kickers had created across decades on the bodies and psyches of Black boys and their uncles, dads, and neighbors. And it was that history that made Daniel sign the confession that the police wrote for him.

He repeated what they told him he did, and they called in the prosecutor to make it official. They also brought in one of the other suspects to name Daniel as a person at the scene of the crime to seal his fate. All of it felt like being buried alive.

As he was being walked to a holding cell, his confession signed, he remembered a crucial piece of evidence. At the time of the murder, Daniel had been locked away in a holding cell on the disorderly conduct charge.[9] He had been arrested at 6:45 p.m. Police were called to the murder scene at 8:43 p.m., and Daniel wasn't released from jail until 10 p.m.

The police were his alibi. Their own records confirmed his innocence.[10] He begged them to look it up.

But the police now had Daniel's confession, signed and approved by the prosecutor. That was as good as a conviction. They had created a witness. And this inconvenient detail about Daniel being in police custody? . . . Well, they could fix that, too. They just needed officers to say they saw Daniel near the scene, and that was easy to write up. Police didn't worry about whether a jury could or would believe in their narrative, because like Omar and his friends, Daniel was from Black Chicago, which was notoriously dismissed as the leviathan of crime. And that belief, that dark things come from dark places, made even the darkest horror stories seem very real.

## Racism and Fear: Locking Your Door Is Not Enough

Those who lived in Chicago's Grace Abbott Homes knew about the danger in the walls. Exactly six nails held the medicine cabinets in place on the bathroom wall, and even the young residents of the high rises knew that popping the cabinet off of its moorings allowed you to shimmy between the walls that separated adjacent apartments. In some of the buildings, you could use the pipe chase to climb to apartments above or below you.[11]

Ruthie Mae McCoy was a longtime resident of the Abbott Homes. She could hear sounds from the walls, improbable sounds that were more than just rodents or paranoia. Louder and louder, they became.

Ms. McCoy's bathroom was a white cinder block structure, the kind you find in jails, prisons, and mental wards, the sterile kind suited for the projects. She decorated the space with religious magazine pages and made it her own. There was a picture of a girl pointing to her teeth, praising God for being the true dentist that saved her smile. There was another clipping from *The Power of the Holy Ghost* magazine about a woman healed of her thyroid disease during Holy Week. Coincidentally, the woman in the magazine received the miracle when her husband removed the bathroom mirror during remodeling.

Ms. McCoy was religious, and it's possible that she was waiting for some kind of redemption. But she didn't believe the rattling of the medicine cabinet was redemption, rodents, or repairmen. Ms. McCoy often spoke about fearing for her safety, but she also suffered from mental illness and paranoia.

The Abbott Homes, like other public housing locations in Chicago, were largely neglected by police. There was a murder there almost every week. Fear of crime pinned many people to their apartments. Stairwells were built like claustrophobic tubes with almost no light, natural or otherwise.

Abbott was the precursor to other notorious public housing complexes in Chicago: Cabrini-Green, Robert Taylor Homes, Stateway Gardens, and Rockwell Gardens. Abbott was more dangerous than the infamous Cabrini-Green, a housing project that had national notoriety for violence and neglect. Cabrini-Green got most of the media hype because it was a concentration of Black poverty situated close to the wealthiest White Chicagoans on the Gold Coast, downtown, and the lakefront. For Abbott residents, fear was everywhere; crime was endemic, and the darkness was terror. But police were perpetrators rather than protectors.

Whether Ms. McCoy's mental illness was inherited through biology or caused by a daily diet of poverty, segregation, and hypervigilance, on April 22, 1987, she appeared to be completely lucid and living "The Tell-Tale Heart." She called the police and explained that she could hear people tearing down the medicine cabinet. Her claims probably sounded delusional to the police because in any other part of Chicago, houses were not built with corridors between the walls. A dispatcher did send police to the scene, but when Ms. McCoy didn't answer, they shrugged and left.

The next day, a concerned neighbor called the police, but again police left when she didn't answer. The day after that, a neighbor called project officials, who came to Ms. McCoy's apartment with a carpenter to drill through the lock on the front door of the apartment. Once they entered, they found her on her side, lying in a pool of blood. Magazines, coins, and paper littered the floor around her. The medical examiner determined that she had been shot four times and that her death probably had not been immediate. It was unclear whether she had been alive or dead at the moment when the police walked away from her door and gave up on her call.

Her murder confirmed what Abbott residents already knew. This was a dangerous place, and now even locking the apartment door was not enough. There were other routes and corridors that could be accessed to victimize both the body and the mind. In the projects, you had to fear your shadow and your reflection because the hallways of the Abbott Homes, Cabrini-Green, and other notorious places were dark, neglected, and unsupervised. Police had abdicated their responsibility, and residents were left to fend for themselves on even the most basic of things—like lights in the hallways.

White Chicagoans had been primed to fear Black places. Ms. McCoy's death was seen not as an indictment of the city, its policies, and its police but as an indication of dysfunction. Locals asked a familiar question with historical roots: *What kind of place is it when locks are not enough? What kind of people are capable of such monstrosity?*

## Locking the Jailhouse Doors Is Not Enough

Horror movies blur the lines between what is actual and what is imagined. They exploit our cultural fears and, in the process, reveal who we are. Daniel Taylor was arrested for murder one month after the horror movie *Candyman,* a movie based on Ms. McCoy's murder, premiered in theaters in October 1992.[12] *Candyman* became, for White audiences, further proof of the monsters living in Black places. Candyman is a hook-handed killer who is both magical and bestial; he terrorizes the Chicago projects coming through the cabinets to kill. Harkening to the tropes portrayed in *The Birth of a Nation,* Candyman seeks and unrelentingly craves a White woman. Her name is Helen. Helen summons the Candyman by looking in a medicine cabinet mirror and saying his name five times. He eventually appears, but it's his deep voice hissing Helen's name that viewers hear before seeing his form: "I came for you. Be my victim." Helen changes from being a powerful or even defiant woman into a damsel caught in a nightmarish descent. In the psych ward under lockdown, Helen lies in a cell, medicated, on a sterile white bed as Candyman hovers over her: "Allow me at least a kiss—just one exquisite kiss."

*Candyman* transformed Ms. McCoy's victimization into yet another story about Black men's lust for White women, only this time, they conferred their Black monster, born of racial violence, with supernatural powers. He is able to move through walls, even enter and exit a mental ward built like a prison. And this horror fantasy would not remain on the screen; it would be written into the case of Daniel Taylor to eventually narrate his guilt.

Police did not worry about the messy alibi issue with Daniel Taylor. The fact that Daniel was in their custody at the time of the murder and couldn't have possibly committed the act didn't matter. The police narrated him as superhuman, just like the Candyman.

Daniel was made to have magical qualities, the ability to defy time, space, and even the bars of the holding cell. He could transport himself through the city, commit murder, and manifest himself back into his cell. This made him bestial and magical all at once—a police fiction that narrated him as a real-life horror villain.

Police didn't need any physical evidence of his crimes, because the narratives they would create would be enough to grab him and seven other co-defendants. With such terror on the loose, it was better to capture as many as possible—and certainly more than just one.

## The Candyman in the Court

During jury selection for Daniel Taylor's trial, a prospective juror was asked a basic question:

*Do you believe that, as Taylor sits there, that he is innocent and must be proven guilty?*[13]

The potential juror answered confidently: *Yes, I believe he's innocent until proven guilty but if an officer gets up there and says he did something or that he did it, I'm going to convict him.*[14]

What was poignant about the juror's response was that it was an admission of the status of police in our culture: The average person saw the police's word as a *type* of infallible evidence.[15] And that was all they needed. She was excluded from the jury, but Daniel would remember the exchange as a foreshadowing of his fate because the juror who had been excluded was Black. And if a Black woman was so convinced of his guilt and the bulletproof word of the officers, what hope did he have?[16]

At the trial, prosecutors paraded all the things about Daniel that made him seem disposable. Every personal hardship he suffered—his life as a foster kid, his poor upbringing in Black places, his previous arrest for small crimes—made it seem like he was the kind of kid that needed to be vanished.

This trial was a moral test—a character trial—where Daniel's moral standing was placed adjacent to the officers who had scooped him up on this double murder. But it was Daniel who was telling the truth. It was Daniel who believed that his innocence was worth something and that it could protect him.

When embedded in the courts, I saw many public defenders advise their clients in the courtroom lockup.[17] Often, defendants like Daniel would confide in their attorney that the police were lying. In that situation, most public defenders would advise and reassure their clients of a simple truth about the "law" as it was practiced. The lawyers believe their clients, but the judge and jury would likely not, especially over the word of an officer. Daniel was figuring this out in real time as the trial unfolded.

Prosecutors did not present any physical evidence against Daniel; it did not exist. None of the fingerprints at the scene of the crime matched his fingerprints; neither did the DNA. There was no murder weapon. Instead, they spent a great deal of time trying to convince the jury that it was possible that Daniel could have been at the crime scene at the time of the murder. They put an officer on the stand to testify that he had seen and spoken to Daniel near where the murders had happened. The prosecutors had seen the paperwork confirming that Daniel was in police custody, so they must have known that the officer was giving false testimony. In fact, the paperwork that police had submitted confirming that they saw Daniel was crafted one month *after* the double homicide and nearly two weeks *after* his confession. No police supervisor ever signed off on it. It was a clear case of police fabricating evidence to "fit" their claim about Daniel.

Prosecutors presented a new narrative in court, claiming that the officers who arrested and released Daniel on the night of the murder must have made a mistake in their paperwork. And since the word of the officer is a piece of evidence, the officer's lie (both on paper and on the stand) was the foundation of Daniel's conviction. The prosecutor's job was to convict at all costs: "Testilying" and rigging of evidence was just the cost of doing business.[18]

Daniel's defense attorney fought the case, telling the jury that "there isn't one reasonable doubt in this case; the whole case is one big doubt."[19] The jury deliberated for a few hours, and in the character trial of Daniel Taylor versus the Chicago Police, Daniel was convicted. The jury saw their murderer and believed that Daniel was the type of teen who ran in packs and left victims in his wake. He was convicted and sentenced to life in prison.

One juror said that "the only piece that didn't seem to fit was that stuff that he'd been in jail at the time. He could have walked out the back door, for all we knew."[20] Did the jurors believe that Daniel was capable of magical things? Did they imagine him to be so monstrous that the doors of the jailhouse were not enough to contain him and so imbecilic that he would choose to sneak back into jail again? Racism can be sloppy and contradictory.

Daniel was not the first Black teen to have the police project magical, monstrous qualities on him. In fact, one memorable case was the famous U.S. Supreme Court decision's *In re Gault* ruling (1967) mandating that juvenile criminal defendants are entitled to basic due process rights, including the right to counsel, under the Fourteenth Amendment of the Constitution.[21] The ruling described the case of a twelve-year-old boy, referred to simply as "Gregory W." by the court,[22] who was arrested in New York City in 1964.[23] It wasn't just the same decade as Lee Hester's tragedy; it was the same type of imagined crime.[24] The New York Police Department accused Gregory and a friend of sexually assaulting two elderly White women from Brooklyn and killing one of them. The surviving victim described the suspect as a twenty-year-old Black man with a deep voice.

Instead, police brought in two children.

Gregory had been diagnosed with schizophrenia. And yet police relentlessly interrogated Gregory on three separate occasions as if they were stalking the boy.[25] The first interrogation session lasted for twenty-four hours, and he continuously told them that he wanted to go to sleep. Even for a healthy individual, sleep deprivation of this type can cause hallucinations and disorientation.[26] For Gregory, such tactics were enough to press him to confess to an unbelievable narrative of guilt: To commit murder and rape, he escaped from a locked security ward at the hospital, the sterile kind with cinder block walls, similar to the kind portrayed in *Candyman* when he hovers over Helen.

During Gregory's trial, the defense called a psychiatrist to the stand in order to explain the medical reason for his false confession. Given Gregory's disability, the psychiatrist said, he would have said anything to stop the interrogation. The court ignored this expert testimony in favor of the police's fiction: that Gregory had escaped the security ward using a broken spoon to open a locked door, ran 3.5 miles to commit the crime, only to run 3.5 miles back and sneak back into the ward, all without any adult noticing.

Ultimately, Daniel Taylor, like Gregory before him, was convicted because the narratives about Black boys were more convincing than expert testimony. And, in Chicago, there were other cases like Daniel's where the confessions were absurd or inaccurate. A *Chicago Tribune* investigation found that between 1991 and 2000, there were at least 247 cases where police obtained "incriminating statements that were thrown out by the courts as tainted or failed to secure a conviction."[27] Of course, only the tainted cases were thrown out; others, like Daniel's, advance through the courts unnoticed. Judges often refuse to suppress confessions, tending to side with the police's account of how the confession was obtained, making the courts complicit in miscarriages of justice.[28]

Even more alarmingly, Chicago Police at this time were securing an "admission of guilt in 7 of every 10 murder cases they solved."[29] Some would look at these statistics and think that police were great at their jobs. But that's only true if the job was "getting confessions" rather than ascertaining the truth. Given everything we know about the street file system and the prevalence of torture and manipulation, these numbers suggest the potential for an alarming number of errors in these "closed cases."

What happened to Daniel wasn't a one-time error, either. The *Chicago Tribune* investigation found that the Chicago Police had obtained confessions from three people who were able to produce records confirming that they were in police custody when the murder occurred.[30] By any standard, what this truly revealed was that "solving cases" meant closing them at all costs—and there would be casualties. While there were 247 defendants who eventually managed to dodge a wrongful conviction, Daniel, like an untold number of other Black teens, was one of many people whose lives were ruined by these practices.

When the police rigged Daniel's case, they coached someone into saying what the police had written in the confession. This "witness" later said police had told him that no one would care about Daniel because he had no family—it would be "nobody's loss."[31] Other orphaned Black boys, wards of the state, and abandoned children—both historically and in the future—would be criminally discarded as well. Black "dependent" children had often been labeled as criminal "delinquents" and routed to carceral systems. Now, the police could informally handle these kids—the defuturized "nobodies"—through wrongful conviction.[32]

After his conviction, Daniel was numb, and in a state of shock. He described it as a "pain" that made him "dull," unable to connect with anyone.[33] Daniel knew that the state had given him a life sentence; for a person that young, not even twenty, he was less fearful of confronting the prison setting than he was terrified of the prospect of living and serving slow time, a fear hauntingly similar to what Malik describes in his writings as "death by incarceration."[34]

Soon, Daniel was transported to an Illinois prison, but he was not riding the regular bus with defendants who had "out dates"—a date that guaranteed freedom. He was now a "lifer," and guards put him into a van for his final ride through the free world. Daniel was shackled around his waist, his hands, and even his feet. They had a "doggie chain" looped around his waist so that they could tether him like an animal and walk him wherever they wanted him to go. They also chained him to the floor of the van. And, with such conditions, he lost his will to live.[35]

Daniel would serve more than twenty years in prison and in that time, Daniel wrote to anyone he could for help. It wasn't until 2001, nine years after he was arrested, that journalist Steve Mills would begin to see the holes in his case and the fight to exonerate him would begin.[36]

Throughout his incarceration, he had more than enough time to wonder how this could happen to him. How could the jury believe a police narrative despite the lack of evidence and an alibi provided by the police themselves? He would contemplate whether the confession mattered.[37] Was that the biggest mistake he ever made? But in all, wolf pack cases were prosecuted on an idea that juries understood. Confession or not, Daniel's dark skin and his neighborhood acted as a type of evidence against him. For prosecutors who wanted a simple and clean narrative for the public and—most importantly—a jury to understand, these cases were easy to win. All they had to do was "perform" the narrative in the courts.

At the time of Daniel's conviction, Omar Saunders had already served seven years of his sentence. He was now a man in his mid-twenties. Like Daniel, he had had time to wonder how and if things would ever be okay. Like Daniel, he spent time fighting his case from the inside.[38]

Marking time on a life sentence can be numbing. The word *indefinite* may be the most apt.[39] However, there are still events that mark the time; for Omar, it was a news story that a little girl named Ryan Harris had been murdered and sexually assaulted. Normally, that type of news may come and go; lots of tragedies can happen in a city, even the death of a young girl. And many of these cases, especially the ones occurring in Black neighborhoods, go unsolved by the police.[40] But this tragedy came with details that caused Omar to catch his breath. The accused suspects were seven- and eight-year-old boys, and the police claimed that they had also sexually assaulted the girl. As the narrative went, they did these horrendous acts just to steal her bike and then went home to play.

Omar knew he and his friends were innocent. But here, in this new case, he could see that some of the improbable stories told about him were now being placed upon those little boys—boys who hadn't even been born when Lori Roscetti was murdered. And it was this awakening—that Omar's personal troubles were spreading like a virus to other Black boys—that was the true horror story. Omar knew how low the police could go. And that realization, that his tragedy and trauma was one of many, was a heavy burden to bear.

And in the most profane place, Omar did the most sacred thing. He dropped to his knees in his cell and begged God to help those little boys.[41] He prayed long and hard, asking God to give them protection against the police, the kind of protection that he and his friends never had.

7

# The Final Question

*The children are always ours, every single one of them, all over the globe; and I am beginning to suspect that whoever is incapable of recognizing this may be incapable of morality.*

—**James Baldwin**[1]

## A Calling

Attorney R. Eugene Pincham was settling for sleep when he heard the news of Ryan Harris's death.[2] The devastating violence of the murder made it a heater case (he knew that for sure), one the media would jump on and exhaustively cover. His first reaction was to talk with his wife, Alzata, a woman who was his everything: his confidant in court, before trials, and in life.

"I certainly hope that they won't find some junkie in Englewood who's defenseless and pin it on him to clear up the case," he said.[3]

Mr. Pincham was a legal legend in Chicago. He was a human rights activist, lawyer, former judge of the Circuit Court of Cook County, and justice of the Appellate Court of Illinois. In his years on the bench at the main courthouse at 26th and California, he estimated that he disposed of no less than eight felony cases a day. Ninety-nine percent of the defendants who came before him were Black.[4] During his time as a trial attorney, he learned what the Chicago Police were capable of doing and how they viewed Black people. He even defended Robert M. Harness, Chicago's second Black police commander and the namesake of the police station at 51st and Wentworth, after Harness was pushed out of the force by his brothers in blue. It was the same station where Elijah, Romarr, and so many others were interrogated and where the street files were hidden under their feet. Mr. Pincham was often responsible for vindicating and defending the police's victims, and he had seen it all.

Mr. Pincham was one of the attorneys on Anthony Porter's legal team. Anthony was a man who was wrongfully convicted. Despite the errors in his case, his life was saved hours before his scheduled execution. His was a case that was so egregious that it helped bring the death penalty in Illinois to an end.[5]

Anthony struggled in life. That much Mr. Pincham knew. But he also knew that the Chicago Police made that suffering worse. For example, long after his exoneration, Anthony would get arrested for stealing four dollars' worth of deodorant. Another customer tried to pay on his behalf, but once the police were called, Anthony was charged with retail theft and routed back to prison.[6] Anthony's petty crime was never categorized as a faulty charge or the like. Few would ever believe that it was a charge tied to retaliation. However, the police had a monopoly on creating case narratives and could, as they often did, blow up the small theft of a common self-care item and use it to route people back to where they thought they should go—like a modern-day slave patrol.

For the deodorant offense, Anthony would be held on a $10,000 bond, which he could not pay, and therefore he would once again languish behind bars. At his bond hearing for this new charge, the prosecutors listed the homicide as part of his criminal background.[7] Anthony had to ask his attorney to clarify to the court that he had been exonerated, that he was innocent of the homicide charge. One headline read, EXONERATED DEATH ROW INMATE GOING BACK TO PRISON FOR STEALING DEODORANT, reaffirming that it couldn't be possible for such a man to be truly innocent for long.[8]

Mr. Pincham knew that the Chicago Police always had a way of getting in the last word. In Anthony's case, as in others, fighting the police involved winning many battles, both big and small, but never winning the war. He fought for those charged with crimes and even for Commander Harness when the Chicago Police were forcing a Black police leader into retirement. Mr. Pincham did this work relentlessly and on many fronts, but he had to be discerning about which fights to choose.

Mr. Pincham's knee-jerk reaction to Ryan Harris's death was born of both seeing and experiencing the racist wrath of the Chicago Police. He knew that the Chicago Police would have media pressure on them to clear and then close this case at all costs. It also meant that as the case grew colder, the pressure on the police to find a scapegoat to pin this crime on would rise. But even Mr. Pincham, a man who had seen it all, was floored when he learned the identity of the defendants charged with Ryan's murder.

Nearly two weeks later, Mr. Pincham received a sobering call. It was a young man named Andre Grant, another Black lawyer he respected and mentored.[9] Like others in the legal community, Andre affectionately called him "Judge."

*Judge, they've arrested two seven- and eight-year-old boys and charged them with Ryan Harris's murder. And my mother and the grandmother of the eight-year-old boy grew up together as friends, and I want you to come help me on the case.*[10]

This was how close the Black Chicago community was. Grandmas and moms, friends and families, legal legends and upcoming stars, they were all connected to the boys by a degree of separation or so. But Mr. Pincham was not having Andre's request. It was the kind of request that could occupy him for years.

*Andre, you don't need me on the case. Hell, you know, anybody knows, no seven- or eight-year-old boys did this. You got to be an idiot not to know this; you don't need me on this.*[11]

Andre continued to push. *But Judge, I need you.*

Andre begged and pleaded and then begged and pleaded again. It was Sunday night; the boys had been arrested that afternoon. Andre had received the call from Ms. Rosetta, a woman who took care of him like her own son when he lived in the Washington Park housing project. Now her grandson, Elijah, was in trouble.

Earlier in the day, Andre had met Elijah and his family at the station. He was a former prosecutor, and so he was keenly aware of what the police could do to this boy and his seven-year-old friend. When he found Elijah in the interrogation room, there were still officers swarming about. The eight-year-old boy was crying. Andre told them to leave so that he could talk to Elijah in private.[12]

Andre started by explaining that he was his lawyer and that his grandmother had hired him.[13] Andre had to ask the question: *Do you know what a lawyer is?* Elijah said no, and he could not stop crying. Andre asked if he knew who he was, and Elijah said, "Yes, you're another police."[14]

Both Elijah and Romarr had been interrogated by Detectives James Cassidy and Allen Nathaniel, a Black officer. In total, there were five officers who had helped question little Elijah.[15] By the time Elijah saw Andre, he was a different boy from the one who entered the station. He was terrified of everyone.

Andre was in uncharted waters, representing a child who could not even understand who a lawyer was, what a lawyer did, let alone the concept that he had rights under the law. What are rights to a child when their days are controlled by adults?

Andre's voice was soft as he tried to reassure Elijah. "No, I'm not the police. I'm here to help you. I'm going to fight for you."[16]

Andre knew that he had to change course for this young boy, because he was himself the father of a five-year-old boy, and because Elijah was in clear emotional distress. He leaned over and asked him: "Do you like the Power Rangers?"[17] Elijah looked bewildered by the question, but he was calmer; he was listening now. "Who's your favorite Power Ranger?" Andre asked. "The Blue Power Ranger," Elijah answered, his mind evidently drifting to the TV show and away from the police station.

"I'm the Blue Power Ranger," Andre said conspiratorially. "I'm going to fight for you."

Many superheroes have secret identities. By day they masquerade as ordinary people, and when danger calls and the bad guys come, the superhero transforms into their true self. Andre confided in Elijah in a way that an eight-year-old could understand. And by revealing his true identity, Andre built trust with this traumatized boy.

Andre knew that he had promised to protect this boy, but there were no guarantees when defending someone from the Chicago Police. He had no choice but to call for backup. If Andre was the Blue Power Ranger, then Mr. Pincham was the Black one—a mentor and leader who knew the Chicago Police's playbook and knew how to fight it on a grand scale.

Andre tried to convince Mr. Pincham that this case was as significant as any death penalty case or brutality case that he had ever fought because the lives of two tiny boys were at stake. And it wasn't just one officer attacking, but an entire institution, police officers unknown and unidentified working different angles.[18]

But Mr. Pincham could not be convinced, and he just left Andre with reassurances that he could call him for help.

*You can handle this.*[19]

And that was how Mr. Pincham left it, hanging up and readying himself for bed. He was a prayerful man, getting out of bed to humbly pray on his knees the good way—the way grandmas teach boys when they are young.

He got into bed, and just as clear as Andre's voice had sounded was the voice of a spirit who spoke to him directly after his prayer.

*Why would you tell such a big lie?*[20]

Mr. Pincham had hung up and said no to helping two children.[21] He was a believer in the Good Book. He had read and recited it throughout his life, and the Bible was very clear about how one should care for and treat children. As he would later tell it, "It is better that you be cast into [the] sea with a yoke on your neck than to harm one hair on a child's head. The book says, 'Suffer little children that come unto me and forbid them not, for such is the kingdom.'"[22] And Mr. Pincham knew: Andre's call was a *calling*.

Mr. Pincham was known by many to possess the sharpest legal mind in the business; he was one of the great trial attorneys of his time. But he didn't just practice the law with his mind; it was a spiritual practice born of a calling to do righteous work where such work was needed. And that was the most admirable thing about Mr. Pincham. He said that he "never lost the zeal for standing up for the downtrodden, the abused and the accused."[23]

He often cited an adage: "I'm using my life to help others, to make life better for others, 'cause I don't want no debate at the gate. I don't want no mess out of Peter. When he sees me coming, I want him to open the gate and say, 'Come on, brother.'"[24]

A few minutes later, Mr. Pincham called Andre back and accepted his calling to protect the children.[25] Indeed, Andre promised to protect Elijah, and Mr. Pincham promised that Andre wouldn't have to do it alone. And there was hope in that intergenerational bond and the calling that brought them all together in a defense of something good against something so evil.

Mr. Pincham would meet his youngest client ever at the Hartgrove Hospital, where he and his friend had been ordered to be confined. When Mr. Pincham set eyes on Elijah, this tiny child for which a spirit had summoned him to protect, Mr. Pincham wept. It was the first time in forty years that he had cried. He could only ask himself and maybe God: *How could anybody do this to this kid?*[26]

He knew God was on his side to help answer this question, but the "anybody" was not a single person. It was an entire institution. The Chicago Police. And for that, he assembled what Andre had begun: a legal Dream Team of Black attorneys, all Power Rangers in the eyes of Elijah. He gave each of them their superhero colors. Lew Myers Jr. (Green), Berve Power (Red), and, of course, Andre (Blue) . . . they would be by Mr. Pincham's side.[27] They were men who loved their people, who saw the Chicago Police for what and who they were; men who were ready to punch up to save a baby who could have been their own child or grandson. Indeed, a child who was theirs, a child who was them.

## The Helpers

Catherine Ferguson was one of only a handful of public defenders working when the arrest was made in the Ryan Harris case.[28] It was the dead of summer, and so many attorneys, judges, prosecutors, and investigators were off on vacation. A skeleton crew was left to manage it all. When Catherine heard that two arrests had been made in the case, she knew one of them was going to be her client. And that's how she was paired up with, possibly, the youngest murder suspect in the nation, little Romarr.

Catherine was a seasoned public defender and had seen a lot. Her clients would come into the lockup beaten and bruised. She would get her investigators to take pictures, at first, and when she went to her supervisors, they just threw their hands up. The cases would go nowhere. No officers were held accountable. There was nothing they could do. Just too many young defendants were brought in that way.

Certainly, Catherine thought, there had to be some database of the cops who were doing this. There was no such database: There were just too many of them to track and not enough time to track the enormity. When she was at the Markham Courthouse in Cook County, where she started her career as a lawyer, she learned about the "jump out boys," a group of Chicago Police who would pull up to playgrounds and just start beating kids up. And it was an open secret: Officers would take their identification and let their presence be known. The Chicago Police were watching them.

In her career as a public defender, she saw so many injustices. However, no amount of legal experience could have prepared her to see her client, Romarr, in the distance, being brought to her in the police station as if she were his caregiver. Romarr held the hand of an officer, and his other hand was in his mouth as he sucked his thumb. Romarr was crying, and it was clear that he wanted out of the police station. He looked exhausted and wanted his mom.

Because Romarr was visibly scared, Catherine asked him if he wanted some candy. Romarr's answer was a repeated mumbling that had Catherine looking around for a translator. With some help she realized that Romarr was asking for a pack of honey buns, but she also realized that this child could barely assemble a sentence, let alone confess to a murder. She spent more time with him, babysitting and coloring. Catherine invited a talented supervising public defender named Darron Bowden, who was Black, in on the case so that Romarr could feel some sense of protection from a person who looked like him.

Catherine was left to pursue the case with an investigative reporter from the *Chicago Tribune* named Maurice Possley. In those days, police reporters were typically more like cops than reporters. All of their sources were cops. And the expectation was to just report what the police said without scrutiny, because scrutiny could get you ostracized from the inner sanctum of the police station. The reporter was more like an extension of the police's public relations machine—without being on the books.

Maurice was different. In the scrum of reporters who filled the courthouse, he was the only one who was curious about meeting Romarr's family. The rest didn't think of asking for such permission; their assumption was that the parents must be some kind of crack addicts. But it was Maurice who knew there might be a story to tell about Romarr's parents and grandmother and the Black residents of Englewood. Maurice asked permission to interview the Gipsons, and Catherine agreed—so long as she was present. They became an unlikely pair, journeying to Englewood to talk to potential witnesses and the Gipson family.

When they arrived in the neighborhood, most folks weren't home.

They learned that everyone was at church. Maurice said, "Well, we go to church." So Catherine and Maurice headed to the church and tried to take seats, inconspicuously, in the back.

There are no strangers in a Black church. Newcomers are greeted and welcomed appropriately with warmth. But this was a tense time, a time of shared tragedy when a pastor may struggle to find the words that will ease the congregation's suffering. The pastor acknowledged their presence and invited Catherine up to the pulpit to say a few words.

Catherine looked over to Maurice as though she could pawn off the request to him. She felt like a mess. It was the dead of summer, and the thick air was hot and soupy. Here she was, a White woman in a mustard-stained shirt while the Black congregation was dressed to the nines: proper dresses, nylons, hats, and ties. Maurice told Catherine that she had no choice but to go up there. What was clear from the congregation was that Romarr had more than just his mom, dad, and grandma on his side. His family was all of Black Englewood. It had already lost one of their precious girls. And in that church, everyone had a stake in knowing that their little boys would be okay. They couldn't lose them too. Not Shannon's son. Not Iris's grandson. Not the Hendersons' little baby boy Elijah, who had the same name as the prophet known for experiencing God as a "still small voice"—appropriate for a tiny eight-year-old who was well mannered, quiet, and painfully shy.

For Catherine, it was a long walk to the altar because now, instead of looking at the pastor for faith and hope, they were looking to her. She needed what Isaiah 50:4 described as a "well-trained tongue," so that she "might know how to answer the weary a word that will waken them"—even if it meant going to the altar in that mustard-stained tee.

After scanning the audience in front of her, she said, "This would not have happened to a White mother in Wilmette. Never. People will see this now." It was the best opening statement she ever made. The congregation responded with applause and affirmation. Catherine just said what everyone in that congregation knew. And with that, she kept going for it. "A Black kid in Englewood is not equated to a White kid in Wilmette."

Little Romarr and Elijah were just two more Black victims wronged by the police. Catherine's awkward but bold performance ended with the elders of the church praying for truth and protection. For Catherine to see that justice could be done for their sacred son and for Maurice, the reporter who bothered to spend time listening to Black residents as though their words mattered because there was no Black mother nor father nor auntie and uncle who believed that such tiny boys could do the unthinkable, with such force and rage. They knew their kids. They knew how small a seven-year-old was, and they could see it all so clearly.

And yet, Catherine and Maurice were the only two White people who were present among them. The church community surrounded these two helpers in prayer. What a sight it was: At a time when grief and rage was palpable, it was Black people who could still rely on hope and faith as a source of protection against their perpetrators—the police.

## Public Relations and Due Process

Police know the importance of public relations. Part of creating a convincing narrative for a case is ensuring that it reaches the public. Indeed, public relations (PR) is so important to policing work that Chicago's spending on in-house PR has increased dramatically since this era.[29] Between 2011 and 2023, the in-house PR professionals working for the Chicago Police Department went from around four people to fifty.[30] This amounts to a cost of about $3.85 million per year on interfacing with the media and the public.[31] If that lavish budget is any indication, the business of policing is managed like a business.[32] The PR professionals are protecting the reputation and the standing of the police in the hearts and minds of the public, even if it means creating fictions and fantasies about policing itself.[33]

Press conferences are television moments and, as in all politicking, the stage, message, and performance are well crafted.[34] The press conference must glorify the police's work, place a mystique around their investigation, and show that they can close the all-important heater cases that seize the spotlight. Theatrics and staging are involved: The seal of the city. Uniforms. A small group of officers looking solemn and confident. A high-ranking officer at the mic behind a podium. And the entire event must end with the detectives being praised for their work solving the case. For most people, the accusation *is* the resolution, regardless of how the court rules or whether the case is dropped.[35] It was this sensibility that framed the press conference for the Ryan Harris case.

Five detectives stood shoulder to shoulder. In their suits and ties, they looked like prep school graduates. In front of them was Sergeant Stanley Zoborac. His tone was measured, confident, and proud as he explained the arrest of Romarr and Elijah, hiding their real names due to their young ages. "Their statements indicate that they are perpetrators, and we have some physical evidence that is corroborated by their statements." This was not true. And yet, Sergeant Zoborac made a point of saying that the officers had acted "magnificently" in gaining confessions from the boys.[36]

Media and public persuasion are essential to policing, and Detective James Cassidy used his power to persuade the public as an essential part of his policing tactics. In his op-ed about A.M., he warned Chicagoans about a new breed of small children who were poised to kill others like Anna Gilvis unless we toughened the laws governing their crimes.[37] Four years prior to his experiment of interrogating and charging Romarr and Elijah, he had started stoking fears in the public.

The entire Ryan Harris case rested on the confessions of two young boys who had been interrogated by multiple officers. And those statements were all they had to close this case. Police had no physical evidence. Like other cases, the police would narrate both the victim's story and the perpetrators' stories. Their narratives would complement each other and make the case seem cohesive for the press and the public. By the time the police took to the mic, all the shaky details and inconsistencies would be sorted out into an ironclad story that went like this:

The fictional motive for this case centered around Ryan's blue Road Warrior bike. Such a bike might be a dime a dozen in the richer neighborhoods of Chicago, but it was highly coveted among poor kids in Englewood. Little Ryan had it all. Honors student. Ambitions of being a doctor or basketball player, a kind heart, and a loving family.[38] Repeatedly, the press would note that Ryan was only *visiting* Englewood from the suburbs, rather than being *from* Englewood. The mention of the suburbs connected her to White spaces, White people, and manicured middle-class lawns. Her portrayal was similar to Lori Roscetti, who was canonized as the hardworking, aspiring doctor whose only "crime" was going to medical school in proximity to the projects. The police hammered the racist idea that Ryan was one of the good ones: She may have been Black, but she was different. She was Black but suburban. She was Black but had a future. She was Black but not from Englewood.

The police constructed Ryan's innocence in opposition to the so-called predators that she would encounter in Englewood—a tried-and-true trope about the neighborhood that had been planted decades earlier in the Lee Hester case. The police said that Ryan had the bike that the two young predators wanted, and they were willing to get it, by any means necessary. This narrative fit the racist expectation that Black children were willing to kill for the items they wanted, whether it be Nikes, jewelry, or a bicycle.[39] These kids weren't just influenced by the bad elements in Englewood; they *were* the bad elements. The children would be demonized as being both born to do wrong and born in the perfect environment to do it.

According to the police's media spin, the boys cornered Ryan next to an abandoned lot and Romarr threw a rock, striking her in the head. Ryan fell, and the two descended upon her.[40] They molested her and stuffed clothing in her mouth.[41]

Questions came in from the press. "Did they, Sergeant, indicate an understanding of what they'd done?"[42] The press only questioned the idea that such young boys understood the gravity of their acts, not their capacity to do it.

In front of the media, Zoborac would try to shape the media's collective conclusion: "You would have to use conjecture or logical thoughts. . . . We're being set off on two various tangents by one of the children involved. You would have to suspect that they knew what they had done and that they were coming up with various accounts to point the blame towards someone else."[43]

The young boys were portrayed as not only understanding what they had done but also as having the "street smarts" of knowing how to cover it up and deceive grown men. For the police, the boys were not just lying kids but conniving criminals. And this narrative allowed all the holes in the confessions and physical evidence to be explained away with a short response that adultified and racialized the boys and made the story believable to the press.

This was the explosive narrative that greeted the boys in court the day after they were charged with the murder of Ryan Harris. Thirty years later I spoke to one of the White reporters who had been there and ventured that the media and public had "almost" believed the police's lies; he quickly corrected me: "No, we did believe." This was a powerful admission. While Englewood was skeptical at the absurdity of two little boys being murderers, much of the predominantly White media bought the entire thing hook, line, and sinker. The public was primed to see these boys as guilty until proven innocent well before any court, hearing, or ruling on probable cause had taken place.

Maurice was in the scrum of reporters in the court. He received an abrupt and unexpected call notifying him that a hearing in the Ryan Harris case was about to happen. One of the few reporters who had bothered to meet the families involved, Maurice sensed something wasn't right. That intuition likely came from years of covering numerous wrongful conviction cases, some involving suspects headed to death row.

He remembered the case of fifteen-year-old Eddie Huggins, who had supposedly confessed to stabbing someone—but the police found no stab wounds on the body.[44] When Maurice questioned the then-elected State's Attorney, Richard A. Devine, about whether he was going to proceed with prosecuting Eddie's case just before it went to trial, Devine said "No comment" and that he would look into it. However, the trial proceeded anyway, with a young boy's life at stake, despite science that contradicted the confession. And there were so many more cases that were that absurd.

It seemed like every reporter in the city was packed into the courtroom. The sea of faces, from the reporters to the judge to the prosecutors, was majority White; the view was similar to the one that Lee Hester would have seen during his trial.

Maurice got one of the precious seats and sat, shoulder to shoulder, with his peers. "The press was waiting to see the demons. . . . We were waiting to see John Wayne Gacy or some serial rapist. We'd been told the story by the police. I think we were expecting to see burly oversized kids with glinty eyes. We were not expecting to see what we got."[45]

But this is exactly what the Chicago Police wanted.

The boys were brought in through the loading docks after a night at Hartgrove Hospital. They had been wailing before they came into the court; when they saw the crowd, they seemed dazed and lost. Their families were there, occupying the front row—parents, grandparents, even a great-grandmother. Romarr's father was notably missing. Jeremy, Romarr's dad, disassociated, an understandable trauma response to what he and his family had been through. He got into his 1988 Ford Taurus and drove away. He drove so long that he ended up in Milwaukee, still not far enough away to cope with the idea of his baby, who shared his braids and features, being charged with murder.[46] The soundtrack of this traumatic trip was Al Green's "Love and Happiness," a song he and Romarr shared as a favorite.

When the crowd got its first sight of the tiny children, there was an audible gasp. And yet, law enforcement operated with the formalities and security protocols as though they were grown men. For instance, Judge Gerald Winiecki called the boys "Mr. Gipson" and "Mr. Henderson." The boys' parents were waiting at the front of the gallery and tried to hug their boys, but this natural action was treated as a security threat.

Maurice would remember just how tiny they were and how surreal it all was. The sheriff's deputy who led them into court towered over the boys; their hands seemed to be swallowed by his long fingers.[47]

Elijah sat next to Andre, the Blue Power Ranger, who handled the first day of the hearing on his own. Romarr sat next to his team of public defenders, which included Catherine, Elizabeth Tarzia, and Darron Bowden, who did their best to comfort the boy. The boys stayed occupied by drawing and coloring. On a yellow legal pad, Romarr drew a house with heart-shaped balloons flying overhead. And then his pictures turned to doodles. He wrote his name and his father's name, over and over, as though his sketches could manifest him in the room. Romarr kept asking Catherine, "Am I going to jail, or am I going to see my mommy?"[48]

This was a preliminary hearing where the judge first determines whether there is probable cause that an offense was committed by the defendants, and importantly, whether or not to keep the boys locked up pending their trials.[49] Such hearings are usually brief and more of a formality, often occurring in empty galleries. But in this heater case, with the media packing the courtroom and the defendants being so young, both sides knew that this hearing would be a show with the purpose of shaping public opinion.

The hearing was not a fight over facts or to discern some kind of truth. Indeed, Andre and Catherine would contend that they didn't even have the same records and evidence that the prosecutor had, and they begged the judge to consider postponing the hearing. What became very clear was that the state was going to put an officer on the stand, one who was ready to testify and must have been prepped by someone, almost certainly a prosecutor. But both defense teams had no police report or other documents. And yet, by some clandestine process, the state was ready to question a detective on the case even as the defense had no papers, notes, or reports to go by.

Andre Grant: *I am asking the court, pleading with the court, that we not proceed with a probable cause hearing until the State has given us what they used to prep their witness and charging a seven- and eight-year-old child with murder. It's not an ordinary case. Those boys should be given everything the State has. . . . We should not proceed until they tender those documents.*[50]

A veteran of the Cook County State's Attorney's Office, Michael D. Oppenheimer did not deny that there were documents in his possession that had not been shared with the defense. And yet, Oppenheimer's response was merely to dodge the issue.[51]

The judge asked: *State wish to respond?*

The state used a common refrain that I heard often in my time clerking in the prosecutor's office.

Oppenheimer: *State is ready for probable cause hearing right now today, Judge. We have the detective here. We're ready to go.*[52]

The evasion worked. The judge overruled the objections from the defense, any claims about the boys' best interests or that they were so young and vulnerable. Andre argued that a fair playing field was in the best interests of the boys and society alike. The system runs like a meat grinder, and it's expected that everyone (regardless if the "everyone" includes a child) proceeds in an orderly fashion to conviction: no objections, no protests, no nonsense.[53] As I found in my research, this production ethic favors police and their availability.[54] Preferentially accommodating police as VIP witnesses comes at the expense of the defendant. The judge in the Ryan Harris case was fine with that courtroom norm.

The hearing was much more than a fight over whether the state had "probable cause"; it was the first battle over whether the boys were innocent, and it was a fight for their freedom. In order to detain the boys, prosecutors had to convince the judge that jailing them was a matter of "immediate and urgent necessity" because they posed such a dire threat to other people or their property.[55] To meet this standard the prosecutor's job was to paint the children as monsters who needed to be contained.[56] In a sense, this was a character trial, where the morality of the little boys would be litigated for the media in the room.[57]

The defense was there to show that these innocent boys were the true victims—victims of the real monsters, the Chicago Police. This was a battle over the way we see innocent Black boys and the way we see the police. From the start, the defense was at a disadvantage.

The Cook County State's Attorney's Office knew how to create drama in the courtroom, just as the Chicago Police Department knew how to use a press conference to forge a compelling narrative. It is why one of the few people to testify in the preliminary hearing was Detective Allen Nathaniel.

Black officers were an integral part of the business of the Chicago Police. They were present during Burge's torture. Black police leaders played a legitimizing role for policing as an institution.[58] One example was Milton Deas, the Black past commander of Area 2. Despite his higher rank and leadership role, Burge relegated Deas to an office far from the interrogations of Anthony Williams, Andrew Wilson, and the many others that were tortured, so that he could plausibly deny torture when confronted by defense attorneys and the Black community.[59] Beyond their roles in leadership, Black officers were used as lures, to deceive the likes of Lee Hester. And certainly, that was Nathaniel's role in interacting with Elijah and Romarr. Nathaniel's purpose on the stand was to serve as a racial veil that masked the racist intent of framing innocent Black children. And he was ready to perform his role on behalf of the Chicago Police.

Nathaniel's appearance to the mostly White crowd had the effect of making their police work and tactics appear nonracial. Former federal prosecutor Paul Butler has described how he, as one of the few lone Black prosecutors in his office, has played an important role for the White establishment. The presence of Black officers and prosecutors legitimized the punitive tactics that were weaponized against Black people, making their presence a display of virtue signaling that made the police seem race-blind.[60] How could one accuse the police of being racist when a Black face was the ambassador of their work?

This was a high-stakes performance for Chicago Police, and they were not about to leave this testimony to chance. The performance had to be both accurate and consistent with the confession and the other reports the police had created. And such accuracy required coaching, sharing notes and timelines, rehearsal, and teamwork. In another heater case, where Detective James Cassidy had been involved, the Englewood Four, he had been instrumental in constructing and propagating a narrative for the detectives and prosecutors to recite during their testimonies.[61]

In my time clerking in the prosecutor's office, prosecutors allowed police to confer with their partners before prosecutors could question them on a case.[62] Prosecutors would leave the room "to get coffee" while the police got their story straight. The police were allowed to study the police reports so that they could perform them in court.

Cassidy was a throughline for these practices. He was instrumental in extracting the confessions but also ensuring that the officers in the case's orbit spoke in lockstep with the narrative. If Cassidy wasn't on the stand, then it was safe to assume that whoever was testifying would be both well rehearsed and prepared to act as the parrot of Cassidy and all the "unknown and unidentified" officers who manufactured the case.[63]

Nathaniel stayed close to the talking points of the press conference but twisted the emphasis. He testified that the boys had thrown rocks at Ryan, also describing Romarr as the aggressor. But the point of Nathaniel's testimony was to suggest something more insidious than death. He testified that they dragged the body and tore off Ryan's clothes and played with her "softly"—rubbing leaves and foliage on her.[64]

There were no formal criminal charges of sexual assault, but the story sounded similar to the police fiction that Lee Hester laid down on top of Mrs. Keane while he exposed himself. The language was coded and childlike but tapped into racist logics that transcended history and time. If the racist lie is that Black men are bestial and crave the bodies of White women, it begs the question: When does a Black boy become a monster?

Romarr and Elijah were the police's answer to that perverse curiosity. And that the message had come from a "good" Black cop made it more believable—seemingly race-neutral—and thus absolved the White room from feeling any discomfort over such grotesquely racist thoughts.

After Nathaniel's testimony, the judge determined that there was probable cause and ordered the two boys to be held at Hartgrove Hospital for a psychiatric evaluation to see if it was safe for them to be home with their parents. Both sides, the prosecutors and the defense, would gear up for the second phase of hearings and would up their game, because all sides saw the high stakes of their cause.

If the boys were innocent, then the police were guilty. And that was something that the police establishment and prosecutors would not concede.

## Enter R. Eugene Pincham

Cases can be won in the opening statement. At least, Mr. Pincham could win them this way. He was a revered trial lawyer and a powerful orator. Attorneys used to flock to the courtrooms when he was cross-examining a witness or giving an opening or closing argument. To him, the law wasn't just about logic and reasoning; it was also about creating a performance. And Mr. Pincham was a master showman. He had no intention of losing this case. Elijah's life was on the line. There *would be* a performance, and a performance was about gravitas, connection, attitude—everything to bring the jury, judge, and gallery with you to see what you see and to know what you know. In Elijah's case, Mr. Pincham didn't let any details go unattended. For the second day of hearings, he would join Andre and shift the wind.

Mr. Pincham walked into the court with stature; indeed, juvenile court is the domain of the poorest of children and, therefore, many lawyers see it has a noble but lesser status of law.[65] It's often a stepping stone, not a destination. Mr. Pincham's presence ignited the room with a crackle. He knew this case would be a persuasive battle to see the boys *as* boys. And the battle would be won by performing such truth.

Romarr's mom grasped the stakes as well. From her seat near the Hendersons, she was kept from comforting her child, clinging instead to the hope that this performance might deliver justice for the boys. In her possession was her evidence that her baby boy was a good kid. She brought it in a folder like an attorney would. It contained Romarr's certificate of achievement for a science project (a model of a lever made from cups and spoons); perfect attendance awards he received; and photographs of him in his Easter Sunday best. When Maurice Possley interviewed her, she said, "I look at him and I don't see a murderer. I see my baby. He is my baby."[66]

This quote summed up Mr. Pincham's entire legal strategy and message. He and the Dream Team knew these boys were babies and not murderers. If they were seen as the tiny boys they were, then the police's lies—both in the legal case and the media spin—would begin to unravel. It was the police who were up to something wicked and deceitful in their "offical reports."

Mr. Pincham was dressed in his signature black Stetson, black boots, and a crisp suit, like an old-time sheriff, a man of the law.[67] He had a mischievous smile on his face, as though he knew something the prosecutor didn't know—which was true.

After Mr. Pincham agreed to represent Elijah, his doorbell rang in the dead of the night. He came to the door in his bedclothes, but there was no one to be seen. He looked down at his feet, and placed inside the screen door were police reports that had been withheld from Andre and Catherine.[68]

It appeared to be a whistleblower in the police department or maybe a lawyer from the State's Attorney's Office who took their ethics seriously. Whoever it was, they wanted to do the right thing, but they didn't want to end up like Frank Laverty—labeled a "dead on the streets" troublemaker—so they remained anonymous. Mr. Pincham, along with his wife, thumbed through the files. He shook his head at the lies, embellishments, and reports that didn't make sense.[69]

Mr. Pincham's air of confidence was born of the knowledge that the police reports were all lies. He was so confident that he was both a performer and usher in his own show. In the courtroom, he demanded seats for the crowd of reporters and began his performance like a magician, revealing the illusion right before their very eyes.[70] He brought out a simple prop into the court, one that didn't, on its first appearance, make sense. It was a medical scale.

He placed the scale before the judge and weighed his client. Elijah was fourteen pounds lighter and five inches shorter than the police estimates.[71] The police lied on the little details and the big ones. Indeed, their little lies helped shade the picture into focus and painted the boys as being deviantly large or abnormal seven- and eight-year-olds.

But Mr. Pincham wasn't done. He made Elijah into a prop to save him. Mr. Pincham was an elder, in his seventies, and to show Elijah's "featheriness" he lifted Elijah a foot off the ground by the armpit, like Moses commanding the Red Sea.[72] When he waved Elijah around in the air, Mr. Pincham smiled knowingly. At one point during the drama, Elijah smiled at his family. It was all going to be okay. The Black Power Ranger was on the case.

Mr. Pincham lectured the judge and the courtroom on the Constitution and quoted the Bible. He sparred with the judge while posturing and turning his body to the gallery of people. He questioned witnesses as he leaned casually by the judge's bench, as though he could intimidate with his coolness.

Catherine was a "courtroom regular," masterful at the everyday, knockdown, drag-out delirium that was juvenile court.[73] She consistently saw the lack of regard that judges had for Black children and their families. She understood the thorns of the system and fought every day for the kids she represented. She had the weight of the world on her shoulders, trying to protect Romarr, while she continued to distract Romarr from the adult exchanges in front of him. But the theater? The man handling a child and holding him up like a rag doll in court? For her, it was too far and too much.

And perhaps that was the difference between the Black Dream Team of lawyers and Catherine. All of them had law degrees, years of experience, and polished exteriors, but unlike Catherine, every Black man defending Elijah and Romarr (even Darron Bowden—the supervising public defender on the side of Romarr[74]) had been falsely accused or profiled because of their race. Many of their fathers, uncles, neighbors too. Scrutinized. Followed while shopping. Stopped by an officer for no reason. Some as young children. Just like W.E.B. Du Bois, who almost went to jail for taking a handful of grapes with his boyhood friends. Some of it was the police, but some of it was just the constant surveillance and possibility of accusation.[75] At stake in this nearly five-hour courtroom exchange was a way of seeing these little boys as boys.[76] And winning the battle and their short-term freedom to return to their parents' houses while awaiting trial was a battle they could not or would not lose . . . courtroom norms be damned. This was a heater case of the utmost importance, and the case would be won in the public, the media, and of course, by the persuasion of the judge.

For their part, prosecutors are not known for backing down. And this case was no exception. To beat Mr. Pincham, even in the later part of his life, would be a huge notch in the belt of any prosecutor, a surefire way to get promoted out of juvenile court.

In my time embedded in the prosecutor's office, Assistant State's Attorneys would celebrate their victories—"victories" meant convicting "mopes" but especially "monsters." They would memorialize their victories, saving the mug shots of their convicted defendants crying or the ties of the new prosecutors to publicize their first trial win. The objects would be placed on a community bulletin board like an honor roll list or a football team celebrating tackles, sacks, and touchdowns with stars on their helmets.[77]

When Mr. Pincham transformed the court into *his* show, the prosecutors were prepared to take it back. They were here to win, and winning meant keeping Romarr and Elijah in custody by arguing that they were a safety hazard to the community, monsters in the midst. And what they established in this early hearing had staying power in the mind's eye of the public. This *was* the trial.

Patti Sudendorf was one of the prosecutors who took the lead in this "mini-trial." Sudendorf had just transferred from the adult court to the juvenile court, and she brought that mindset and gusto to her approach.[78] Prosecutors like her had a way of seeing their mission and purpose as a moral calling. I interviewed and worked alongside many of them. In their view, prosecutors served a higher duty because they were the "good guys" doing what was morally righteous in society. Morality was like picking teams: You were either a good guy or a bad guy, and there was nothing in between. And of course, putting away "monsters" was the height of their responsibility.[79] In their view, a prosecutor's office was the "one place" where a lawyer can do what is "right," and they were doing "God's work on earth," which sounded reminiscent of Rudyard Kipling's poem "The White Man's Burden."[80] Indeed, prosecutors got promoted by how many trial wins they got, with little discussion of whether the convictions were legitimate or accurate. Questioning such matters would require questioning the veracity of the police, and such actions were career suicide.

Sudendorf, along with her colleagues, jumped into the sparring with Mr. Pincham, and the jousting went on for hours. One prosecutor interrupted the defense so much that the judge threatened to expel her.[81] The prosecutors argued that the two therapists who evaluated the boys in Hartgrove had not spent enough time with the boys to do their evaluations; later, they challenged the credentials of one of the therapists.[82]

At 5:45 p.m., well after court would normally adjourn, the prosecutors dramatically announced new evidence that would show just how dangerous the boys were. It was the school records of the boys.[83] The grandiose announcement of such surprise evidence made it seem like a twist in an episode of *Law & Order.* Sudendorf was given a chance to describe that evidence, but it fell flat. It had none of the punch of Mr. Pincham exposing the lies of police with a medical scale and lifting Elijah up in the air.

She could only show the records of the eight-year-old, which revealed he was an ordinary, good kid. They showed no discipline problems, eight and a half days of missing school, and solid grades that included an A, two B's, and a C.[84]

Without any smoking gun of danger, Sudendorf had to bring the fire to her concluding remarks. Many prosecutors believe that they do "God's work," so if Mr. Pincham was going to quote scripture, then Patti would match his moral vibrato. As she spoke, she turned toward the defense attorney's table, wagged her index finger right at the boys, and chastised them on behalf of the entire city: "Thou shall not kill." This made Romarr bow his head and start to cry. He still mumbled and maintained his innocence, "I din't do nothing"—this was Romarr's muffled rebuttal to the final argument.[85] A functionally nonverbal child, terrified of what they were doing to him, but still resolute in knowing he was a good boy who had done nothing wrong.

Ultimately, Judge Winiecki came to a decision that was something of a compromise. The boys would be confined to their homes with ankle monitors. No leaving the house. No backyard. No school. It was house arrest. Court officials would have to customize the ankle bracelets to fit the tiny kids. When Romarr got home, he would try to pry it off.[86] Ultimately, it would take three weeks for the presiding judge to rule that it was inappropriate to detain such young children, even in their home, and the monitors were removed.

In the end, Mr. Pincham and the Dream Team got what they wanted for Elijah, at least in the short term; he would not be detained in a prison-like setting. He got to be home with his parents. Romarr too.

But the Dream Team got something more. They began exposing the Chicago Police and their investigations for the scams they were. Andre started using the word *framed* in the media.[87] They started putting a spotlight on the Chicago Police, and, in turn, police started lawyering up with more prosecutors, to fight their fight, more theatrics to validate their crime fictions, the mayor and chief prosecutor standing behind them.

Normally, courts rule in favor of police narratives. As law professor Susan Bandes has written, "The sad reality is that judges almost never second-guess police testimony. They give police more than just the benefit of the doubt—they practically give them a free pass."[88]

And worse yet, there is a finality to the trial courts. What they rule is often the last word in most people's guilt or innocence.[89] Mr. Pincham's confrontation was an assault on the entire infrastructure upon which these "commonsense" beliefs were built, beliefs that made it so easy for police to accuse, charge, convict, and punish Black boys with impunity—a process that made closing cases "easy" as long as one was not concerned with accuracy. A process that is governed by "finality" because the system itself is weighted in favor of keeping prosecutors' convictions in place.[90]

What was different was that Mr. Pincham's performance helped the media second-guess the police. After the hearing, media pieces created a sympathetic picture of the Gipsons and the Hendersons. Articles focused on the absurdity of the young boys being murderers and rapists. Some raised concerns about how negligent police work that focused on these little boys meant that a real murderous pedophile was on the loose in Englewood. And soon, the national headlines that marveled at this case took a new turn. A *USA Today* headline read: SHOCK TURNS TO DOUBT IN CHICAGO.[91] By Friday of that week, the police seemed to be the ones under scrutiny and suspicion. And that unsettled some in the media establishment.

One of those journalists was pop-culture guru Richard Roeper, who would become known to many Chicagoans and audiences nationwide for co-hosting a movie review TV program with the legendary Roger Ebert. The two of them had the authority to give movies a "thumbs-up" or "thumbs-down"—a verdict that carried significant weight on whether a given film was worth seeing. Before his national fame, Roeper was a well-known opinion columnist and film critic for the *Chicago Sun-Times*. And Roeper felt compelled to chime in on the real-life drama that was the Ryan Harris case.[92]

In his commentary, he expressed sardonic skepticism on how there could be such a quick turn of events in the case: the sympathetic pieces about the boys and their families, the audible gasps from reporters as the boys entered the court, the sketch artists' renderings of the tiny boys with their faces blurred to protect their privacy, and the "courtroom theatrics" of Mr. Pincham.[93] The word *theatrics* made Mr. Pincham seem more like a con man than a former Illinois Appellate Court judge and a masterful litigator.

Roeper claimed that Mr. Pincham continued to "play the media," as though he was a snake oil salesman dealing in lies and deception. He called out one of the public defenders representing Romarr who had communicated an important public safety message for the Chicago Police: "Keep searching for the real killer," as "there's no way these two little tykes could have done this." Roeper dismissed all of this as "noise" from the defense—a distraction without substance and merit.

Roeper then gave his "review" of this drama: "Forgive me if I don't yet join the chorus. You say it's an obscene fairy tale that two little boys could perpetrate such violence; I'd say it's even more difficult to fathom that a team of police investigators would have proceeded with a case they knew would come under intense scrutiny if they didn't have solid evidence beyond what's been revealed in the media. Just because the defense team has been making almost all the noise doesn't mean one side is right and the other is wrong."

Roeper stood firm in his belief in the Chicago Police and essentially gave them his "thumbs-up" approval that they had it right. As he ended, it could be the case that some "hardened thug or thugs" were responsible for Ryan's murder; surely, "all leads should be explored. But that doesn't mean the cops haven't already gotten their men, no matter how small those men might be." This was the hold that the Chicago Police had on the media and the public.

It was much more probable that the Chicago Police were working in good faith than that two little Black boys from Englewood were innocent. Indeed, he deployed the word *thugs*—the same language that Richard A. Devine has used in the media to rationalize his behavior and that of his army of assistant prosecutors when he was the elected Cook County State's Attorney.[94] The media and the prosecutors were speaking the same language, in which there was only one way to understand their would-be killers: They were little "men" with murderous intent, regardless of how small they appeared to the eye.[95]

To say that Roeper was an outlier would be misleading. He was harnessing a popular sentiment that spoke to the city. On the same day that he ran his op-ed, the *Sun-Times* did a poll on Chicagoans' views on the Ryan Harris case.[96] Readers were invited to call in with their vote. Such polls weren't scientific, of course, but the poll did reveal something of the pulse of the city at that moment. The question was simple: Should the two boys linked to the Ryan Harris murder have been sent home?

YES: 29% NO: 71%

The police were litigating and winning their case in the public. The city had spoken.

## The Final Word

On Friday, September 4, 1998, four weeks after the boys' arrest, a new judge, Andrew Berman, called all the parties to a hearing but allowed Romarr and Elijah to be absent. Prior to the hearing, the state asked for a small recess, and when everyone returned to court, something seemed to have shifted. After the recess, Judge Berman called the court to order.[97]

Prosecutor Patti Sudendorf would be the mouthpiece for her colleagues Michael D. Oppenheimer and Kip Owen. Her demeanor was different from the last time she took center stage. There was no performance nor vibrato, just a small trembling in her voice and little inflection. She stood as she read a statement to the court:

> Yesterday afternoon, we received a telephone call from the crime lab advising us that semen was present on the panties of the victim, Ryan Harris. . . . After we received that information, we were informed by medical experts that the possibility of semen coming from seven- and eight-year-olds is highly remote. At ap-

> proximately 11 this morning, we received the report from the crime lab. . . . Therefore, your honor, as a result of the crime laboratory's findings, we seek to *nolle pros* [drop] the charges against both minors.[98]

The statement had dense official language and some legal jargon to boot. It was hard to see where it was going, and certainly, there was no insinuation that anything had gone wrong. The statement led to a hush, a long silence as the room settled into the truth. The prosecutors were forced to drop all charges because the physical evidence showed that Romarr and Elijah were innocent. The boys were free. Mr. Pincham and Catherine made their official statements of "concurrence for the record," and applause erupted.[99]

Mr. Pincham embraced Andre, who broke down in tears; after all, they were not Power Rangers, nor superheroes, but real men, Black men, with broken hearts.[100] They understood that Elijah's fate could have easily been lost as quickly as it had been won—just like so many other clients they knew.

As Judge Berman dismissed the case and officially adjourned the court, Catherine's eyes welled up with tears as she embraced her co-counsel. "Oh, my God, these kids went through hell. Thank God they found something."[101] Moments later, this release would transform into anger—anger at what Romarr had been through, anger at the moments in the police station when she first met Romarr in terror, and anger at the prosecutors dragging their feet on getting the news out that it was semen on the underwear. This was the type of exonerating information that the Chicago Police had a history of burying.

As she spoke to the media moments later, her happiness was tempered with anger. "At first, I was thrilled," she said. "Then I became furious. It couldn't possibly take that long to find out it was semen."[102]

The pandemonium of the moment, the relief and exhilaration for the boys, and the dramatic twist obscured the quiet truth lurking in the room. The police had framed two innocent children. They had filed charges without physical evidence to corroborate it; they had extracted confessions from two tiny boys who couldn't understand their rights, one of whom was disabled and barely verbal. They never looked in the boys' homes for clothing that might have tied them to the crime. They never found Ryan's bike. And they never considered the gory details of the crime, the violent sexual violation of Ryan's body. How could the police possibly believe that two prepubescent Black boys could do such a thing?[103] Andre said this quiet part out loud. The case was a "vile, vicious prosecution"; the boys had been "framed." As he described it, "False evidence had been arranged in such a way as to make young children look guilty. . . . We stand by that."[104]

Mr. Pincham would decry the Chicago Police's actions: "There was a rush to judgment to the extreme deficit to two young innocent babies—children, their families, to the community."[105] The Chicago Police, the prosecutors, anyone who touched this case had failed the babies, the families, and the Black community. A murderous pedophile was still on the loose, and the police were playing with the lives of two innocent children.

And then Mr. Pincham said out loud the question that he likely asked himself, privately, from the moment he wept upon seeing Elijah detained at Hartgrove: "If a police officer would do this to two children, what would he do to me?"[106]

There it was. Mr. Pincham asked the question we must all ask. He asked it on behalf of himself but also Andre, Berve, and Lew—the other Black Dream Team members. He asked the question on behalf of all the young Black children and teens in the community he mentored, for whom his wife baked cookies. He asked the question for all his clients as well as for all those innocent souls, known and unknown, free or still unjustly serving time. Because Mr. Pincham knew that what had happened to Elijah and Romarr was a threat that faced every Black child and family. *What could the police do to us? To my child? To me?*

What made matters worse was that James Cassidy—the experienced detective with almost a thousand cases under his belt who took such a role in extracting and coordinating with other officers to target the innocent—did not have a record of brutality or verbal abuse in his history.[107] His hands were clean. One prosecutor described him as a "gas pumper"—a detective who kept his nose down, went about his business, and got his work done without a rogue agenda.[108] And that quiet admission, that Cassidy was an ordinary, run-of-the-mill detective, was perhaps the most frightening truth about him. He had no rogue agenda but was merely a cog in the Chicago Police's machine of justice.

When Cassidy came under fire for his role in the Ryan Harris case, Eileen O'Neill, who had been a prosecutor in the A.M. case, came to his defense. O'Neill praised Cassidy as the "nicest, slightest man," which was "why they have him interview kids."[109] After A.M. was convicted, she stated, "Our juvenile criminal act was written at a time when kids were knocking over outhouses, not killing people. We're looking at a whole new breed here."[110] In his *Tribune* op-ed, Cassidy used almost identical language in calling for harsher punishment for children who commit violent crimes: "Illinois' Juvenile Code is long overdue for change. The juvenile offender today is far more dangerous than the kid who thirty years ago stole a car's hubcaps. Our present-day Juvenile Code was meant for just such an offender, not for today's vicious criminals."[111]

Alarmingly, the prosecutor who praised him, now Eileen O'Neill Burke, would politically benefit from her loyalty to Cassidy and the Chicago Police. She would be elected judge and ultimately be elected as the new Cook County State's Attorney, replacing the first Black woman prosecutor—a progressive reformer named Kim Foxx. In some of her first acts in office, she would roll back prosecutorial oversight on gun crimes coming out of Area 2. Police would no longer need prosecutors to oversee charges of felony gun possession, effectively giving them a blank check to criminalize. In addition, her predecessor had a public "do not call list" of over 280 police officers who the office deemed so "unreliable" that they should never be government witnesses at a criminal trial.[112] This included officers who were "accused of planting drugs on public housing residents, coercing dozens of Chicagoans into false confessions, and committing high-profile shootings of teenagers." O'Neill Burke made a reversal from her predecessor. She shortened the list and made it only an internal document, a policy move that had symbolic resonance and showed that she was in the business of protecting officers.

Eventually, R. Eugene Pincham and his team would seek justice in civil court, so Elijah and Romarr could get a monetary settlement to help with their lingering trauma and care. Elijah and Romarr would have separate legal teams for that. The Dream Team would represent Elijah, and one of George Jones's attorneys, Flint Taylor, would help represent Romarr. This time, the boys would be plaintiffs who were wronged, and the police would be the defendants. Mr. Pincham's complaint filing to the court on behalf of Elijah and his family was no sleepy, esoteric legal document. Instead, it read like an open letter from the Black Dream Team to the City of Chicago, its police, and its people:

> In spite of their aforesaid sworn duties, responsibilities and obligations, the Defendants, Officers Nathaniel and [Cassidy], unlawfully, immorally, wickedly, wantonly, and maliciously, and with evil and malignant hearts, agreed, confederated, conspired and combined together and with each other and with others, unknown and unidentified . . . to infringe upon, derogate, denigrate, break, disobey and violate Plaintiff Henderson's constitutional rights, privileges and guarantees.[113]

This was an indictment of Cassidy and Nathaniel and those who had conspired together. But there was no doubt that Mr. Pincham was indicting the entire institution, those "unknown and unidentified," the nameless, faceless officers who paid their allegiance to the code of silence and wrongful conviction. Beyond what they had done to the boys in the interrogation room, there was also missing evidence in this case. By choosing to unlawfully "create, concoct, fabricate and present" false evidence, as further alleged in the complaint, they illegally detained, framed, arrested, and imprisoned Elijah.[114]

In reading this civil complaint, Mr. Pincham was unrelenting in his language, with an overt tone of indignation and even rage directed at the Chicago Police and prosecutors. Mr. Pincham would name all the men who would not apologize nor even admit to harming the boys, their families, and the Black community: Mayor Richard M. Daley, Richard A. Devine, Michael D. Oppenheimer, Superintendent of Police Terry Hillard. And Mr. Pincham, a man of great faith, would name them as immoral, wicked, artfully deceptive, even diabolical in their everyday, ordained "work crimes" against Elijah and Romarr.[115]

Such indignation might seem unprofessional; certainly, as a Black lawyer, Mr. Pincham was no stranger to such insinuations—like Richard Roeper's dismissal of his work in the probable cause hearing as "theatrics."[116] However, Mr. Pincham was no longer willing to hold back his punches. The Chicago Police were operating outside of the law, and the tyranny was aimed at his people, his neighbors, and two tiny boys named Elijah and Romarr.

Indignation was the tone of the entire legal complaint, because at the core of that indignation was an expectation of—indeed, a demand for—dignity. Dignity for Elijah and Romarr but all Black people who were subjected to the practices of the Chicago Police. Perhaps it all sounded so radical because a Black lawyer had the audacity and power to demand it for a Black child.

## Payback

Elijah Sr. made a promise to his son in the dark moments before Elijah Jr. was taken away to Hartgrove. He promised Elijah Jr. that, like Simba, the little lion king, he too would be strong so he could be vindicated.[117] He was a father, and he was going to make good on his promise. The police and prosecutors were forced to free his boy because of new evidence; that was obligation, not vindication.

No one in the Chicago Police, Mayor Richard M. Daley's Office, or the State's Attorney's Office, led by Richard A. Devine, would admit that the detectives had done anything wrong. There was still a chorus of supporters who called these officers "trustworthy."[118] A former Assistant State's Attorney, who eventually became a judge, even defended the reputation of the officers, especially James Cassidy. The commentary described Cassidy as "honest, fair, compassionate and tough." He went "above and beyond the call of duty. . . . Our city should feel safer with him, and others like him, on the job."[119]

Elijah Sr. was going to do his part to ensure that there would be public vindication for his son. He told the *Lion King* allegory to the press and pointed out the parallels to his son's terrifying ordeal.[120] The police had cornered his son just as Simba had been left clinging desperately to a tree branch in the movie. "Everybody tried to trample him," said Elijah Sr. "For what reason: power."[121]

And Elijah Sr. didn't stop there. He said that he was angry at how the police could so easily turn his boy from a witness into a suspect and then he gave the police and the city a message: "Some authorities got too much power. . . . They got lazy and didn't do what they were supposed to do."[122] And finally, Elijah Sr. invoked God. It was only through the family's faith that they were able to survive what had happened to their boy.[123]

The Gipsons said their piece to the media as well.

"I can't say I'm happy," said Romarr's mom. "There is still a child dead. I am a little bit disgusted. I'm empty. Sad. I'm real sad because the Chicago Police Department is supposed to serve and protect people. And they didn't give these boys a chance."[124]

The Gipsons and the Hendersons said out loud what the Chicago Police wanted covered up. The families demanded vindication for their boys, and they also demanded that people understand how the police had failed their families, Ryan Harris, and everyone in Englewood.

And grieving Sabrina Harris, who was enduring the unthinkable loss of Ryan, a baby she called "Cookie," was enraged at the police.[125] The police had done their part in exacerbating her pain: "They had me hating those little boys. You never would have believed I was a parent for the hatred I had for them. . . . I was looking dead on, looking at them and I told my mother they didn't do it. I fell on my mother's lap crying, and I told her they didn't do it. . . . I know my daughter fought for her life."[126] How empty it feels, as a victim, to think that the police could solve your child's murder, only to realize that they victimized two other families in a sham. Sabrina would eventually conclude that the children deserved to receive $1 million for each day that they were labeled as the killers.[127] They were charged on August 9, and the charges were not dropped until September 4, and each day was worth something.

## The Terror That Never Sleeps

In every horror movie, there is a moment when such peace and resolution are fleeting, and the viewer is tricked into thinking that the terror is over, but the reality is that it is just gaining strength. For Daniel Taylor, it happened shortly after his exoneration, when he was stopped nearly twenty-five times for traffic violations. They would cuff him before even telling him why they were pulling him over. Officers even stopped his girlfriend when she was driving his car. It was so unrelenting that Daniel finally had to move away from Chicago.[128] Anthony Porter was exonerated and saved from execution, only to have the Chicago Police arrest him again for stealing four dollars' worth of deodorant.

Larry Ollins was falsely accused of shoplifting shoes by two Chicago police officers moonlighting as security guards at a Burlington Coat Factory in a neighboring suburb.[129] Larry approached the counter to pay for the clothes, only to be grabbed from behind. The guards twisted his arm, took him by the throat, and dragged him into a "detention room" in the store—just as he had violently been handled when he was falsely accused of the Lori Roscetti murder. As this violence unfolded, Larry was berated in front of the other patrons and called a "motherfuckin' thief." An empty box from the shoe department was found, and Larry was accused of stealing the shoes on his feet—a shoe brand that the store did not even carry. The tragedy was that this was no regular shopping trip. Larry Ollins and Omar Saunders were there to shop for new clothes to wear to their clemency hearing.[130]

What the Gipsons and Hendersons didn't know, at this moment of peace, was that the Chicago Police were not done with their families. The Chicago Police's memory is long, with new officers carrying the torch across the generations. Like Larry and Omar, it is hard to know when and where they will be, so hypervigilance and fear become a whole new form of torture.

There would be payback in the short term and the long term, and the payback would come as slow, prolonged violence.

## Fighting for a Freedom Dream

Romarr was ready to celebrate and just be a kid. There was a flurry of activity at Catherine's house on Labor Day. Bunches of kids were waiting on the edge of her swimming pool like little ducklings craving the water.[131]

"What are the rules?" an adult asked the little ones.

Romarr burst out with an answer. "I know the rules. . . . No fighting and no cussing."[132]

He smiled proudly, revealing a toothless grin.

This was a celebration. A celebration of freedom but, certainly, there was a shadow of grief and pain. Romarr was there to jump, swim, and run free with his siblings and family, but the adults were still catching their breath.

Catherine was hosting at her South Side home; the Gipsons traveled from Englewood to be there. The entire legal team that supported Romarr and his family during those dark days in the police station, Hartgrove, and the courthouse were now sharing a summer barbecue. While the kids splashed and played, the adults were getting ready to toast to what had transpired and the collective effort to help Romarr. He was now free.

Catherine's supervisor, Darron Bowden, was there. He was a quiet presence during Romarr's case. A Black supervisor with an exceptional professional record, but also a Black man who knew what it meant to be profiled as a child. When he was ten years old, he was riding his bike home from Abbott Park and a police car drove up and cut him off.[133] Within seconds, their handguns were drawn and pointed at him. They called him everything but a child of God, searching his body and pockets. Once the police decided to let him go, Darron was so shaken that he could barely walk his bike home. From the moment Romarr was arrested, all these memories came back fresh. He knew that his role as a Black lawyer was to make Romarr feel safe and cared for. Darron was as relieved as anyone, but his heart was also heavy. His childhood trauma wasn't history; it was present in Romarr and Elijah. Celebration? Yes. But forget this? No.

While the celebration was taking place, two uninvited guests rolled up to the party. It was the Chicago Police and they invited themselves.

The Chicago Police do not do public apologies, and they were still on the hook to close the Ryan Harris case.[134] Romarr was still on their radar. Surely, the police noted that Romarr's mother was speaking to the press. To them, Romarr was still a witness, even if they could no longer call him a suspect. But, perhaps, the distinction was just a matter of time. The police were there to question Romarr at his party, and Darron jumped into action. He took Romarr and his entire family, and they all hid in Catherine's office in total silence. They were imprisoned and hiding out at their own freedom party.

Darron wasn't just their lawyer; he was their physical protector. Catherine was the forward-facing negotiator with these two cops. In familiar form, one officer played the good cop and seemed to be appeased by eating the Gipsons' grilled food. Catherine kept serving him burgers.[135]

Every time Catherine would go to check on Darron and the Gipsons, all she saw was Darron, Romarr, and the entire Gipson family sitting there, wide-eyed and silent. It was the type of silence that can only happen when you hold your breath—a stark contrast to the pandemonium of a house full of children.

Purportedly, the police were there, again, to get Romarr to talk, to get more information and a statement. But their presence was a message in and of itself. The Gipsons could try to celebrate; they could even hide in their attorney's house. But the police knew exactly where they were. And there was a cruelty to sending this message at the exact moment they were toasting to freedom.

Once the police finally left, Darron lifted his glass in relief. "This is a time of mixed emotions," he said. "We are celebrating a family back together that was devastated for almost thirty days. . . . And we must remember that there is still a family who's missing a little girl. . . . Bless them and keep them in peace."[136]

Catherine was next. She gestured reverently at Romarr's mom. "Here's to a woman who has impressed me more than anyone with her strength and how she protected her child." And as the adults spoke, Romarr jumped in and out of the pool, ran through the sprinkler, passed out lollipops, and asked an adult to open a can of pop. And for a moment, the flurry of activity and the sheer pandemonium of childhood was at peace.[137]

The *Chicago Tribune* would report that since Ryan's murder, Romarr was getting harassed by someone nicknamed the "toy guy."[138] He would get near Romarr and try to give him toys, and the bizarre nature of it all (coupled with Romarr being one of the first children to find Ryan) meant that Romarr may have seen the murder or, worse yet, may have seen the murderer. And that could make him a target for the real killer, who was still on the loose. In such terrifying circumstances, one would have to call the police for protection. For Romarr, that was not an option—the police were the perpetrators. Making it worse, when they were so publicly exposed, Romarr and Elijah committed a new offense: They embarrassed the Chicago Police, and there would be payback.

Catherine would reflect later that the urgency to get a statement from Romarr, unannounced and in the relative protection of his lawyers, was a form of intimidation.[139] They wanted that statement, but the subtext was that they thought they would find more evidence to re-indict the boy.

There was also another possibility. The police were there just to have their presence known: *We know where you are. You can run or hide, but the Chicago Police will be there.* Catherine ended up giving the Gipsons a set of keys to her house in case they needed to flee for safety.

The police also had eyes on the Hendersons. Days after the police charged Elijah, his grandmother was told by a police officer that "he had been assigned to guard her family."[140] According to the grandmother, the officer said, "I was told to watch your house because there was a threat on your family," but the officer would not say anything more about the threat. There was just police, sitting and watching. This officer, tasked with "protecting" them, was an extension of the police trying to charge and criminalize her grandson. The officer tasked with protecting them could also arrest them—a latent threat whether there was someone after them or not. Regardless, the police were responsible. The false accusations against the boy were the reason for the threat in the first place.

But there was more. So much more. For the police, arrests are not just for fighting crime. Arrests are a tool. They can be a warning, a message, a solution to a problem, or a preemptive strike. Disorderly conduct charges are a perfect "law on the books" to make an arrest, a true weapon that police can use at will.

Elijah Sr. was vocal about the police wronging his boy, and he was able to distill the total failures of the institution with passion and emotion. His way with words put a target on his chest. A few days after he talked to the press, Elijah Sr. found himself being hunted by the Chicago Police. The "official report" said that officers spotted the father standing in the street and blocking traffic. A foot chase ensued, and the police caught the father. Andre Grant, who was still there to help the Hendersons, told the press that the father was charged with disorderly conduct for "whistling"—a peculiar offense that sounded very close to "whistleblowing."[141] It also had an Emmett Till quality to it. In this instance, whistling served as a dog whistle, a signal that a Black man was out of line and mouthy in a White world. It implied danger and even death, and there would be death.

If what happened to Detective Frank Laverty, one of their own, was any indication of how the Chicago Police handled whistleblowers, then the arrest of Elijah Sr. for "whistling" may have been the first sign that more was to come for an outspoken Black man. And the reporting of this harassment was not a headline; it was just a small detail buried in the articles on the Harris case.[142]

But within the year, more tragedy would befall the Hendersons. In June 1999, a fire swept through the house of Elijah Sr.'s mom.[143] The police found an accelerant in the hallway of the building that ignited the apartment around 3 a.m. The fire killed everyone in their sleep, including Elijah's paternal grandma, two aunts, two cousins, and a family friend. Their deaths would be investigated, by the Chicago Police, as homicides.

"When a whole family is wiped out in a fire, it's a tragedy," said police spokesman Pat Camden,[144] the same spokesman who had defended the actions of the Chicago Police in the Ryan Harris case. The police would claim that they had no reason to suspect the fire was linked to the Harris case, but one had to ask: *How much tragedy could befall a single family?*

Police encouraged the community to reach out to 51st and Wentworth for any leads in the arson case,[145] the very same place where police buried street file evidence and interrogated the victim's grandson. In the end, all the roads still led back to 51st and Wentworth and to the Chicago Police. Even if this was just a random act of violence, the Hendersons were forced to depend upon the police to investigate the case in good faith.

The Hendersons moved away from Englewood to what they hoped would be a safer part of Chicago. In 2005, with the Dream Team fighting for them, the Hendersons accepted a settlement. Ironically, the attorneys for the city and police would argue that Elijah's trauma did not derive from the police interrogation or imprisonment but from the father's arrest and the arson.[146] In the end, the Hendersons received a $6.2 million settlement.[147] That may have seemed like another ending to the story—a vindication that his father wanted for his boy.

But this is not the end of the story, only a pause when Elijah went from being a boy to a man. A pause and a passage of time in which Mr. Pincham would pass away, in 2008, and would no longer be able to play superhero for the boy. The tragedy was on pause until Elijah was grown.

## The Final Question

In 2008, nearly ten years had passed since the Chicago Police made their first hit on Elijah Henderson. Elijah was eighteen years old—a young adult.[148] He was also marked.

On this day, police were checking for seat belt use at a traffic stop and tried to pull Elijah Sr. over for a seat belt infraction. Elijah Jr. was in the car with his dad. Unaware that he was being pulled over, Elijah Sr. drove back to the family home. Such confusion is the perfect foundation upon which the police could engage in a chase with a legitimate pretense that would not raise any eyebrows. I have seen it myself. Police giving directions to keep people in compliance with the law, only to have another officer give the opposite instruction to make an arrest. Police yelling "Stop resisting" as they tighten their headlock around a man's neck to make him flinch. Bait and switch. Chaos. Arrest. Conviction.

Andre Grant was still supporting the Henderson family. As he described it, Elijah Sr. "was unaware that somebody was following him or stopped him. They kicked in the door. They tore a screen off the door. And when they came in with guns blazing is when they met his family."[149]

Elijah's maternal grandmother was there to see it all unfold. The officers came into the house after they had Elijah Sr. in the car, and they came ready to fight. She later recalled that the police came in the form of an army, twenty-five deep. They threw Elijah's sister up against the wall; she hit her head and dropped down to the floor. They used their hands and their knees to pin, push, and punch like a gang fight.

When twenty-five armed officers burst into the house unexpectedly or over a supposed seat belt infraction, there is bound to be yelling and protesting, chaos and trauma. This was especially true given the events of over a decade earlier.

Sonya Crawford, Elijah's mother, went down screaming and fighting to keep her other children safe. Elijah Jr., now a young man, did the same. As officers beat Elijah in the dining room, his sisters lay on top of him to try to prevent the officers from harming him.

Resistance to the Chicago Police is easily classified as a crime, even if an officer suffers only small bruises. In the melee, Elijah Jr. was accused of striking a police officer and was charged alongside his mom with aggravated battery to a police officer. His father faced a seat belt violation. Elijah's teenage sisters were cuffed and arrested like adults, dragged from the house in their underwear and pajamas and stripped of their dignity out on the front lawn for all the neighbors to see. In all, police would arrest six people, including two children.[150]

Lew Myers, one of the Dream Team, would tell the media: "It's not a coincidence that they ran into a Black home on the South Side of Chicago with no probable cause."[151]

The narratives that the police create become unbending truths that define people for their whole lives. In the end, a Cook County jury would deliberate for ninety minutes before finding Elijah and his mom guilty of aggravated battery to a police officer.

Surely their neighbors wondered:

*Could a poor Black family such as the Hendersons get the truth and a six-million-dollar settlement without payback from the Chicago Police?*

# Conclusion

*Well, if one really wishes to know how justice is administered in a country, one does not question the policemen, the lawyers, the judges, or the protected members of the middle class. One goes to the unprotected—those, precisely, who need the law's protection most!—and listens to their testimony.*

**—James Baldwin, *No Name in the Street*[1]**

Historian Melanie D. Newport's book on the history of incarceration in Chicago gives us a glimpse into this origin story of America's wrongful conviction system.

As she describes it, in 1842 Edwin Heathcock was arrested for being "unconstitutionally free."[2] He was held in what was then called the Cook County Jail for six weeks, the amount of time that would allow his master to come forward to claim him as property. If no one came forward, he would be sold at an auction. If no one purchased him at auction, Edwin could be imprisoned indefinitely—an open-ended punishment for the sole "crime" of being both Black and free in Chicago.

By the 1920s, Black people and Black spaces were seen as a social threat that required containment, and the criminal justice system was an essential part of that solution. The historical throughline is the belief that the criminal justice system is needed for the "adjustment, containment, and discipline" of Black people—with cops, courts, and corrections working in concert to such ends.[3] Historical records show that judges treated Black defendants with callous levity. Like a precursor to the "Two-Ton Contest," one judge even had a habit of rolling dice during hearings for Black people as though their fate and freedom was in his hands like a rigged game.[4]

And that enduring prejudice, that crime of being both Black and free, was what all of these supposed blameworthy boys had in common.

Child saving was never meant for Black children in the juvenile justice system, a fact that many journalists and policy makers failed to realize. The orphaned Black child was not a dependent of the state but was labeled a delinquent.[5]

I thought through this history when I talked to Romarr in 2021.[6] He was a grown man and had struggled throughout his life. He was bullied as a "baby killer" when he went back to school. His trauma endured, and as a boy, he self-harmed and lashed out. He rolled with the wrong crowd and was convicted of felonies and sent to prison.

One day many years later, Catherine was representing her clients and was shocked to hear an older teen yelling for her from the lockup.[7] It was Romarr calling her name, and her heart sank for him: for all that was done to him, for the irreparable harm that she had seen with her own eyes, back when he was still sucking his thumb.

Now in his thirties and with a new baby and partner, Romarr was hopeful to start a new life with his family. Given all that had transpired and all that he had survived, the most important question I asked him was: "Why you? Why Elijah?"

Implied in the question was that they never deserved this, any of this, any of them.

Romarr: I guess they were just trying to close the case.

*How did you come to that conclusion?* I asked.

Romarr: When I was in prison . . . I been around a lot of guys that ain't never come home and got framed.

For Romarr, it was that simple. To understand and maybe to heal all that had happened to him, he had to meet others like him, other innocent people who were in prison because the police had put them there without regard to accuracy, fairness, public safety, or the law. They were in prison because the police needed them to be there. They were there as the solution to a problem. They were there because, as the police saw it, they *were* the problem. The astounding part is that this number, this systemic error in the criminal justice system, is unknown.[8] As Daniel Taylor would conclude, "Mark my word. I won't be the last one to be proved innocent."[9]

"Waiting can be a weapon."[10] It is a way for "the state to tell you that your time and thus your life, is neither yours to control nor worth very much."[11] It is a daily lesson in remaining "neglected, unattended to, or postponed."[12] As Malik would later say: "My entire life has [consisted] of me waiting. It feels like my life has been shattered into a million pieces of waiting. It hurts to wait for justice, to wait on something you can not afford to give up on with the hope it will arrive soon!"[13]

During the course of this research, I went to exoneration clinics and civil rights firms to see their process of weeding through all the desperate letters from incarcerated people who claim their innocence. One firm said that the average wait period to read a person's application to review their case was two years.[14] This was just the time it took to have someone, anyone—a student or clerk or volunteer—open the application.[15] If the incarcerated person hadn't filled out the application, their letter was ignored, thrown out, or routed back to them in prison, where they had to start the entire process over again.

I thought back to Daniel Taylor and his words about the prevalence of innocence behind bars. He begged an investigative reporter to help him, and that reporter admitted to getting myriads of letters and requests of similar urgency. I get them as well, a groundswell of need. And it was an accident that Daniel was both heard and helped. To be clear, the accident wasn't the wrongful conviction—that part seemed patterned and predictable. The accident—left to chance and luck—was whether someone *would* or *could* save him.

And that waiting, that horrendously slow violence, is the most shocking part of this system. The lie that we all accept is that the innocent will go free and that the "mistakes" will be rectified. But the reality is that accusation and conviction are nearly one and the same, and accuracy is an afterthought.[16]

"In 2018, the National Registry of Exonerations reported a grim milestone. Exonerated defendants had collectively served 20,000 years in prison for crimes they did not commit. Just three years later, in June 2021, we reached another: Time lost to false convictions exceeded 25,000 years."[17] As of January 13, 2026, time lost to wrongful convictions reached 35,163 years. That is an average of over nine years in prison for each of the 3,771 exonerees in the Registry. And it is innocent Black defendants who serve a majority of that time—a total of 21,072 years of life lost to wrongful conviction.[18] And these statistics, these numbers of those waiting for freedom and justice, should be sobering because they do not even include someone like Malik Muhammad, who is still imprisoned and is likely innocent.

Astoundingly, none of the officers, in any of these cases, were ever substantively punished by the Chicago Police Department.[19] The city paid to represent them in all the civil cases, and only Jon Burge faced federal perjury and obstruction of justice charges related to over one hundred torture cases—an unsavory outcome akin to Al Capone getting tripped up on tax evasion charges.[20] Burge retired in sunny Florida. James Cassidy, like Burge before him, also retired to Florida and published books in the true crime genre. With all his years of experience, he literally made himself into an author of crime fiction.

But more than that, Cassidy would write a moral tale of being a good, righteous Catholic servant, where God would call upon people to be heroes and saints in this world. His work in a religious genre may have harkened back to his time holding children's hands and explaining how the police would forgive them, as God would do. The police officer who did get punished by the Chicago Police was Frank Laverty—the mythical "good cop," the whistleblower, who was turned into a cautionary tale of why every officer must obey the code of silence and violence to be blue.

As for the prosecutors, few could say they were truly "clean" of these practices. The number of people implicated is astounding. As Flint Taylor writes in *The Torture Machine:*

> One hundred and ninety-three ASAs [Assistant State's Attorneys], including sixty-seven supervisors and Chiefs, and two State's Attorneys, have been directly involved or otherwise significantly connected to the torture cases since the first allegations arose almost thirty years ago. Among this group of one hundred and ninety-three ASAs, there are forty-one Felony Review ASAs who took statements from defendants who alleged that they were tortured or otherwise physically abused by Burge and his men, and one hundred and fifty-four more, including Richard M. Daley, [Richard A.] Devine, and their Chiefs and Deputies, who have been involved in the prosecution or appeal of these cases, the defense of Burge and his associates, who have been witnesses for the State or Burge, and/or who directly supervised one or more of the interrogations and prosecutions in question.[21]

Many of these prosecutors were even elected to the bench. Beyond that, an unknown number of prosecutors are connected to cases involving junk science, withholding of evidence, psychological coercion, deception, and false confession—other wrongful conviction tactics that are all but required to win cases and advance in the office. These are, in the words of Mr. Pincham, the "unknown and unidentified" people who knowingly "infringe upon, derogate, denigrate, break, disobey and violate" constitutional rights, privileges, and guarantees.[22]

It seems that nearly everyone in the office who worked in the felony courts was one degree of separation, in friendship or professional ties, to those who tortured, coerced, or hid evidence. Even Catherine Ferguson's brother was neighbors with James Cassidy. I tried to imagine them waving to each other over the fence or grilling out in the summers. I thought back to how Romarr's celebration barbecue was interrupted by two of the police's henchmen, while in a nearby neighborhood Cassidy lived a quiet existence as though no harm was ever done.

Indeed, it was hard to meet any courtroom insider who didn't have some ties to this system. I unknowingly tested this theory while at a professional mixer on the East Coast where I met a family who had moved from Chicago.[23] This news launched a game of "Who do you know?" It turned out that both the husband and wife had been Chicago attorneys in a past life. I told them about my work and my book and mentioned false confessions, the street files, Candace Gorman, and other details that I thought they may know.

Turns out, I was telling the husband about his own career. He was colleagues and co-counsel with Dan Norland, the attorney who fought Candace Gorman in the Nathson Field case—the case that revealed to the world that the street file system was alive and well. My unfiltered reaction was to blurt out: "I've got to know. How did the police move a metal file cabinet? Did they use a forklift?" In his response there was exasperation—an equally matched defense of Dan coupled with anger over a troublemaker like Candace who was overreacting about the hidden files. There was also a doubling down of denial.

Sociologists don't believe in accidents. We believe in process. We believe in odds. And the odds of randomly making this connection demonstrate just how far-reaching this system was. That even as I researched this book in New England and commuted to my hometown of Chicago, I was standing shoulder to shoulder with Candace Gorman's opponent, a man who represented and therefore protected the lawlessness of the Chicago Police.

As for Malik, he was still being punished by these practices.

A special prosecutor was assigned to review cases where new trials were sought "due to alleged police brutality under disgraced former Chicago Police Commander Jon Burge."[24] The problem was that despite this formal mission, the system was informally designed to protect itself: The special prosecutor assigned to review Malik's case was named Robert Milan. Milan was a longtime prosecutor and part of the machine.

He served as supervisor of the Felony Review Unit and later rose to

First Chair Felony Trial Division, followed by First Assistant State's Attorney (second in charge of the office), and he ran for State's Attorney in 2008 with a powerful endorsement from his old boss, Richard A. Devine. At the time of his campaign (he eventually lost the election primary), he was a twenty-year veteran of the office—the second largest prosecutor's office in the nation—and supervised nine hundred attorneys and investigators.

Milan's appointment bucked years of previous court rulings that found an inherent conflict of interest in letting the State's Attorney's Office review its own convictions. Milan had recently left the office for a job with a corporate security firm, a move that made him technically eligible for the appointment, even though to most laypeople this could appear to be a significant conflict of interest.[25]

On the surface, Milan was an establishment guy. He was one of the prosecutors tied to the Dixmoor Five case, a wolf pack case in which police grabbed Robert Veal, a fourteen-year-old disabled boy, and forced him to sign a confession that he couldn't read—an insidious move that eventually subsumed five boys in all. Anita Alvarez, the prosecutor who beat Milan in the primary and eventually won the election, would never acknowledge the boys' innocence. It was only a court that would do that.

Despite his connection to the prosecutor's office, Milan had developed a reputation as a reformer. He used the Dixmoor case and the abundance of exonerations emerging from DNA technology to have an awakening of sorts. He published an article written to educate other prosecutors on the "warning signs" of wrongful conviction, which he saw as a "national problem."[26] While he worked under Devine, Milan created training videos on how prosecutors could detect false confessions as well and began mandating the videotaping of all homicide interrogations (even though police often censor the full duration of what suspects and witnesses endure).[27] Milan was even invited to speak at exoneration clinics for law students to help educate budding lawyers on the proper cross-checks to avoid wrongful conviction. While in the State's Attorney's Office, he even dropped charges in at least six Cook County cases.[28]

However, I was still skeptical; six cases are merely a drop in the bucket when considering the enormity of wrongful conviction cases. Was Milan a true reformer or another variation of smoke and mirrors—like the sham of "reforming" the street file system by the police themselves?

Looking deeper, the idea that he would reform this system is absurd. Despite his reformist reputation, in 2015, Milan wrote an op-ed in the *Chicago Tribune*[29] that was reminiscent of Cassidy's 1994 op-ed, warning the city of an impending threat.[30] Milan warned that with school out for the summer, thousands of teenagers were now "on the streets" on the "South and West sides." South and West sides was a proxy for race and denoted Black communities in Chicago. He even proposed that the city should call in the National Guard. Two years later, as president, Donald Trump was deploying a similar rhetoric to "send in the feds" to manage Chicago's crime.[31] At the time, this article was tinged with a type of racial politics that suggested racial bias, which Milan refuted. When questioned about the article, Milan fought back: "People try to paint me as racist. . . . But I would do it in my own neighborhood."[32] Beyond Milan's views on crime control, he exhibited a strong allegiance to certain members of the Chicago Police. The same year the op-ed was published, the *Tribune* was reporting on Kenneth Boudreau, a detective who had been a part of getting confessions from more than a dozen defendants in murder cases in which the charges were dropped or the defendant was acquitted. These outcomes were the tell-tale signs of false confessions, but Milan claimed it would take too much manpower to formally review Detective Boudreau's work. "There's no reason to review every single case of a detective," Milan said. "This detective has had a long career, a good career."[33] He seemed more aligned with the system than reform, reflecting the enduring pull of institutional loyalties over reformist intent.

And when he was in the office, Milan had significant power to impact policy and practice. Milan had once been a prosecutor and supervised approximately nine hundred prosecutors in the same office that signed off on so many wrongful convictions—many of the cases tied to mental and physical abuse. Moreover, Milan was also notified about the use of torture, deception, and abuse in his department in 1999 by a fellow Assistant State's Attorney named Clarissa Palermo.[34] In a letter, Palermo details meeting a defendant who had a lump on his forehead with a small abrasion on it. His jaw appeared swollen, and there was fresh, bright blood on his shirt. The defendant explained that he was kicked and beaten while he was sleeping, just before his interrogation. Milan took no apparent action. It was under his watch that such practices continued—affecting Malik and many others.

Malik's legal team expressed concern that Milan's connection to the original investigation could complicate his role in reviewing it. He had served as supervisor of felony review during the period Malik was arrested and was now in the position of reviewing the actions of his former subordinates.[35]

Malik's case also had *Brady* violations and torture claims.[36] According to Malik's attorney, it was Milan's prosecutors who worked in tandem with Michael McDermott, an officer known for being in Jon Burge's inner circle. The Illinois Torture Inquiry and Relief Commission (TIRC) would implicate him in several cases where there was "sufficient evidence of torture to merit judicial review."[37] Malik would allege that McDermott and at least four other officers denied him food and water and forced him to urinate and defecate in the interrogation room because a bathroom was withheld from him. Officers also allegedly hit Malik during the interrogation.[38] According to Malik's attorney, it was Milan's teams of prosecutors who impersonated defense attorneys[39] to trick Malik into a confession.[40]

When Candace brought her case on Malik's behalf, to the special prosecutor, it brought her to Milan. The same supervisor who had been head of the felony review office that worked hand in glove with the police who were accused of violating Malik's rights. With Milan in that role, the buck literally stopped with him. Malik's claims of torture were denied.

As special prosecutor, Milan sought to dismiss the proceedings. The circuit court granted Milan's motion without an evidentiary hearing.[41] That meant that Candace would not be able to present evidence of

Malik's alleged abuse and coercion before a judge. Milan's office argued that what happened to Malik did not meet the criteria of a "tortured confession" as it was narrowly defined in the Illinois Torture Inquiry and Relief Commission Act because he had not made a direct confession during the abuse. This interpretation disqualified him for relief—another example of the process and letter of the law denying even the chance of exoneration.

Candace did what Candace did best—she fought. In 2020 she filed a "motion to rescind" Milan's appointment as special prosecutor, a move that, if successful, would eventually force Milan to recuse himself from Malik's case.[42] She cited conflicts of interest—Milan's prior supervisory role of the prosecutors implicated in Malik's claim—but also noted the appearance of impropriety. Milan wouldn't budge, denying the conflict and claiming that Candace was engaging in "gamesmanship."[43]

And like the back-and-forth games she played with Dan Norland over the street files, Candace began a new game on behalf of Malik. A battle began to get Milan to recuse himself from Malik's case (and others)—and Milan fought it every step of the way. Candace didn't hold any punches. In her filing she explained the overt conflicts of interest that he never mentioned during his appointment process. She argued that keeping Milan in that role "violates [Malik's] right to a prosecutor unencumbered by conflicting loyalties and potentially prejudicial inclinations . . . [which] undermines the integrity and legitimacy of the entire process."[44] An Appellate Court of Illinois would rule in Malik's favor and say that Milan had a conflict but in the end the Supreme Court of Illinois would overturn that lower court and allow Milan to remain on the case.[45]

There was another injustice, too. The back-and-forth with Milan delayed Malik's case, prolonging the time he remained incarcerated. Legal scholars often use the phrase "the process is the punishment" to describe the arduous nature of being accused of a crime and having to fight the case—often from the inside of a jail cell awaiting trial.[46] What I was seeing was that even on the back end of the system, there were processes that could punish, transforming good faith avenues for remedies and relief into arduous processes that could continue to punish people even when they had credible claims of innocence.

Doing the research for this book made me ponder the way that people were wrongfully routed into the criminal justice system. In Malik's case, I could now see how a whole set of legal actors and processes could act like back-end gatekeepers that could keep the innocent inside.

The "principle of finality" is a legal doctrine that makes it nearly impossible, except in the narrowest of situations, to appeal cases and reverse a conviction.[47] Beyond that, prosecutors could literally hold the innocent under lock and key—even when there was a credible route to having cases reviewed. Creating delays, explaining away conflicts of interest, fighting small details like whether someone had confessed or had made smaller, incriminating statements under physical abuse. The back-and-forth, the twists and turns, the dizzying number of hearings: All it did was prolong the punishment for so many who were possibly innocent and were just waiting for any semblance of impartial oversight. Over five hundred other defendants were waiting, and it would take decades to hear them all.[48] Many of them would die waiting in prison, and perhaps that was the point of Milan and other back-end gatekeepers like him.

After the appellate victory that temporarily rescinded Milan's appointment to his case, Malik could only reflect on both the joy and the emptiness of the short-term win. He was still in prison and not much closer to freedom. As he said, "The opinion itself causes so much emotion. It is a very big win, and yet I am still sitting here for an unknown amount of time. After spending twenty-four years in prison, there is a vacancy in my life that will never be filled."[49]

I followed Malik's story as he graduated from Northwestern University via their college education program in Illinois prisons. Award-winning author Ta-Nehisi Coates was his commencement speaker. Candace was there, too. She was fighting for his life but showed up to celebrate his living.

I received a letter from Malik describing the pride he felt to wear a cap and gown. And, in that graduation event, he noted the disdainful glares of prison guards as he and his cohort celebrated their intellectual freedom. Their power as thinkers and scholars. Their piece of being Black and free on the inside. They were being seen for who they really were: people with potential, talent, and power—not the "defuturized" or "disposable" boys that the police once saw. This ceremony, behind prison walls, was a radical and defiant act.

Those who have suffered trauma, like the many boys in this book, know that the event will replay in the mind. But the secondary trauma is not being believed, having the reality of your injury denied, being told or gaslit into thinking that what happened is what you deserved or something you welcomed or caused. Let this book defuse that injury. Let those who claim their innocence know that we see the clandestine system that targets and violates Black people. Let those who are innocent know we see how police can rig justice in their favor and at the expense of those who are most vulnerable. Let those who are innocent and imprisoned know that their stories will be believed and be heard.

In the end, all we have is our time, so it may not be surprising that time is the currency through which we inflict punishment. We call it "doing time," and delays are weaponized to take more time from those who have already lost so much. We take away their childhoods and youth. We take away their innocence. We take away their dignity. We take away their narrative in favor of the police's version of truth, and no matter how the police's media spin colors it, none of us are safer for it.

I once asked a colleague, Princeton professor Laurence Ralph, how researchers can remain objective in the face of egregious injustices. His answer was poignant and powerful: If we cannot pick a side in matters as grave as torture, for instance, then who are we as a people?[50] So perhaps that is the final question, the one that is hardest to reflect upon:

Now that we know and see what justice is in this country, *What side are we on?*

# Epilogue

*And once you realize that you can do something, it would be difficult to live with yourself if you didn't do it.*

**—James Baldwin**[1]

Mr. Cole must have known that Omar Saunders, now Omar Muhammad, was destined to be a teacher and a truth teller. As a free man rebuilding his life, the teaching and truth telling, for Omar, would reach beyond the classroom and take many forms.

Omar fought relentlessly for his innocence. He spent nearly fifteen years in prison before his and his friends' convictions were vacated. New evidence and DNA testing showed, definitively, that none of the boys—Omar, Calvin, Larry, and Marcellius—were involved in the death of Lori Roscetti. In 2002, Governor George Ryan pardoned the men. Ultimately, all four received a compensation, settling with the City of Chicago for the harms they had endured and the years they had lost. But money can't buy peace, and it can't give purpose.

Even after Omar's exoneration, lies were still told about his case, and about his friends. And just as Mr. Cole had taught him so many years ago, he knew that his calling was to be a truth teller and fight back with his words.

Omar became an author to set the record straight; that was how I first met him, through his memoir and his reflections on all he survived. His book, *The Kids Who Cried Wolf,* dissected every facet of the case and demonstrated his innocence. And there was freedom in being the writer of his own story and knowing that he, and not the police, would have the last word. As he said, "As I was writing the book, I realized that it freed me up and at the same time, I realized that it was about time to tell the truth."[2]

Omar moved to Rockford, Illinois—far enough away from the city and all the pain that he had endured. With his family, the simple joys of freedom are easy to savor after being incarcerated for so long. He is now a father, and the beauty that he sees in his children is to be nurtured by him, teaching them how to be good, just citizens of the world. A type of light that can disinfect the darkness. Indeed, he named one of his children Justice as though her name would anoint others with that virtue, making her into a hopeful ambassador. A righter of wrongs.

Omar was a teacher to his kids, but he also earned a reputation for teaching government and civics classes to local children, including lessons from the Constitution.[3] And despite all he had been through, he still saw the Constitution and all its rights and privileges as sacred. There was not a cynical bone in his body.

It was in this rich and principled intellectual home that his one son learned about a little boy named George Stinney, a child who in 1944 was executed for a crime he did not commit. He was fourteen years old. Certainly, the violence of it all was what set off the outrage and tears from Omar's young son, Supreme.

The White folks of Alcolu, South Carolina, accused an innocent Black child, George, of the sexual assault and murder of two White girls. They created a sham of a trial with a lynch mob serving as the jury. Through a rigged game of due process, he was sentenced to death.[4]

White folks had affectionate names for their electric chairs. South Carolinians called theirs "Old Sparky." George walked into the execution chamber with the Bible. There were about fifty witnesses in the room, and the most prominent leaders of the lynch mob were given the prime seating they had demanded. Reportedly, the Bible was used as a booster seat because the electric chair was not imagined for a person as tiny as George. A hood was put over his head—loosely. This allowed the hood to fall off his face once the powerful jolt of electricity was administered—giving the viewers a better look at the gruesome specter of it all.

Supreme questioned how something so horrible could happen to a boy who looked as young as him, with Black skin like his and a small frame. George's death made the tears flow down his face, the kind of tears where the child is seeing the true nature of the world for the first time.

But for Omar, George's story was so much more than his tragic death. The path of so-called justice that led fourteen-year-old George Stinney to sit on a Bible on the electric chair was a familiar set of steps and techniques that Omar knew too well.

Omar felt those tears as a father, but he felt something else deeply.[5] He knew boys like George, young ones who faced similar injustices. What was in the past was in the present. Wiping his son's tears felt insufficient to remedy it all. Indignation had to come with action, and there was power in that righteous cause, a power to expose injustice, even when truth was meant to be buried like the dead.

George was a beloved and benevolent boy, wronged by lies, lies told by people who didn't see him as worthy of having a future. And what happened to George was a blueprint of sorts, an original sin of the system itself that could incriminate and vanish Black boys across history. Indeed, there was a hint of young George's case in all the wrongful convictions that came after. It was Omar who was called to tell that truth.

Omar told Supreme not to worry. That he would do something for George Stinney.[6] So he started small, creating a memorial page on Facebook that told the truth about George's life and death and the false accusations that killed him. With impressive speed, the groundswell of people calling for George's exoneration grew beyond Omar's original efforts. Lawyers and law schools took interest, and soon a group that began as a humble promise to Omar's son ended up creating the considerable groundswell of public support to exonerate George, posthumously.

Discussions began about a headstone to replace the unmarked grave.

The headstone would have George's name and the dates of his birth and death. And below that, a profound admission: "Wrongfully Convicted. Illegally Executed by South Carolina."

From my research and experience, police and the state rarely admit when they are wrong. In fact, they often double down on their errors, create new narratives, and block the back-end review of cases.

However, Omar was a force, a man who had learned from his teacher, Mr. Cole, that those with great authority and power must be held to a higher standard. This vindication, this truth telling, began with Omar. He did it for George; he did it for his son; and indeed, he did it for himself. Because Omar *was* George and George *was* Omar. They were brothers across time.

# Acknowledgments

James Baldwin argues that the supreme animating force of the writer is the irrepressible impossibility of not-writing or creating: "Something that irritates you and won't let you go. That's the anguish of it. Do this book, or die." He goes on to dismiss talent and emphasize something more: "Beyond talent lie all the usual words: discipline, love, luck, but, most of all, endurance."

From the day Steven Drizin called me about studying wrongful conviction, I had that terrible anguish that Baldwin described. In fact, I hung up the phone and was angry; I had no choice but to write this book. It wasn't just a call; it was a calling, and I knew it would take years, tears, and a profound amount of grief and healing to complete. But as my dear friend, Professor Zandria F. Robinson, taught me, "we are not meant to do this work alone."

To be sure, this book was an endurance test, but I was surrounded by friends, informants, messengers, students, colleagues, family, ancestors, and angels—a whole village surrounding me in love, strength, and care. Let me introduce these people to you as I give them my thanks.

I thank Steven Drizin for believing that I could do justice to this work and trusting me as I went beyond false confessions into the underbelly of wrongful conviction. He was a true and constant presence during this journey, and I am forever grateful for his generosity. I thank Flint Taylor, who encouraged me when this project seemed too big and unwieldy to complete. He believed in me before I could believe in myself. I thank my dear mentor, Professor Stephen Daniels, who advised me on my undergraduate thesis project (that turned into my first book, *Crook County*). He continues to be a source of wisdom and support for nearly 27 years.

I thank all the experts that sat down for an interview but also allowed me to mine their archives (and memories) in order to generate the breath of data, stories, news articles, and legal documents in this book: Andrew Berman, Judge Darron E. Bowden, Locke Bowman, Donald Kizza-Brown, Christopher Coleman, John Conroy, Catherine Ferguson, Thomas F. Geraghty, H. Candace Gorman, Steve Mills, Joey Mogul, Laura Nirider, Maurice Possley, Wesley Skogan, Joshua Tepfer, and Alexa Van Brunt. I honor all the wrongfully convicted men whose stories are profiled in this book and especially those who generously gave their time to speak and correspond with me: Romarr Gipson, Abdul Malik Muhammad, Omar Muhammad, and Daniel Taylor. Mr. R. Eugene Pincham was a man that I never had the honor of meeting, but I give him thanks and heavenly respect. He left 14 tapes of his oral history that, I believe, he intentionally left so that someone could continue investigating his work fighting the Chicago police. I just happen to be that *someone.* Mr. Pincham's favorite quote from the Bible was Joshua 24:14–15: "*As For Me And My House, We Will Serve The Lord.*" I hope that I did justice to his ethos. In this book, I honor you, Judge.

Writing a book requires an "elsewhere"—a space or place, physical or metaphorical, for the mind and spirit to retreat into imagination, peace, and whatever emotions emerge from research and writing. I had two main "elsewheres" but really, it was the people who made these places both sacred and safe.* In 2021, the Radcliffe Institute for Ad-

* Eddie S. Glaude Jr., *Begin Again: James Baldwin's America and Its Urgent Lessons for Our Own* (New York: Crown, 2020).

vanced Study at Harvard University (also known as the "Harvard Radcliffe Institute") generously awarded me a fellowship for this project, where I held the title, Elizabeth S. and Richard M. Cashin Fellow. Dean Tomiko Brown-Nagin of the Harvard Radcliffe Institute was enormously supportive of this work. I was surrounded by amazing colleagues—hard scientists, social scientists, poets, musicians, journalists, and novelists. The "MIG," our not-so-secret scholarly association, created fun, music, dancing, and thematic parties that gave us joy. I thank: W. Ralph Eubanks, Elena L. Glassman, Amelia M. Glaser, Ariela J. Gross, Faren Humes, Pardiss Kebriaei, Suki Kim, Margaret Litvin, Robin Mitchell, Steven Phelps, Sandra Susan Smith, Anne Whiston Spirn, Lysley Tenorio, and Chidi Ugwu. I also thank my Harvard Undergraduate Research Assistants: Nina Chandra, Tahj Johnson, and Maddie Proctor. While at Harvard, Sociologist Michael Burawoy was a Hutchins Fellow, and we met for what was our last conversation before his passing. His spirit and humanity are represented in this work, despite him never seeing the final project.

Brown University is another place that has been "elsewhere" with supportive colleagues and a dreamy campus where I could retreat. I spent countless hours working in the reading room of the John Hay Library with its sprawling wood tables, library lamps, and books. Spring and summer allowed for working on the Main Green. In this beautiful environment, I have benefited from supportive colleagues and friends: Librarian Karen Bouchard, Pembroke Center Archivist Mary Murphy, my wonderful colleagues in Brown University's Department of Sociology, Professors Prudence Carter, John B. Diamond, John Eason, Scott Frickel, Patrick Heller, and José Itzigsohn. This also includes faculty in the Department of Africana Studies at Brown University, like Professors Ainsley LeSure and Tricia Rose. Finally, I am thankful for supportive leaders like the Deputy Provost Janet Blume and Dean of Faculty Leah VanWey. Special thanks to the Center for the Study of Race and Ethnicity in America at Brown University, which hosted me as a Faculty Fellow and supported this project through a Mellon Foundation Grant.

This work was generously funded by the Brown University SPRINT Undergraduate Teaching and Research Awards, which is managed under the leadership of Associate Dean for Undergraduate Research and Inclusive Science, Oludurotimi O. Adetunji. Through this program, I had a powerhouse team of undergraduate research assistants that rotated, semester by semester, to support my work. We had a war room with an old chalkboard where we mapped out ideas, tracked cases and officers, and had lively discussions about theory and data. To write and animate these sacred stories, I held the weight of the pain of each of these boys, families, and attorneys, but it was my research assistants who held these cases alongside me. Sometimes they would be messengers of hope and grace. Like, one student, Christie Cadette, who scrawled this beautiful note and shared it with me when we realized how many people (attorneys and the falsely accused) prayed during the weight of their despair. She said: "When things are hopeless, all that is left is a man and his God." And with such wisdom, I could cry and keep going. Together, we held the grief of this book and did it as a community. With their permission, I thank the core team of brilliant students whose tenure on this project went from Spring 2022 to Spring 2026: Phobe Grace Aseoche, Sophia Block, Jenifer Bonilla, Christie Cadette, Samantha Chambers, Julian Cohen, Léo Corzo-Clark, Tessa Rose Crowley, Alexander Dufort, Brayson Freeman, Eliot Geer, Ayla Kattler, Anjoli Mathew, Meleah Neely, Ariana Palomo, Reina Salama, Riya Srinivasan, Helena Stacy, Willow Stewart, and Talia Yett. Additional thanks go to Presidential Fellows Serenity Hamilton, Caroline Cordts, Ruhma Khawaj, and my thesis advisee, Anna Brent-Levenstein.

Sophia Block was one research assistant who became like a "Chief of Staff," working three years with me even after graduation. She now works for the Innocence Project Delaware. If this research inspires a new generation of students to begin striving to free people, then this would be an unintended (yet joyous) consequence of the community that we started and will continue at Brown. I send these students into the world, but each one of them changes me. Like student Helena Stacy once wrote to me, "we show up differently in the world" because of what we learn . . . together. May they know their brilliance and power and never give up their desire to change the world for good. I am waiting and watching with admiration and hope.

Books come into the world with a team of dedicated literary professionals who believe in both the work and the author. I am so grateful that my agent, Margo Beth Fleming, believes in me. She tirelessly worked to match me with a press and editor(s) that could share and support my vision. Thank you to Random House (the House that Toni built) for believing in this work and to Hilary Redmon who acquired it and stewarded it through the early days of editorial work prior to her move to Knopf as Editorial Director of Nonfiction. Since then, I have worked with the talented Marie Pantojan who completed the process with great care. We have benefited from the support of Assistant Editor Azraf Khan, a rising star in my opinion.

Peer review is an essential part of research, and I want to honor and thank those who vetted this work. I thank the anonymous reviewers at Harvard Radcliffe Institute who vetted this work at the proposal phase, as well as the generosity of Professors Michael Burowoy, George Lipsitz, Osagie Obasogie, and my past academic editor, Michelle Lipinski. I thank the professors who peer reviewed the final version of this book: Professors Stephen Daniels, Susan Bandes, and Michael Kennedy.

As described in the "author's notes on research and analysis," this work was fact-checked by Heather Kreidler. She held the citations, sources, and legal cases in this book, but she also held the emotional weight of finishing this book alongside me. I am forever grateful for her exceptional work and her emotional investment. Benjamin Gerstein did the legal review and vetted every case and law cited in this work. Matthew Martin at Random House did the final legal review of all these stages of fact-checking. This was like a 12-hour mini-trial where he was the auditor, and I was the audited. It was arduous for us all, but I am grateful for his hard work.

On the wall of my office is a piece of paper that says, "Who's got you?" That is, who are the friends, scholars, and spiritual advisers that I carry with me as I write unafraid. Here they are: Ellen Berrey, Karida

Brown, Paul Butler, Brittnay Friedman, Andrea Freeman, Laura E. Gómez, Amin Ghaziani, Maria Gaspar, Saida Grundy, Elizabeth Hinton, Marcus Anthony Hunter, Nina A. Johnson, Armando Lara-Millán, Melanie Newport, Anthony Perguero, Laurence Ralph, Malcolm Rich, Victor Rios, Zandria F. Robinson, Mary Pattillo, Heather Ann Thompson, and Robert Vargas. Also included are the "Petritoli Writers and Creators" brought together by Janice and Reuben Jonathan Miller, especially Joyce M. Bell, Waverly Duck, Lisa Eason, Michael Walker, Susan Burton, Shaun Ossei-Owusu, and Ronald Simpson-Bey.

On a personal level, I thank Pastor Jason Ferris, Rebecca Ferris, and the Old Pine Church. I thank lifelong friends: Puja Chunduri, Barbara Gorder, Julie Groll, Kellie MacDonald Freeze, David Harb, Marissa Mazzoncini, Carrie Nelson, Bonnie Solomon, and Ethelbert Williams. I acknowledge my earliest teachers: Bonnie Diamond, Marilyn Frank, Tammy Lathan, Carol Levin, Frank Mattucci, Tori Price, Mary Roth, and "Coach" David Santee.

I honor the Gonzalez family: My grandparents, Soledad and Jorge Medina Gonzalez and Esther Rico Morgan. My father, Joel Gonzalez, and my aunts and uncles: Ortencia, Veronica, Robert, Martha, George, and Gina. My cousins: Joaquin, Valerie, Gina, Samuel, Krystle, Ruben, and Katrina. I also thank my in-laws, Jane and Roger Van Cleve, for their support and care. I honor the love and sacrifice of my great-aunt and great-uncle, Marie and Salvatore Valenziano.

My two children, Dylan and Micah, are my joy and my reason for persisting. In my work, I try to show them who I am, but who they can be, young people of moral standing and strength. As I wrote this book, my children have been Romarr's age, Elijah's age, Lee's age, Calvin's age, and are now approaching the ages of teens like Omar, Marcellius, Daniel, or Larry. My children were often my muse, reminding me to narrate the universal joy and innocence of childhood, helping me see the boys and teens in the book with the same reverent lens that I apply to my own children. Micah and Dylan, I love you and pray for you, whether you are near or far.

I thank my husband, Andrew Van Cleve, my soulmate and love. We met at Northwestern University and have grown up together. In our 25 years of marriage, he has loved every version of me and always believes in my dreams. For all you have sacrificed and gifted me, thank you. I love this adventure with you.

I honor the loving memory of those dear ones that I have lost but live in my heart, soul, and spirit: Bryan Monroe, Barbara Winslow Boardman, "Coach" John F. Jones Jr., Thomas (Reem) Cottom, Michael Burowoy, Julie and Mark Van Cleve, Grant Freeze, and Mark Wiwatowski.

Finally, it is easy to acknowledge the heroic lawyers who fought tirelessly for the children, teens and young people in this book. But we cannot forget the parents who never gave up on their children—who were the first to know and maintain that their boys' innocence was worth the fight. Some parents passed away and never got to see the child's exoneration. These were the first champions of justice, the quiet ambassadors of truth. And to the victims whose stories are told in this book, whose parents and families demanded justice, they deserved more than what the police gave them. They deserved truth, peace, and a just and accurate verdict. Both types of families are victimized by this wrongful conviction system; they deserve to be seen, acknowledged, and repaired. *You have not always been acknowledged in the archives or the data, but I know and see your story, and now others will as well.*

# Notes

## Introduction

1. *Trevon M. Yates v. County of St. Clair et al.*, No. 14-CV-00934-MJR (S.D. Ill. July 27, 2015), Plaintiff Trevon Yates' Response in Opposition to Defendants' Motion for Summary Judgment. "Psychologically Coercive Interrogation by St. Clair County Sheriff's Officers Results in $900,000 Legal Settlement," news release, Bluhm Legal Clinic, Roderick and Solange MacArthur Justice Center, September 29, 2015, Northwestern University School of Law, Evanston, Illinois.
2. *Yates v. County of St. Clair et al.*, No. 14-CV-00934-MJR (S.D. Ill. Aug. 27, 2014), Complaint, 7; Joel Currier, "Mentally Impaired East St. Louis Teen Gets $900,000 Settlement in False Confession Lawsuit," *St. Louis Post-Dispatch*, September 29, 2015, www.stltoday.com/news/local/crime-and-courts/mentally-impaired-east-st-louis-teen-gets-900-000-settlement-in-false-confession-lawsuit/article_26605f3d-6b97-531d-a50c-175976f350cd.html.
3. *Yates v. County of St. Clair et al.*, Complaint, 5.
4. *Yates v. County of St. Clair, Response in Opposition.*
5. *Yates v. County of St. Clair, Response in Opposition.* This citation misidentifies Kenneth McHughes as "Kevin McHughes."
6. "American police in the modern era have succeeded in eliciting confessions by developing interrogation methods that rely on fraud, persuasion, and impression management. Their goal is to elicit incriminating statements from suspects in order to build the strongest possible case against them and thereby assist the prosecution in securing conviction and incarceration." Richard A. Leo, *Police Interrogation and American Justice* (Cambridge, MA: Harvard University Press, 2008), 6.

   ". . . police proclaim truth as the goal of interrogation, yet interrogators regularly rely on deception and sophisticated forms of trickery; while confessions are presented as reliable indicators of a suspect's culpability, interrogation is a social process through which culpability is orchestrated and constructed (not always accurately)." Leo, *Police Interrogation and American Justice,* 6.

7. Baer argues that Miranda was a smoke-and-mirrors protection that allowed the public to believe the people's rights were protected even if officers engaged in misconduct—and violent interrogations. It's a "false performance of protection." Andrew S. Baer, *Beyond the Usual Beating: The Jon Burge Police Torture Scandal and Social Movements for Police Accountability in Chicago* (Chicago: University of Chicago Press, 2020), 54.
8. *Yates v. County of St. Clair, Response in Opposition,* 13.
9. Joseph Bustos, "'Appalling': St. Clair County to Pay $900K to Teen Who Says Confession Was Coerced," *Belleville News-Democrat,* September 29, 2015, www.bnd.com/news/local/article36954897.html. The page contains a video depicting part of the interrogation.
10. *Yates v. County of St. Clair et al.,* No. 14-CV-00934-MJR (S.D. Ill.), Deposition of Scott Toth, March 11, 2015, 156 & 177.
11. *Yates v. County of St. Clair et al.,* Deposition of Scott Toth, 177–78.
12. *Yates v. County of St. Clair et al.,* Complaint, 8.
13. *Yates v. County of St. Clair et al.,* Complaint, 8.
14. Bustos, "'Appalling.'"
15. *Yates v. County of St. Clair et al.,* Complaint, 9.
16. Armando Lara-Millán and Nicole Gonzalez Van Cleve, "Interorganizational Utility of Welfare Stigma in the Criminal Justice System," *Criminology* 55, no. 1 (February 2017): 59–84.
17. *Yates v. County of St. Clair et al.,* Complaint, 10.
18. While conceding that substantive perjury is "far more destructive" to the criminal justice system mechanism, Russell Covey explains that procedural perjury is still too often used by the police "to punish those who are believed to be committing or to have committed crimes." For Trevon, forcing him to wait in jail while the courts reviewed the abuse utilized in his case was yet another way to punish an innocent child. See Covey, "Police Misconduct as a Cause of Wrongful Convictions," *Washington University Law Review* 90, no. 4 (2013): 1177.
19. In Chicago, the elected prosecutor is called the Cook County State's Attorney. The attorneys who work in courtrooms throughout Cook County are referred to as Assistant State's Attorneys. In this book, we use these official terms to refer to people's professional titles where necessary; for simplicity and for the ease of the reader, I also use the general term "prosecutor."
20. In 2021, Illinois became the first state to ban police from using deception during interrogations of minors. Illinois also requires the electronic recording of all juvenile interrogations. See "Illinois Becomes the First State to Ban Police from Lying to Juveniles During Interrogations," Innocence Project, July 15, 2021, https://innocenceproject.org/illinois-first-state-to-ban-police-lying/.
21. W.E.B. Du Bois, *The Souls of Black Folk: Essays and Sketches* (Chicago: A. C. McClurg & Co., 1903), 173.
22. Nicole Gonzalez Van Cleve, *Crook County: Racism and Injustice in America's Largest Criminal Court* (Stanford, CA: Stanford University Press, 2016), 74.
23. Lawyers and legal scholars would say the proper term for the information gathering period (the investigation) between arrest and conviction is *discovery.*
24. Gonzalez Van Cleve, *Crook County,* 114.
25. "Exoneration by Year," National Registry of Exonerations (Michigan State University

College of Law, Michigan Law, University of Michigan Law School, University of California, Irvine Newkirk Center for Science & Society), n.d., www.law.umich.edu/special/exoneration/Pages/Exoneration-by-Year.aspx, accessed January 4, 2026.

26. The National Registry of Exonerations keeps a running total of "years lost" by people exonerated since 1989. See "Explore Exonerations," National Registry of Exonerations. Within these numbers lies an under-discussed category of wrongful convictions known as "no-crime convictions," in which a person is convicted of a crime that, in fact, never occurred. No-crime convictions tend to occur in the aftermath of a medical tragedy, when criminal blame is projected onto a caretaker or parent. These cases often target women who miscarry babies or parents who have a child with an undiagnosed condition that results in the baby's sudden death. See Jessica S. Henry, *Smoke but No Fire: Convicting the Innocent of Crimes That Never Happened* (Oakland: University of California Press, 2020); Kaitlin Jackson and Samuel Gross, "Female Exonerees: Trends and Patterns," September 27, 2014, www.law.umich.edu/special/exoneration/Pages/Features.Female.Exonerees.aspx.
27. "Report: Black People 7.5 Times More Likely to Be Wrongfully Convicted of Murder Than Whites, Risk Even Greater if Victim Was White," Death Penalty Information Center, September 30, 2022, https://deathpenaltyinfo.org/report-black-people-7-5-times-more-likely-to-be-wrongfully-convicted-of-murder-than-whites-risk-even-greater-if-victim-was-white. On disparities in the criminal justice system more broadly, see Mike Wessler, "Updated Charts Provide Insights on Racial Disparities, Correctional Control, Jail Suicides, and More," *Prison Policy Initiative,* May 19, 2022, www.prisonpolicy.org/blog/2022/05/19/updated_charts/. See also Samuel R. Gross et al., "Race and Wrongful Convictions in the United States, 2022," National Registry of Exonerations, September 2022.
28. Author interview with intake staff at Loevy + Loevy.
29. Cook County State's Attorney's Office, "The Final Report: The Kim Foxx Administration, 2017–2024," Cook County State's Attorney, Chicago, Illinois, November 30, 2024, www.cookcountystatesattorney.org/sites/g/files/ywwepo351/files/document/file/2024-11/Foxx%20Administration%20Final%20Report%2011%2030%2024.pdf; "2024 Annual Report, National Registry of Exonerations," April 2, 2025, www.law.umich.edu/special/exoneration/Documents/2024_Annual_Report.pdf.
30. "Exoneration by Year," National Registry of Exonerations.
31. Police "referred to [such cases] as a 'heater' or a 'special,' the kind of case that attracted media attention and sent added pressure down the chain of command." Baer, *Beyond the Usual Beating,* 55–56.
32. While the wider field of wrongful conviction research increasingly acknowledges that wrongful conviction is a systemic issue rather than a collection of inadvertent errors, it also tends to absolve the guilt of the criminal justice officials responsible. Professor of law Jon Gould, among others, refers to wrongful convictions as "erroneous convictions," suggesting that, rather than being intentional, such convictions are the unfortunate product of an imperfect system. This reframing reflects the sincere fiction of the benevolence of the American justice system. See "Wrongful Convictions: The Latest Scientific Research and Implications for Law Enforcement," video, National Institute of Justice, March 1, 2013, https://nij.ojp.gov/media/video/24066#0-0. See also Jon B. Gould and Richard A. Leo, "One Hundred Years Later: Wrongful Convictions After a Century of Research," *Journal of Criminal Law and Criminology* 100, no. 3 (2010): 825–68.

33. In the Melvin Jones case, which was later recognized as a wrongful conviction, Lieutenant Jon Burge was quoted as saying, "You see, it's just me and you, you know. No court and no State are going to take your word against a Lieutenant's word." See *People of the State of Illinois v. Melvin Jones,* No. 82-1605, Motion to Suppress Statements, Circuit Court of Cook County, Criminal Division, Aug. 5, 1982 (before Judge Roger J. Kiley Jr.), 71.

    For instances of defense attorneys warning defendants about this issue of the police's word over that of a defendant, see Gonzalez Van Cleve, *Crook County.*
34. Susan A. Bandes discusses the role that popular culture plays in valorizing the violence in policing, claiming, "There is a powerful dominant narrative about policing . . . a claim of unprovoked police violence must be one of three things: an aberration, a lie, or a reasonable response to provocation." See Bandes, "Video, Popular Culture, and Police Excessive Force: The Elusive Narrative of Over-Policing," *University of Chicago Legal Forum 2018,* no. 1 (2019): 2.
35. Author interview with Steven Drizin, March 11, 2025.
36. While legal remedies for wrongful conviction do exist, they more often serve as theoretical safeguards against unlawful detention than as a practical means of overturning wrongful convictions. This shifts the focus away from the issue of innocent people being in jail to center the identification of unconstitutional practices in a trial. According to Daniel S. Medwed, "It doesn't violate the constitution to imprison or execute an innocent person." See Medwed, *Barred: Why the Innocent Can't Get Out of Prison* (New York: Basic Books, 2022); Daniel Medwed, "Barred: Why the Innocent Can't Get Out of Prison," Harvard Law Library Book Talk, YouTube, February 1, 2024, 13:23, www.youtube.com/watch?v=np_hKNe_-NY.
37. "Sentinel Event Review (SER)," University of Pennsylvania Carey Law School, www.law.upenn.edu/institutes/quattronecenter/sentinel-event-review/.
38. Author correspondence with Reuben Miller.
39. James Baldwin, *The Evidence of Things Not Seen* (New York: Holt, Rinehart, and Winston, 1985).

## Chapter 1: The Question We Must Ask

1. DeNeen L. Brown, "As 2 Boys Face Murder Trial, South Side Neighbors Voice Disbelief," *Washington Post,* August 16, 1998, A03.
2. Brown, "As 2 Boys Face Murder Trial."
3. Alex Kotlowitz, "The Unprotected," *New Yorker,* February 8, 1999, 53.
4. John Carpenter and Lorraine Forte, "Killed for Her Bike: Police Charge Boys 7 and 8," *Chicago Sun-Times,* August 11, 1998, 1.
5. *Elijah Akbar Henderson, a Minor, by and Through Rosetta Crawford and Sonja Crawford v. City of Chicago, Illinois; the Chicago Police Department; and Chicago Illinois Police Department Officers Allen Nathaniel and James Cassidy,* No. 99L01886. Cir. Ct. Cook Cnty., Ill., Cnty. Dep't, Law Div., 1999, Plaintiffs' Complaint at Law, 29 (hereafter "Elijah Henderson Civil Case").
6. Maurice Possley and Steve Mills, "Police Questioning Others in Ryan Harris Case More Open Than Shut; Suspect's Relative Latest Interviewed," *Chicago Tribune,* Chicagoland final edition, August 16, 1998, 1.
7. Marla Donato, "Englewood Neighbors Find Body of Missing Girl," *Chicago Tribune,* north sports final edition, July 29, 1998, 3.

8. Possley and Mills, "Police Questioning Others," 1.
9. Brown, "As 2 Boys Face Murder Trial."
10. Brown, "As 2 Boys Face Murder Trial."
11. Kotlowitz, "Unprotected."
12. Author interview with Flint Taylor, September 1, 2022; author interview with Catherine Ferguson, October 16, 2023; Maurice Possley, "Ex-Murder Suspect Is Busy Being a Boy; Probe in Harris Case Focusing on 'Toy Guy,'" *Chicago Tribune,* September 8, 1998, 21.
13. Author interview with Romarr Gipson, November 5, 2021.
14. Kotlowitz, "Unprotected."
15. She goes missing on July 27, 1998. It's July 28 when they find the body, and August 9 when the boys are charged. Sheila Washington, "Body May Be That of Baby Missing," *Chicago Defender,* July 29, 1998, 4:1.
16. Tera Eva Agyepong, *The Criminalization of Black Children: Race, Gender, and Delinquency in Chicago's Juvenile Justice System, 1899–1945* (Chapel Hill: University of North Carolina Press, 2018).
17. Gonzalez Van Cleve, *Crook County,* 127.
18. Jeannene M. Przybylski, quoted in Bruce Jackson, *Pictures from a Drawer: Prison and the Art of Portraiture* (Philadelphia: Temple University Press, 2009), 8.
19. Elijah Henderson Civil Case, 50, 147, 151. "Henderson was frightened, traumatized, panicked, physically, emotionally and psychologically distressed, and severely injured and damaged." Elijah Henderson Civil Case, 74.
20. Romarr Gipson, letter to the author, April 8, 2021.
21. Floyd Durr was ill and was petitioning to die outside of prison. The request was denied due to Sabrina Harris's advocacy. See Evelyn Holmes, "Floyd Durr, Convicted in 1998 Rape, Murder of 11-Year-Old Chicago Girl, Ryan Harris, Dies in Prison," ABC7 Chicago, April 9, 2024, https://abc7chicago.com/floyd-durr-ryan-harris-englewood-chicago-news/14638214/.

    Floyd Durr died in prison in April 2024. See Todd Feurer, "Floyd Durr, Guilty in Rape and Murder of 11-Year-Old Ryan Harris, Dies in Illinois Prison," CBS Chicago, updated April 10, 2024.
22. Steve Mills and Maurice Possley, "Cops Ignored Clues That Case Was Weak," *Chicago Tribune,* September 6, 1998.
23. Catherine Ferguson interview; Carlos Sadovi, "Killing of Girl, 11, Detailed," *Chicago Tribune,* August 12, 2005.
24. Maurice Possley, "How Cops Got Boys to Talk," *Chicago Tribune,* August 30, 1998, 1.
25. Possley, "How Cops Got Boys to Talk," 1.
26. DeNeen L. Brown, "The Accused: For Two Little Boys, Wrongful Murder Charges Could Stick for Life," *Washington Post,* October 31, 1998.
27. Kotlowitz, "Unprotected."
28. Ben A. Franklin, "Lie Detector's Use by Industry Rises; Rights Peril Feared," *New York Times,* November 22, 1971.
29. Historically, third-degree interrogation was characterized by overt physical brutality to break a suspect's will and extract confessions from interrogatees. In contemporary investigations, third-degree tactics have expanded to include psychologically manipulative methods, in light of increased contemporary awareness of police brutality. Law enforcement utilizes these tactics for the purpose of securing confessions as opposed to seeking the truth. See Leo, *Police Interrogation and American Justice.*

30. "Troubling Questions Demand Answers," editorial, *Chicago Tribune,* October 24, 1999, 58.
31. Flint Taylor, *The Torture Machine: Racism and Police Violence in Chicago* (Chicago: Haymarket Books, 2019), Kindle ed., loc. 300.
32. "A confession produced by a trained interrogator is like a Hollywood drama. Scripted by his or her theory of the case, rehearsed during hours of interrogation, and enacted on camera by the suspect. Often the result is a compelling but false illusion." Saul M. Kassin, "Videotape Police Interrogations," *Boston Globe,* April 26, 2004.
33. John E. Reid and Associates, Inc., rightfully want to use interrogation in order "to learn the truth." They don't acknowledge, however, that the police utilize vast discretion to turn their interrogation techniques into something more dangerous. Reid knows that "when questioning juveniles and individuals with significant mental or psychological disabilities the investigator has to make a number of modifications to their approach." There is evidence that shows that police do not abide by the expectations set by Reid, instead circumventing these safeguards and using harmful techniques against innocent and vulnerable individuals. See John E. Reid and Associates, Inc., "Clarifying Misrepresentations About Law Enforcement Interrogation Techniques," February 2022, 18–19, https://reid.com/pdfs/Clarifying-Misrepresentations-of-Law-Enforcement-Interrogation-Techniques-Feb-2022_2022-03-18-140724_nabu.pdf.

    The technique was not called the Reid Technique until Joseph Buckley refined it and reduced it to nine steps. Chicago Police would not easily adopt these techniques. They would use promises of leniency ("If you say you did it, you can go home") and threats of harm ("If you don't confess, the cops will throw your head through a wall") to get children to confess. These tactics were not approved by the Reid Technique. Steven Drizin, text exchange with the author, August 28, 2024.
34. Leo, *Police Interrogation and American Justice,* 11–12.
35. Leo, *Police Interrogation and American Justice,* 12.
36. Richard Leo refers to American police interrogation as an "adversarial model," with police "committed to the goal of incriminating the accused in order to assist the state in its prosecution." Leo structures this model as enveloping two types of "fraud": first compelling the suspect to confess despite one's perceived self-interest, then legitimizing these statements to the public, shadowing over their own interrogative methods. Leo, *Police Interrogation and American Justice,* 12–13, 20.
37. Baer, *Beyond the Usual Beating.*
38. Kotlowitz, "Unprotected," 47.
39. "The open secret is what people in power know but refuse to say about police torture." Laurence Ralph, *The Torture Letters: Reckoning with Police Violence* (Chicago: University of Chicago Press, 2020), xi.
40. During this era she was Eileen O'Neill.
41. Burke said this in a 1999 *Nation* magazine article. See Amy Bach, "True Crime, False Confession," *The Nation,* February 8, 1999, 21. See also Erick Johnson, "Black Leaders Step Up Support for Harris After Reports," *Chicago Crusader,* January 18, 2024, https://chicagocrusader.com/black-leaders-step-up-support-for-harris-after-reports/.
42. Susan A. Bandes, "The Lone Miscreant, the Self-Training Prosecutor, and Other Fictions: A Comment on *Connick v. Thompson,*" *Fordham Law Review* 80, no. 2 (2011): 715–36.

Bandes discusses the need to break away from the idea of a "lone miscreant" or bad actor as the explanation for systemic practices that violate the law or its spirit. She uses the example of *Brady* violations to show that such practices are "group work." But police practices are extensions of the entire institution.

43. Phoebe Mogharei, "Untrue Confessions," *Chicago Magazine,* January 16, 2019.
44. Mogharei, "Untrue Confessions."
45. James Cassidy, "The Ugliness of Being a Kid of the '90s," *Chicago Tribune,* December 28, 1994.
46. He was ten years old at the time Anna Gilvis died.
47. Maurice Possley, "Boy Convicted of Slaying at Age 10 Appeals," *Chicago Tribune,* January 11, 2000.
48. Bach, "True Crime, False Confession."
49. Bach, "True Crime, False Confession."
50. Steve Mills, "Boy's Conviction Thrown Out," *Chicago Tribune,* June 21, 2002.
51. *A.M., a Minor v. Jerry Butler, Superintendent of the Illinois Youth Center,* 360 F.3d 787 (7th Cir. 2004).
52. Ta-Nehisi Coates, "Fear of a Black Avenger," *The Atlantic,* September 25, 2012.
53. Gonzalez Van Cleve, *Crook County,* 96.
54. Brown, "Accused."
55. Brown, "Accused."
56. Brown, "Accused."
57. Brown, "Accused."
58. Brown, "Accused."
59. Brown, "Accused."
60. Possley, "How Cops Got Boys to Talk," 1.
61. Possley, "How Cops Got Boys to Talk."
62. The accounts of the crime differ depending on the source, complicated further by the boys' shifting versions of events, which reflected the suggestive questioning by the police.
63. Brown, "Accused."
64. Kotlowitz, "Unprotected."
65. Kotlowitz, "Unprotected," 46.
66. *Mother and Father, on their own behalf and as guardians of the estate of R.G., a minor v. Det. James Cassidy, et al.,* No. 01 L 7637 (Consolidated with *E.H., a Minor, by and through Rosetta Crawford, E.H.'s Maternal Grandmother, et al. v. City of Chicago, et al.,* No. 99 L 1886) (Cir. Ct. Cook Cnty., Ill., Law Div., Judge Mulhern, [2003]), and E.H. Plaintiffs' Response to the Defendants' Motion for Summary Judgment, item 144 (hereafter "Romarr Gipson Civil Case").
67. Brown, "Accused."
68. Author interview with Romarr Gipson, November 5, 2021.
69. Brown, "Accused."
70. *Miranda v. Arizona,* 384 U.S. 436 (1966).
71. *Miranda v. Arizona,* 384 U.S. 436 (1966).
72. James Cassidy's one-page, handwritten "General Progress" report, dated August 9, 1998, purportedly of his interview of Elijah Henderson, Exhibit No. 9, Elijah Henderson Civil Case, 33–34.
73. Maurice Possley and Judy Peres, "Fight Looms over Boys' Confessions: 7- and 8-Year-Old's Grasp of Police Questioning at Issue in Slaying of Girl," *Chicago Tribune,* north sports final edition, August 12, 1998, 1.

74. Brown, "Accused."
75. Elijah Henderson Civil Case, 33–37.
76. Elijah Henderson Civil Case, 11.
77. Romarr Gipson Civil Case, items 149, 160, 163.
78. "Instead, Cassidy walked down the hall to Area 1's Juvenile Division to obtain two Chicago police youth officers to witness further questioning of R. G. Cassidy Dep. 359, 362, 373." Romarr Gipson Civil Case, item 187.
79. Ken Armstrong, Maurice Possley, and Steve Mills, "Officers Ignore Laws Set Up to Guard Kids; Detectives Grill Minors Without Juvenile Officers, Parents Present," *Chicago Tribune,* December 18, 2001.
80. "While Cassidy and Nathaniel were interrogating R.G., I. James, who had a headache and was exhausted from working the night before and going to church in the morning, dozed off and on." Romarr Gipson Civil Case, item 126.
81. Armstrong, Possley, and Mills, "Officers Ignore Laws," 1. See also Romarr Gipson Civil Case, items 307–18.
82. One article claims that the phone call occurred on August 8, the day before the boys confessed, while the civil case and James Cassidy's depositions imply that it occurred after the boys confessed prior to their being charged. Regardless of this inconsistency, this moment reveals how Cassidy had the discretion to use the medical evidence in whichever way he wanted, disregarding it for the sake of bolstering the false narrative he created. See Sadovi, "Killing of Girl, 11, Detailed," 3; Romarr Gipson Civil Case, items 276–77, Cassidy Deposition, 707–10.
83. Maurice Possley and Steve Mills, "Police Tried to Fire Cop in Ryan Harris Case: Boys' Interrogator Accused of Framing Man in '92 Arrest," *Chicago Tribune,* June 14, 2001; Elijah Henderson Civil Case, 43–44.
84. "Defendants Cassidy and Nathaniel and other detectives and supervisors then met, discussed the case and the report from Dr. Kalelkar and agreed that it was impossible for Ryan Harris to have been killed in the manner alleged by Nathaniel and Cassidy, so they constructed another version of events which Cassidy and Nathaniel knew to be false—that E.H. and R.G. bludgeoned her to death with a brick, with one holding her down and the other bludgeoning her, and that these little boys then falsely said that they had killed her with a thrown rock. They made this conclusion despite Cassidy's assertion that he thought that R.G. and E.H. were open, honest, good kids, and that the murder was brutal. Nathaniel Dep. 707-20, Cassidy Dep. 707-10, 751-52, 756." Romarr Gipson Civil Case, item 293; Maurice Possley, "Harris Autopsy Doctor Testifies; Deposition Taken in 2 Boys' Lawsuit," *Chicago Tribune,* August 10, 2003, 1; Steve Patterson and Monifa Thomas, "Harris Head Injury Unlikely Caused by Rocks: Medical Examiner," *Chicago Sun-Times,* August 12, 2005.
85. Romarr Gipson Civil Case, item 8. See also Nathaniel Deposition, 707–20; Cassidy Deposition, 707–10, 751–52, 756.
86. "I was pretty agitated with the headline news that came out after my conversation with Detective Cassidy where it said that two boys were charged," Kalelkar testified. "And I was aghast. . . . I said, 'Oh, my God. This is totally different from what I told him.'" Possley, "Harris Autopsy Doctor Testifies."
87. Romarr Gipson Civil Case, item 287.
88. Possley, "Harris Autopsy Doctor Testifies." "Dr. Kalelkar related to Cassidy that Ryan Harris did not die the way he was telling her the scenario occurred, and when she heard next morning that the boys had been charged she was upset, agi-

tated and surprised. Kalelkar Dep. 151, 163, 172, 202." Romarr Gipson Civil Case, item 290.

89. Possley, "Harris Autopsy Doctor Testifies."
90. Possley, "Harris Autopsy Doctor Testifies," 17.
91. *Crook County*, 53–54.
92. Steve Patterson, "Mother in Ryan Harris Case Recounts Son's Harrowing Ordeal: She Testifies Boy, 8, Was Lied to by Cops, Locked in Dark Room," *Chicago Sun-Times,* August 30, 2005.
93. Maurice Possley, "Anguish Grips Mom of 7-Year-Old Held in Killing," *Chicago Tribune,* August 13, 1998, 1.
94. Kotlowitz, "Unprotected," 47.
95. Kotlowitz, "Unprotected," 47.
96. Brown, "Accused."
97. Possley, "Anguish Grips Mom."
98. Brown, "Accused."
99. Romarr Gipson Civil Case, item 128.
100. Possley, "Anguish Grips Mom."
101. Brown, "Accused." See also Romarr Gipson Civil Case, items 316–17; Possley, "Anguish Grips Mom."
102. Brown, "Accused." On abusive and punitive practices of the child welfare system, see Dorothy Roberts, *Shattered Bonds: The Color of Child Welfare* (New York: Basic Books, 2002).
103. Lara-Millán and Gonzalez Van Cleve, "Interorganizational Utility."
104. Dorothy Roberts, *Killing the Black Body: Race, Reproduction, and the Meaning of Liberty* (New York: Pantheon Books, 1997), 18.
105. Gonzalez Van Cleve, *Crook County,* 64.
106. Romarr Gipson Civil Case, items 310–18. In this book, when I mention an "Area" (like Area 1 or Area 2), I am referring to the geographic location that processed that case at that time in history. These boundaries are fluid and may have changed since then, as they are periodically revised, similar to the redistricting of an electoral map.
107. Romarr Gipson Civil Case, items 310–18.
108. Elijah Henderson Civil Case, 76. See also Possley, "Anguish Grips Mom."
109. Patterson, "Mother in Ryan Harris Case Recounts"; see also Romarr Gipson Civil Case, item 260.
110. Teresa Puente and Janita Poe, "Emotion Washes Englewood," *Chicago Tribune,* Chicagoland edition, September 6, 1998, 14.
111. Puente and Poe, "Emotion Washes Englewood"; Patterson, "Mother in Ryan Harris Case Recounts."
112. Possley, "Anguish Grips Mom," 1. "She told R.G. what the officer had told her about him accidentally killing Ryan Harris, and R.G. repeatedly said, 'I didn't do it grandma.' James Deposition, 152–56." Romarr Gipson Civil Case, item 128.
113. Possley, "Anguish Grips Mom," 1.
114. Elijah Henderson Civil Case, 76. See also Carlos Sadovi, "Mother Tearfully Recalls Boy's Arrest for Murder; Charges in Harris Case Changed Son, She Says," *Chicago Tribune,* August 30, 2005, 2C.1; Patterson, "Mother in Ryan Harris Case Recounts."

## Chapter 2: A Blueprint

1. In April 2020, Hester was also granted $236,095 in compensation from the State of Illinois. "Lee Arthur Hester," Center on Wrongful Convictions, https://cwc.law.northwestern.edu/freed-exonerated/lee-arthur-hester/.
2. His family, friends, and teachers knew he was innocent. This was defined by a declaration from the state.
3. Steven Drizin, "Mourning through writing," email message to author, November 17, 2022.
4. See Brian Palmer, "Why Do So Many Assassins Have Three Names?," *Slate,* January 9, 2011, https://slate.com/news-and-politics/2011/01/jared-lee-loughner-gabrielle-giffords-suspected-shooter-has-three-names-so-do-lots-of-famous-assassins-what-gives.html.
5. Richard Wright, *The Man Who Lived Underground* (New York: Library of America, 2021).
6. A censored version of *The Man Who Lived Underground* was published by the literary journal *Accent* in 1942. This version specifically removed "unbearable" scenes of police brutality central to the original manuscript, with over fifty pages of content removed. Author interview with Donald Kizza-Brown, email, February 19, 2025.

   As Christopher Borrelli remarked, "The readers (all White) who read the manuscript found it an unsettling clash of realism (police abuse) and surrealism (life inside a sewer)." Borrelli, "Richard Wright's Novel of Police Brutality: The Most Relevant Book of 2021 Was Written 80 Years Ago," *Chicago Tribune,* April 15, 2021.
7. Brittany Friedman, *Carceral Apartheid: How Lies and White Supremacists Run Our Prisons* (Chapel Hill: University of North Carolina Press, 2025). Karl E. Taeuber and Alma F. Taeuber, *Negroes in Cities: Residential Segregation and Community Change* (Chicago: Aldine, 1965).
8. "The draft siphoned off many of these men, while the turmoil in Europe disrupted the flow of immigrants from that area. Desperately in need of additional workers, northern businesses looked southward for new sources of labor. Because Afro-Americans made up a large portion of the unskilled work force in the South and because of social conditions there, they became the targets of aggressive recruitment campaigns. Northern companies offered well-paying jobs, free transportation, and low-cost housing as inducements to Afro-Americans to move North. They also sent labor recruiters into the South who received a fee for every recruit they provided for the company they represented." Spencer R. Crew, "The Great Migration of Afro-Americans, 1915–40," *Monthly Labor Review,* February 1987, 34. See also James N. Gregory, "The Great Migration (African American)," *America's Great Migrations,* America's Great Migrations Project, University of Washington, https://depts.washington.edu/moving1/black_migration.shtml.
9. Bobby Vanecko, "King David and Boss Daley," *South Side Weekly,* November 17, 2022, https://southsideweekly.com/king-david-and-boss-daley/.
10. "Daley was elected president of the Hamburg Athletic Club in 1924 at twenty-two, and he had been a member of the group since his early teen years. He was seventeen in 1919, when the Hamburgs were heavily involved in the deadliest anti-Black race riot in Chicago's history, although Williams notes that it was never confirmed whether Daley himself took part in the violence." Vanecko, "King

David and Boss Daley." See also Lance Williams, *King David and Boss Daley: The Black Disciples, Mayor Daley, and Chicago on the Edge* (Amherst, NY: Prometheus Books, 2022).

11. For more recent reporting on White gang/vigilante violence against Black communities, see Invisible Institute, *You Don't Speak for Me* podcast, hosted by Yahance Lacour, https://invisible.institute/ydsnpodcast.
12. Imani Perry, "The Bleak Prescience of Richard Wright," *The Atlantic,* June 2021, www.theatlantic.com/magazine/archive/2021/06/richard-wright-man-who-lived-underground/618705/.
13. Natalie Y. Moore, *The South Side: A Portrait of Chicago and American Segregation* (New York: St. Martin's Press, 2016).
14. Marcus Anthony Hunter and Zandria F. Robinson, *Chocolate Cities: The Black Map of American Life* (Oakland: University of California Press, 2018).
15. Moore, *South Side.*
16. There is power in movement, and restricting the movements of Black people is a central feature of anti-Black racism. See Hunter and Robinson, *Chocolate Cities,* 171.
17. Marcus Anthony Hunter, *Black Citymakers: How the Philadelphia Negro Changed Urban America* (New York: Oxford University Press, 2013).
18. *Shelley v. Kraemer,* 334 U.S. 1 (1948).
19. Steven A. Drizin, "The Lee Arthur Hester Case and the Unfinished Business of the United States Supreme Court to Protect Juveniles During Police Interrogations," *Northwestern Journal of Law and Social Policy* 6 (2011): 358; Moore, *South Side.*
20. When Blacks attended a union gathering at the home of a nonobservant Jewish resident at 5643 South Peoria Street in 1949, a rumor circulated that Black families were moving into the area. For five days in Englewood, mobs of people attacked Blacks as well as "Jews, Communists, and—apparently worst of all—University of Chicago meddlers," per Arnold R. Hirsch, *Making the Second Ghetto: Race and Housing in Chicago, 1940–1960* (Chicago: University of Chicago Press, 2021), 55. See also Ron Grossman, "In 1949, a Union Official Invited Colleagues to His Englewood Home. Some Were Black. Violence Ensued," *Chicago Tribune,* November 3, 2024.
21. Hirsch, *Making the Second Ghetto.*
22. Jacqueline Serrato, Pat Sier, and Charmaine Runes, "Mapping Chicago's Racial Segregation," FIRSTHAND Segregation, WTTW Chicago public television, www.wttw.com/firsthand/segregation/mapping-chicago-racial-segregation.
23. Chicago Commission on Human Relations, "Non-White Population Changes 1950–1960," *Human Relations News of Chicago* 3, no. 3 (July 1961), www.nlm.nih.gov/exhibition/forallthepeople/img/1234.pdf.
24. John L. Worrall and Frank Schmalleger, *Policing (Justice Series),* 3rd ed. (New York: Pearson, 2018).
25. Baer, *Beyond the Usual Beating,* 13–106.
26. "White Flight, by the Numbers," NBC Chicago, May 6, 2013, www.nbcchicago.com/news/local/chicago-politics/white-flight-by-the-numbers/1951412/.
27. William Lee, "John Wayne Gacy Was Arrested 40 Years Ago in a Killing Spree That Claimed 33 Victims and Shattered the Illusion of the Safe Suburban Community," *Chicago Tribune,* December 16, 2018, https://graphics.chicagotribune.com/john-wayne-gacy-murders-40-years-later/index.html.
28. *People v. Gacy,* 103 Ill. 2d 1, 468 N.E.2d 1171 (Ill. 1984).

29. The "veil" is a concept from W.E.B. Du Bois, *Souls of Black Folk.*
30. Accounts of Lee Arthur Hester's intellectual abilities vary. Affidavit testimony from Jerry Feldman described Hester as "a few grades behind," while Steven Drizin reported he was "three grades behind" and cited school testing that placed him four grades behind in math and five in reading and spelling. Psychological testing by the Chicago Public Schools, two years earlier, assigned him an IQ score of 82. Drizin, "Lee Arthur Hester Case," 132.
31. "Slain Woman His Favorite Teacher: Mother Refuses to Believe Her Son Committed Crime," *Chicago Daily News,* April 22, 1961.
32. Drizin, "Lee Arthur Hester Case."
33. "1,300 Attend Funeral for Slain Teacher," *Chicago Tribune,* April 25, 1961, sec. 2, p. 7.
34. According to Steven Drizin, she was not assigned a regular classroom. In the mid-1950s, the concept of a "master teacher" in Chicago involved providing experienced educators to support new teachers with difficult problems of instruction and discipline, particularly in more challenging schools. Correspondence with the author, July 17, 2025.
35. "Teacher Murdered in School: Find Mother of 6 Stabbed on South Side," *Chicago Daily Tribune,* April 21, 1961, 1–2.
36. "Teacher Murdered in School."
37. "Teacher Murdered in School."
38. Drizin, "Lee Arthur Hester Case."
39. Drizin, "Lee Arthur Hester Case."
40. Drizin, "Lee Arthur Hester Case."
41. Jerry Feldman, Affidavit, *People of the State of Illinois v. Lee Arthur Hester,* No. 61-1251 (Cir. Ct. Cook County), 2.
42. Feldman Affidavit, 2.
43. Oral arguments later presented different accounts of the timing. For example, in *People v. Hester,* 39 Ill. 2d 489, 237 N.E.2d 466 (Ill. 1968), it was reported that Lee was on the balcony for fifteen minutes and then moved to the auditorium. *Hester v. Illinois,* 397 U.S. 660 (argued November 18, 1969, decided April 27, 1970), reported that Lee was on the balcony for forty-five minutes before being turned over to Follis. See also Drizin, "Lee Arthur Hester Case."
44. Drizin, "Lee Arthur Hester Case"; *People v. Hester.*
45. Gaslighting is about more than just playing mind games. It is sociological and "rooted in social inequalities, including gender, and executed in power-laden intimate relationships." Gaslighting is consequential when perpetrators leverage stereotypes and stigmas related to gender, race, and "structural and institutional inequalities against victims to manipulate their realities." In this case, police used the technique to create a sense of helplessness and despair for the victim so that the victim would feel that surrendering their rights would be the only way to save themselves. Overall, the police can "erode [the] reality" of the target. Paige L. Sweet, "The Sociology of Gaslighting," *American Sociological Review* 84, no. 5 (2019): 851.
46. *Hester v. Illinois,* 397 U.S. 660.
47. Drizin, "Lee Arthur Hester Case," 370; *People v. Hester,* 39 Ill. 2d at 493.
48. "Those two officers: Sheldon R. Teller and another officer by the name of Anton Prunckle, who then turned Hester over to another officer by the name of Follis and the principal's office, who kept him for approximately 15 minutes." *Hester v.*

*Illinois,* 397 U.S. 660 (1970), at 4. "The defendant was in the custody of Officers Teller and Prunckle from shortly after 8:00 a.m. until approximately 8:45 a.m. when they turned him over to Sergeant Frank Follis of the youth division." *People v. Hester,* 39 Ill. 2d at 493.

49. Drizin, "Lee Arthur Hester Case," 370; *Hester v. Illinois,* 397 U.S. 660 (1970).
50. *Hester v. Illinois,* 397 U.S. 660 (1970).
51. Drizin, "Lee Arthur Hester Case," 370–71.
52. *Hester v. Illinois,* 397 U.S. 660 (1970).
53. Henry A. Giroux, *Disposable Youth: Racialized Memories, and the Culture of Cruelty* (New York: Routledge, 2012).
54. Tera Eva Agyepong, *The Criminalization of Black Children: Race, Gender, and Delinquency in Chicago's Juvenile Justice System, 1899–1945* (Chapel Hill: University of North Carolina Press, 2018). See also Gonzalez Van Cleve, *Crook County,* 102.
55. Agyepong, *Criminalization of Black Children.*
56. Agyepong, *Criminalization of Black Children.*
57. Black children were also barred from charity homes; the lack of resources in neglected Black neighborhoods meant that there were few options for Black children in need.
58. Using census data, Moses showed the aggressive results of targeting Black children through this system. The proportion of Black children grew from 3.5 percent (in 1900) to 21.8 percent in 1930. This sevenfold increase was in drastic contrast to the threefold increase in the city's Black population. Over this same period, the Black population in Chicago grew from 1.8 percent to 6.9 percent. Earl R. Moses, "Community Factors in Negro Delinquency," *Journal of Negro Education* 5, no. 2 (1936): 220–27.
59. Agyepong, *Criminalization of Black Children,* 43–44.
60. Agyepong, *Criminalization of Black Children,* 43–44. After the Civil War, ex-Confederates migrated north and brought their racist views to Northern cities; however, historians caution us into believing that the North was without its own racial prejudice. Cases of lynching in the North were quite prevalent, and race riots were common. See Samuel Bazzi et al., "The Confederate Diaspora," NBER Working Paper No. 31331 (Cambridge, MA: National Bureau of Economic Research, June 2023), www.nber.org/papers/w31331.
61. *The Birth of a Nation,* directed by D. W. Griffith (Los Angeles: David W. Griffith Corp., 1915).
62. The second variety of anti-Black caricature was portrayed as rebellious, untamed, out to raise havoc. In this view, the lesser, obedient Black man was distorted into a bestial creature known to White people as a brutal Black buck. In *The Birth of a Nation,* the portrayal of Black men as frenzied, savage, and violent dramatized the ties between racism and sex. See also Jonathan Markovitz, "Black 'Brute' and 'Buck' Stereotypes," *Research Starters: History,* EBSCO, 2024, www.ebsco.com/research-starters/history/black-brute-and-buck-stereotypes.
63. Joshua Rovner, "Black Disparities in Youth Incarceration," The Sentencing Project, Washington, D.C., August 12, 2025, www.sentencingproject.org/fact-sheet/black-disparities-in-youth-incarceration/; Margaret Werner Cahalan, with the assistance of Lee Anne Parsons, "Historical Corrections Statistics in the United States, 1850–1984," NCJ-102529, December 1986, Bureau of Justice Statistics, U.S. Department of Justice, Washington, D.C., https://bjs.ojp.gov/content/pub/pdf/hcsus5084.pdf.
64. Amanda Klonsky, "What I Saw at the Cook County Juvenile Detention Center,"

*Chicago Sun-Times,* November 7, 2019, https://chicago.suntimes.com/2019/11/7/20953943/cook-county-juvenile-temporary-detention-center-jtdc-child-offenders-audy-home-amanda-klonsky. See also Dan Hinkel and Kelly Garcia, "For Kids Arrested in Chicago, the City Has Little to Offer," *Injustice Watch,* June 26, 2024, www.injusticewatch.org/juvenile-courts/juvenile-justice/2024/youth-diversion-chicago-failures/.

65. National Council on Crime and Delinquency, *The Cook County Family (Juvenile) Court and Arthur J. Audy Home: An Appraisal and Recommendations by the National Council on Crime and Delinquency,* prepared for the Citizens Committee on the Family Court (Chicago, Illinois, 1963), 127.
66. Amanda Klonsky, "The Lifelong Damage We Do in Cook County When We Jail Kids as Young as 10," *Chicago Sun-Times,* November 7, 2019, https://chicago.suntimes.com/2019/11/7/20953943/cook-county-juvenile-temporary-detention-center-jtdc-child-offenders-audy-home-amanda-klonsky.
67. National Council on Crime and Delinquency, *Cook County Family Court and Arthur J. Audy Home,* 11.
68. National Council on Crime and Delinquency, *Cook County Family Court and Arthur J. Audy Home,* 163.
69. Alan Mills, "The Fight Against Solitary Confinement," The Barbara McDowell Social Justice Center, 2023, www.mcdowellsocialjusticecenter.org/blog/fight-against-solitary-confinement.
70. Feldman Affidavit, 7.
71. National Council on Crime and Delinquency, *Cook County Family Court and Arthur J. Audy Home,* 139.
72. Michael L. Walker, *Indefinite: Doing Time in Jail* (New York: Oxford University Press, 2022), 26.
73. John Irwin, *The Jail: Managing the Underclass in American Society* (Berkeley: University of California Press, 1987), 54–55.
74. Irwin, *Jail,* 67–69.
75. Rob Warden, co-founder of the Center on Wrongful Convictions, suggests that police use three broad tactics in obtaining false confessions: brainwashing, in which the chosen suspect is convinced that they committed the crime and have blocked the memory; desperation, where the suspect has been so worn down they confess to end the interrogation; and inquisitory techniques, which convince the suspect that it is in their self-interest to confess to minimize consequences. See Rob Warden, "Wrongful Convictions," YouTube, TEDx Talks, June 26, 2012, www.youtube.com/watch?v=XA7H5hvaA9g. See also Mary Catlin et al., "Interview and Interrogation Methods and Their Effects on True and False Confessions: A Systematic Review Update and Extension," *Campbell Systematic Reviews* 20, no. 4 (December 2024): e1441.
76. Many studies show that children with a disability are disproportionately impacted by police interrogation and false confessions. Between 1989 and 2020, 69 percent of people who falsely confessed and were later exonerated had a mental illness or intellectual disability. National Registry of Exonerations, "Age and Mental Status of Exonerated Defendants Who Confessed," https://exonerationregistry.org/sites/exonerationregistry.org/files/documents/Age_and_Mental_Status_FINAL_CHART.pdf. It has been estimated that approximately 75 percent of offenders with intellectual disabilities had not been identified when they were arrested (Schatz, 2018). And Johnson et al. (2018) found that exonerees with intellectual

disabilities were more likely to have been wrongfully convicted of murder (69 percent) than exonerees without intellectual disabilities (38 percent). This leads police to further miscategorize innocent suspects as guilty, with no knowledge of pre-existing explanations of presumed "guilty" behavior. Many studies investigating the vulnerability of disabled minors show that signs of disability may be viewed by police as signs of deception and indications of guilt. Aldert Vrij and Samantha Mann (2005) showed that suspect signs of deception such as "showing gaze aversion, displaying unnatural posture changes, fidgeting and placing a hand over the mouth or eyes when speaking" are not found to be reliable indicators of dishonesty. See John E. Reid and Associates, Inc., "Clarifying Misrepresentations"; Fred E. Inbau et al., *Essentials of the Reid Technique: Criminal Interrogation and Confessions* (Burlington, MA: Jones & Bartlett Learning, 2013), ch. 7; Sheri Lynn Johnson, John H. Blume, and Amelia Courtney Hritz, "Convictions of Innocent People with Intellectual Disability," *Albany Law Review* 82, no. 3 (2018): 1031–61; Saul M. Kassin and Gisli H. Gudjonsson, "The Psychology of Confessions," *Psychological Science in the Public Interest* 5, no. 2 (2004): 33–67; Meghan Nguyen, "8 Ways People with Disabilities Can Be Vulnerable to Wrongful Conviction," Innocence Project, July 31, 2023, https://innocenceproject.org/news/ways-disabilities-can-be-vulnerable-to-wrongful-conviction/; Vrij and Mann, "Chapter 4: Police Use of Nonverbal Behavior as Indicators of Deception," in *Applications of Nonverbal Communication,* ed. Ronald E. Riggio and Robert S. Feldman (New York: Psychology Press, 2005), 73; Samson J. Schatz, "Interrogated with Intellectual Disabilities: The Risks of False Confession," *Stanford Law Review* 70 (2018): 643–88.

77. Gisli H. Gudjonsson et al., "A National Epidemiological Study Investigating Risk Factors for Police Interrogation and False Confession Among Juveniles and Young Persons," *Social Psychiatry and Psychiatric Epidemiology* 51, no. 3 (2015): 359–67.
78. Barriers to understanding the legal system may further render disabled youth vulnerable to false confessions. For example, multiple studies have determined that intellectually disabled individuals, similar to youth, may have difficulty comprehending the importance or meaning behind Miranda rights, putting them in jeopardy of self-incrimination. See Karen L. Salekin, J. Gregory Olley, and Krystal A. Hedge, "Offenders with Intellectual Disability: Characteristics, Prevalence, and Issues in Forensic Assessment," *Journal of Mental Health Research in Intellectual Disabilities* 3, no. 2 (2010): 97–116. Further, disabled individuals may not understand that confessions may be used against them in court. Isabel C. H. Clare and Gisli H. Gudjonsson found that intellectually impaired individuals were "less likely to think that a police interview and false confession might have serious consequences." See Clare and Gudjonsson, "The Vulnerability of Suspects with Intellectual Disabilities During Police Interviews: A Review and Experimental Study of Decision-Making," *Mental Handicap Research* 8, no. 2 (1995): 110.
79. During the interrogation process, disabled children have a heightened vulnerability to false confessions due to an increased susceptibility to police interrogation tactics. The Death Penalty Information Center states that "juveniles and those with mental impairments are most likely to succumb to psychological pressure and make erroneous admissions during intense police interrogations." Death Penalty Information Center, "Juveniles and the Mentally Disabled." On the potential impact of PTSD on suspect behaviors in response to minimization tactics, see Hayley Cleary et al., "How Trauma May Magnify Risk of Involuntary and False Confessions Among Adolescents," *Wrongful Conviction Law Review* 2, no. 3 (2021):

173–204. On the links between ADHD and poor memory, which is associated with increased suggestibility in an interrogation, see Gisli H. Gudjonsson et al., "Interrogative Suggestibility Among Adolescents and Young Adults with ADHD," *Personality and Individual Differences* 45, no. 5 (2008): 409–13; Rebecca Milne et al., "Assessing the Effectiveness of the Cognitive Interview for Children with Severe Intellectual Disabilities," *International Journal of Disability, Development, and Education* 60, no. 1 (2013): 18–29; Martine B. Powell and Donald M. Thomson, "Contrasting Memory for Temporal-Source and Memory for Content in Children's Discrimination of Repeated Events," *Applied Cognitive Psychology* 11, no. 4 (1997): 339–60.

80. On the impact of trauma on false confessions, see Cleary et al., "How Trauma May Magnify Risk."
81. *Hester v. Illinois,* 397 U.S. 660 (1970).
82. "Hester at first maintained his innocence. But police were relentless. They lied about the crime scene, about the evidence, about allowing Hester to go home to his mother if he just confessed, the boy testified. After hours spent alone in what Hester called a 'dark dungeon room,' he admitted he had killed and sexually assaulted Keane." Del Quentin Wilber, "Righting a Wrong—and Rewriting a Racist Legacy," *Los Angeles Times,* September 5, 2020, www.latimes.com/world-nation/story/2020-09-05/a-14-year-old-boy-a-false-confession-to-murder-a-racist-legacy.
83. *Hester v. Illinois,* 397 U.S. 660 (1970).
84. Nicole Gonzalez Van Cleve, *The Waiting Room,* Amazon Original Stories, 2018. See also Javier Auyero, *Poor People's Politics: Peronist Survival Networks and the Legacy of Evita* (Durham, NC: Duke University Press, 2001); Armando Lara-Millán, *Redistributing the Poor: Jails, Hospitals, and the Crisis of Law and Fiscal Austerity* (New York: Oxford University Press, 2021).
85. *Hester v. Illinois,* 397 U.S. 660 (1970), at 6.
86. Drizin, "Lee Arthur Hester Case," 371.
87. "The allegations of threatening, spitting, and telling Hester about his fingerprints being found on the icebox were denied at the trial by all four of the officers who were in the room." *People v. Hester,* 39 Ill. 2d at 495. However, police lying on the stand is an ongoing pattern, and the culture within the police department, and known among judges, defense attorneys, and prosecutors. See Gonzalez Van Cleve, *Crook County.*
88. Transcript of Oral Argument at 9–10, *Hester v. Illinois,* 397 U.S. 660 (1970) (No. 82).
89. *People v. Hester,* 39 Ill. 2d at 471.
90. Drizin, "Lee Arthur Hester Case," 375.
91. *People v. Hester,* 39 Ill. 2d at 495.
92. On how juveniles of color are at risk of coercive interrogation, see Iris Blandón-Gitlin, Hayley Cleary, and Alisa Blair, "Race and Ethnicity as a Compound Risk Factor in Police Interrogation of Youth," in *The Legacy of Racism for Children: Psychology, Law, and Public Policy,* ed. Margaret C. Stevenson, Bette L. Bottoms, and Gail S. Goodman (New York: Oxford University Press, 2020).
93. Officer Perkins claimed that he had shown Lee the photographs of the scene following the boy's confession; however, Lee claimed that these pictures were shown prior to the confession and that "he concocted the confession after viewing the pictures of the murder scene, and that the police coached him in portraying the details of the crime." *People v. Hester,* 39 Ill. 2d at 496.
94. Drizin, "Lee Arthur Hester Case," 375.

95. Drizin, "Lee Arthur Hester Case," 375.
96. *People v. Hester,* 39 Ill. 2d at 496.
97. Drizin, "Lee Arthur Hester Case," 372.
98. *People v. Hester,* 39 Ill. 2d at 495; Wilber, "Righting a Wrong."
99. *People v. Hester,* 39 Ill. 2d at 506.
100. *Hester v. Illinois,* 397 U.S. 660 (1970), Transcript of Oral Argument at 7.
101. Drizin, "Lee Arthur Hester Case," 375.
102. *Hester v. Illinois,* 397 U.S. 660 (1970), at 23.
103. "Lee Arthur Hester," National Registry of Exonerations, https://exonerationregistry.org/cases/12677.
104. Drizin, "Lee Arthur Hester Case," 385.
105. Gayatri Chakravorty Spivak has written about culture beyond reason. Here I amend this to "racism is beyond reason." Spivak, *A Critique of Postcolonial Reason: Toward a History of the Vanishing Present* (Cambridge, MA: Harvard University Press, 1999).
106. "Act to Indict Boy as a Killer," *Chicago Daily Tribune,* April 26, 1961, 1–2.
107. Mort Edelstein, "Police Reveal Terror by Youth at School," *Chicago American,* 1961, exact date unknown, newspaper clipping, personal archive of Steven Drizin.
108. "Blood Tests Hit in Murder Trial of Boy: Expert Says Sample Is Too Small," *Chicago Tribune,* October 6, 1961, C10.
109. "Act to Indict Boy as a Killer," 1.
110. "For a boy who was known to his teachers and schoolmates to be 'as strong as an ox' and a bully toward younger pupils, Hester showed a complete lack of bravado. He also failed to show any sign of remorse." "Act to Indict Boy as a Killer," 2.
111. Edelstein, "Police Reveal Terror by Youth at School."
112. "Act to Indict Boy as a Killer."
113. "Act to Indict Boy as a Killer," 1–2.
114. "Act to Indict Boy as a Killer."
115. Edelstein, "Police Reveal Terror by Youth at School."
116. "Lee Arthur Hester," National Registry of Exonerations.
117. "Lee Arthur Hester," National Registry of Exonerations.
118. Ms. Jean Webster came from a family who prided themselves on standing up to power. She was the daughter of the late Milton Price Webster Sr. and Elizabeth Harris Webster, who were "recognized leaders in the labor movement of the 20th century." "In Loving Memory: Jean Elizabeth Webster," Memorial Service, Salem United Church of Christ, October 19, 2024.

    Her father was a founder of the Brotherhood of Sleeping Car Porters Union, which was the first Black labor union to successfully challenge the Pullman Company and others for official recognition. He served as the first vice president and leader of its Chicago division. In this leadership role, he showed how to stand up and resist abuses of power. Ms. Webster undoubtedly was shaped by these formative experiences. Standing up for Lee and against the lies of the Chicago Police was a defining moment in her life and was even written into her obituary. Ms. Webster passed away on February 15, 2024, as the final drafts of this book were edited.
119. "Jean E. Webster Obituary (1930–2024)," Legacy.com, January 18, 2025, www.legacy.com/us/obituaries/legacyremembers/jean-webster-obituary?id=57310366.
120. On the three types of false confessions, see Marissa Boyers Bluestine, "False Confessions, Explained," *The Appeal,* June 7, 2021, https://theappeal.org/the-lab/

explainers/false-confessions-explained/; Saul M. Kassin, "False Confessions," *Wiley Interdisciplinary Reviews: Cognitive Science* 8, no. 6 (November/December 2017): e1439.

121. Harry Swegle, "Teen Who Killed Teacher Sees Freedom in a Dream," *Chicago Daily News,* October 11, 1961, 32. The term *jail* is used to be consistent with the news reporting which described Lee Hester as being held in the "County Jail."
122. Swegle, "Teen Who Killed Teacher."
123. Wilber, "Righting a Wrong."
124. Drizin, "Mourning through writing."
125. Adolph J. Slaughter, "Arrest Janitor at School Where Teacher Was Slain," *Chicago Defender,* May 20–26, 1961. And this was a correction article: "Janitors Set Record Straight," *Chicago Defender,* May 22, 1961. (The correction was that Cooley was an engineer, not a janitor.)
126. Feldman Affidavit, 3–4.
127. Drizin, "Mourning through writing."
128. Feldman Affidavit, 29–30. See also *People v. Hester,* 39 Ill. 2d at 508, which stated: "We do not agree with defendant's view that his confession was inadmissible in his criminal prosecution because of section 1 of the old Family Court Act (now chap. 37, para. 702-9), which makes a minor's confession inadmissible in a criminal proceeding if it was made to the juvenile court 'or any officer thereof.' "
129. Feldman Affidavit, 29–33.
130. Drizin, "Lee Arthur Hester Case," 358.
131. *Hester v. Illinois,* 397 U.S. 660 (1970), Petition for Writ of Certiorari at 2 quoted in Drizin, "Lee Arthur Hester Case," 382.
132. *Hester v. Illinois,* 397 U.S. 660 (1970), Transcript of Oral Argument.
133. Drizin, "Lee Arthur Hester Case," 391.
134. See "Supreme Court Insight Help Files: Glossary," adapted from Steven Gifis, *Law Dictionary,* 7th ed. (Hauppauge, NY: Barron's, 2016), https://proquest.libguides.com/supremecourtinsight/glossary. "On rare occasions, however, the Court interrupts that process by deciding that they do not want to decide the case, after all. In those instances, they dismiss the writ of certiorari as improvidently granted, or DIG the case." Michael E. Solimine and Rafael Gely, "The Supreme Court and the Sophisticated Use of DIGs," *Supreme Court Economic Review* 18 (2010): 156.
135. Drizin, "Lee Arthur Hester Case," 391.
136. Drizin, "Lee Arthur Hester Case," 391–92.
137. *Gideon v. Wainwright,* 372 U.S. 335 (1963); *Miranda v. Arizona,* 384 U.S. 436 (1966).
138. *In re Gault,* 387 U.S. 1, 55 (1967).
139. There were some White justices who frequently joined Thurgood Marshall, including Justice Brennan and Justice Douglas. For one example, see *Haley v. Ohio,* 332 U.S. 596 (1948).
140. Drizin, "Lee Arthur Hester Case," 398.
141. Drizin, "Lee Arthur Hester Case," 398.
142. Tom Geraghty interview, February 13, 2023.
143. Cheryl Corley, "50 Years Ago, Martin Luther King Jr. Fought for Open Housing in Chicago," *All Things Considered,* NPR, August 29, 2016, www.npr.org/2016/08/29/491848087/50-years-ago-martin-luther-king-jr-fought-for-open-housing-in-chicago.
144. Hunter and Robinson, *Chocolate Cities,* 171.

145. "School Killing Brings Plea for Police Guard," *Chicago Tribune,* April 24, 1961, 7.
146. "School Killing Brings Plea."
147. "School Killing Brings Plea."
148. "School Killing Brings Plea."
149. "Police Search Lockers in 9 City Schools," *Chicago Tribune,* May 27, 1961. On Robert E. Lewis, see "Robert E. Lewis, 98," *Chicago Tribune,* May 12, 2001, last modified August 20, 2021, www.chicagotribune.com/2001/05/12/robert-e-lewis-98/.
150. "Police Open Headquarters on South Side," *Chicago Tribune,* March 17, 1970, A8.
151. "New Cop Building Has Full Complement," *Chicago Daily Defender,* daily edition, March 18, 1970, 10; "Police Open Headquarters"; "Replacement of Wabash Station Set," *Chicago Defender,* national edition, April 15, 1967, 1.
152. "District Headquarters to Be Police 'Showplace,'" *Chicago Tribune,* October 6, 1968, SC-A7.
153. "Open Police Heliport," *Chicago Tribune,* September 5, 1970, 4.
154. "Police Open Headquarters," A8; "Replacement of Wabash Station Set," 1.
155. "New Cop Building Has Full Complement," 10.
156. "Police Station Honors Harness, Scott Burnham," *Chicago Defender,* February 27, 1992.
157. Lee D. Jenkins, "Harness Grateful, Lauds Chicago Pioneer Testimonial Honorees," *Chicago Daily Defender,* September 20, 1969, 35.
158. Jenkins, "Harness Grateful."
159. There are many examples of police using family separation or the threat of custodial termination as a coercive tactic. In one case the police threatened to separate witnesses from their children if they did not provide statements implicating Kevin Jackson in a shooting, a man who was then wrongfully convicted for twenty-three years. See "Kevin Jackson," National Registry of Exonerations, June 30, 2025, https://exonerationregistry.org/cases/14350.
160. The Equal Justice Initiative, "The Superpredator Myth, 25 Years Later," *Equal Justice Initiative,* April 7, 2014, https://eji.org/news/superpredator-myth-20-years-later/.
161. Theresa F. Hooks, "Force Comdr. Harness to Retire 'At 61': Force Harness to Quit 'At 61,'" *Chicago Daily Defender,* April 18, 1970.
162. Tom Geraghty interview.
163. Tom Geraghty interview.
164. Drizin, "Mourning through writing."
165. Swegle, "Teen Who Killed Teacher."

## Chapter 3: Building the Case

1. Paul Butler, *Let's Get Free: A Hip-Hop Theory of Justice* (New York: New Press, 2009), 16–17.
2. Flint Taylor interview.
3. "These modern studies thus establish, once again, the problem of false confession remains a leading cause of the wrongful conviction of the innocent." Leo, *Police Interrogation and American Justice,* 240.

4. Unless otherwise noted, the following details about the George Jones case are drawn from the Flint Taylor interview; Jones Street File; *Jones v. City of Chicago,* 856 F.2d 985 (7th Cir. 1988); Steve Bogira, *Courtroom 302* (New York: Alfred A. Knopf, 2005).
5. Jones Street File, 14.
6. Jones Street File, 14.
7. Jones Street File, 48, 55.
8. Bogira, *Courtroom 302,* 152.
9. Jones Street File, 49.
10. Bogira, *Courtroom 302,* 152–53.
11. *Jones v. City of Chicago,* 4.
12. *Jones v. City of Chicago,* 4.
13. *Jones v. City of Chicago,* 5.
14. Jones Street File, 48.
15. Jones Street File, 48.
16. Jones Street File, 52.
17. Jones Street File, 49.
18. *Jones v. City of Chicago,* 5.
19. Jones Street File, 26.
20. *Jones v. City of Chicago,* 5.
21. Jones Street File, 27.
22. Jones Street File, 27.
23. "A white gym teacher told the officers that one 'Negro' boy in particular had been accused of sexual misconduct with another boy off-campus, although nothing came from that accusation. . . . His name was Lee Arthur Hester. . . . Following this conversation, the detectives went straight to the classroom of Jean Webster . . . and asked to speak with Hester." Drizin, "Lee Arthur Hester Case," 370.
24. *Jones v. City of Chicago,* 5.
25. *Jones v. City of Chicago,* 5.
26. Flint Taylor interview.
27. Gonzalez Van Cleve, *Crook County.*
28. Bogira, *Courtroom 302,* 157.
29. Bogira, *Courtroom 302,* 155.
30. Bogira, *Courtroom 302,* 153.
31. *Jones v. City of Chicago.*
32. Bonita Brodt, "Student Who 'Had It All' Charged in Rape Slaying," *Chicago Tribune,* May 18, 1981, cited in Bogira, *Courtroom 302,* 155.
33. Bogira, *Courtroom 302,* 153.
34. Brodt, "Student Who 'Had It All,'" cited in Bogira, *Courtroom 302,* 153.
35. Patrick Reyna, "State's Attorney's Felony Review Bypass Program Hinders Due Process and Gives Police Power to File Felony Gun Possession Charges," *Chicago Appleseed,* April 30, 2025, www.chicagoappleseed.org/2025/04/30/felony-review-bypass-program-hinders-due-process-and-gives-police-more-power/.
36. Gonzalez Van Cleve, *Crook County.*
37. "Prosecutors are also constrained by their ongoing relationship with the police. They rely on police effort, cooperation, and good will for the quality of their cases. Maintenance of such a close, dependent relationship requires both tolerance and tact—tolerance of police misconduct (so long as it is not too outrageous and therefore impossible to ignore) and timidity in confronting police officers with anything

that might seem accusatory or blunt. Prosecutors must always assure police officers that they are on the officers' side. The prosecutor who is too demanding of police officers, too judgmental, too 'by the book' is often despised. The consequence of being despised by the police is that the prosecutor gets very little cooperation." David N. Dorfman, "Proving the Lie: Litigating Police Credibility," *American Journal of Criminal Law* 26 (1998): 476–77.

38. Gonzalez Van Cleve, *Crook County.*
39. Gonzalez Van Cleve, *Crook County,* 152.
40. Gonzalez Van Cleve, *Crook County.*
41. The first Black woman prosecutor to lead the State's Attorney's Office, Kim Foxx, was protested by her own police force when she exercised prosecutorial discretion and dropped charges against first-time offender Jussie Smollett, an actor from the series *Empire.* Police protests were joined by White nationalists. At the heart of the issue was that she didn't defer to the police on "their" case. See *Chicago vs. Jussie Smollett,* documentary film, directed by CNN FlashDocs, produced by Eric Johnson, 2022, www.hbomax.com/movies/chicago-vs-jussie-smollett/a247e23d-a05f-4714-b7cd-26fab49110f0; Tom Schuba and Matthew Hendrickson, "How Groups Tied to White Nationalists Are Targeting Chicago and Kim Foxx," *Chicago Sun-Times,* April 27, 2019.
42. Gonzalez Van Cleve, *Crook County,* 153.
43. *Frazier v. Cupp,* 394 U.S. 731 (1969). "There is, however, a legitimate concern . . . that by accepting some types of deceptive practices as legitimate that the police may fashion a belief that all deception is acceptable." Geoffrey P. Alpert and Jeffrey J. Noble, "Lies, True Lies, and Conscious Deception: Police Officers and the Truth," *Police Quarterly* 12, no. 2 (2009): 242. See also J. P. Crank, *Understanding Police Culture,* 2nd ed. (Cincinnati: Anderson, 2004); Rachel Moran, "Police Go to Court: Police Officers as Witnesses/Defendants," *Annual Review of Law and Social Science* 19 (October 2023): 93–107.
44. Skolnick, "Deception by Police," *Criminal Justice Ethics* 1, no. 2 (1982): 43.
45. Myron W. Orfield Jr., "Deterrence, Perjury, and the Heater Factor: An Exclusionary Rule in the Chicago Criminal Courts," *University of Colorado Law Review* 63 (1992): 75–161. In a separate study by Myron W. Orfield Jr., he found that "sixteen of twenty-one responding officers (76 percent), moreover, agreed that the police do 'shade the facts a little (or a lot) to establish probable cause when there may not have been probable cause in fact.'" See "The Exclusionary Rule and Deterrence: An Empirical Study of Chicago Narcotics Officers," *University of Chicago Law Review* 54, no. 3 (1987): 1050.
46. Susan Bandes, "'It Is an Open Secret Long Shared by Prosecutors, Defense Lawyers, and Judges That Perjury Is Widespread Among Law Enforcement Officers': Why Judges So Rarely Second-Guess Police Testimony," *Salon,* December 16, 2015, www.salon.com/2015/12/16/it_is_an_open_secret_long_shared_by_prosecutors_defense_lawyers_and_judges_that_perjury_is_widespread_among_law_enforcement_officers_why_judges_so_rarely_second_guess_police_testimony/.
47. Orfield Jr., "Deterrence, Perjury, and the Heater Factor." See also Bogira, *Courtroom 302,* 181.
48. "The clearance rate—the share of cases that result in an arrest or are otherwise solved—was 58 percent in 2023, the latest year for which F.B.I. data is available. And that figure is inflated because it includes murders from previous years that police solved in 2023." German Lopez, "Nearly Half of America's Murderers Get

Away with It," *New York Times,* July 6, 2025, www.nytimes.com/2025/07/06/us/murder-solve-rate-louisville.html.

49. Shima Baradaran Baughman, "How Effective Are Police?: The Problem of Clearance Rates and Criminal Accountability," *Alabama Law Review* 72 (2020): 47–130.
50. Weihua Li and Jamiles Lartey, "As Murders Spiked, Police Solved About Half in 2020," *The Marshall Project,* January 12, 2022, www.themarshallproject.org/2022/01/12/as-murders-spiked-police-solved-about-half-in-2020.
51. Li and Lartey, "As Murders Spiked."
52. "Black and Brown Chicagoans disproportionately suffer the consequences of violence in the city, and yet, clearance rates in their neighborhoods are less than half of clearance rates in predominantly white communities. In 2021, the homicide clearance rate via prosecution in predominantly white communities was 45.6%, roughly the 2020 national clearance rate. In Latino communities, it was 25.2% and only 21.7% in predominantly Black communities." "Clearance Rates," Live Free Illinois, https://livefreeillinois.org/clearance-rates. See also Rita Oceguera, "When Fatal Shooting Victims Are Black, Chicago Police Arrest Rates Drop," *The Trace,* May 20, 2025, www.thetrace.org/2025/05/chicago-police-gun-homicide-arrests-race/.
53. "Clearance Rates," Live Free Illinois.
54. There are incentives for clearing cases and pressure to do so. "A related reason for police dissembling is the institutional pressure to produce 'results,' which can lead police to cut corners in an effort to secure convictions." Christopher Slobogin, "Testilying: Police Perjury and What to Do About It," *University of Colorado Law Review* 67 (1996): 1044.

    "Agencies receive cash rewards for arresting high numbers of people for drug offenses, no matter how minor the offenses or how weak the evidence. Law enforcement has increasingly become a numbers game. And as it has, police officers' tendency to regard procedural rules as optional and to lie and distort the facts has grown as well." Michelle Alexander, "Why Police Lie Under Oath," *New York Times,* February 2, 2013, www.nytimes.com/2013/02/03/opinion/sunday/why-police-officers-lie-under-oath.html.
55. "Particularly in high publicity cases and major offenses (but not exclusively so), judges don't want to be seen as 'soft on crime.' Whether elected or appointed, state court judges in particular are subject to significant pressures from the press, the public, and from the political powers that be." David N. Dorfman, "Proving the Lie: Litigating Police Credibility," *American Journal of Criminal Law* 26 (1998): 473.
56. See also Agnew, "Fear and Silence"; Agnew, "Police Perjury"; Chicago Appleseed Fund for Justice, *A Report on Chicago's Felony Courts, December 2007,* https://chicagoappleseed.org/wp-content/uploads/2012/08/criminal_justice_full_report.pdf.
57. "Twenty of 27 judges interviewed said that police perjury occurred, six did not directly respond, and only one said that it did not occur. As for prosecutors, 12 of 27 prosecutors said that police perjury sometimes occurred, seven did not directly respond, and eight said that it did not." Nicole Gonzalez Van Cleve, "Chicago's Racist Cops and Racist Courts," *New York Times,* April 14, 2016, www.nytimes.com/2016/04/15/opinion/chicagos-racist-cops-and-racist-courts.html. See also Gonzalez Van Cleve, *Crook County.*

58. Gonzalez Van Cleve, *Crook County,* 153. See also Chicago Appleseed Fund for Justice, *Report on Chicago's Felony Courts.*
59. Butler, *Let's Get Free,* 14–15.
60. Alisha L. McKay discusses multiple forms of prosecutorial misconduct, noting how "overzealousness" and "the extreme desire to convict the accused" can lead to this distinction. While highlighting the lack of accountability for prosecutorial misconduct, she emphasizes that the uses of disciplinary measures against prosecutors still "provide no remedy for those wrongfully convicted." McKay, "Let the Master Answer: Why the Doctrine of Respondeat Superior Should Be Used to Address Egregious Prosecutorial Misconduct Resulting in Wrongful Convictions," *Wisconsin Law Review* (2012): 1222.
61. Gonzalez Van Cleve, *Crook County.*
62. While it is common that criminal acts are often dubbed "violent" and "nonviolent," this typology was only picked up in the 1980s as a liberal response against the war on drugs to argue for a more lenient treatment for drug offenders. However, these rigid definitions are highly subjective and jurisdictionally specific and are often weaponized for political ends. See Abdallah Fayyad, "The Fallacy Behind Tougher Penalties for 'Violent' Crime," *Boston Globe,* April 1, 2021, www.bostonglobe.com/2021/04/01/opinion/fallacy-behind-tougher-penalties-violent-crime/.

    Since the definition of "violence" is loosely defined by the law, and varies from state to state, this phrasing is often used as coded and racialized language to label individuals as "inherently dangerous or non-dangerous," in order to justify longer prison sentences for small offenses that could be categorized as "violent." For example, purse snatching may be considered a violent offense in some states, and therefore may be used to justify a long sentence, where in other states it is considered nonviolent. See Wendy Sawyer and Peter Wagner, "Mass Incarceration: The Whole Pie 2024," Prison Policy Initiative, March 14, 2024, www.prisonpolicy.org/reports/pie2024.html. See also Eli Hager, "When 'Violent Offenders' Commit Nonviolent Crimes," The Marshall Project, April 3, 2019, www.themarshallproject.org/2019/04/03/when-violent-offenders-commit-nonviolent-crimes.
63. Gonzalez Van Cleve, *Crook County,* 114. This mass exoneration of forty-four people in 2022 is an example of how terrible practices like these were. See Chip Mitchell, "In Cook County's Largest Mass Exoneration, a Judge Tosses 44 Convictions Tied to a Corrupt Cop," WBEZ Chicago, April 22, 2022, www.wbez.org/criminal-justice/2022/04/22/judge-tosses-44-more-convictions-tied-to-corrupt-chicago-cop.
64. Gonzalez Van Cleve, *Crook County,* 114. This was prior to the mass exoneration reported in 2022. See Mitchell, "In Cook County's Largest Mass Exoneration."
65. Gonzalez Van Cleve, *Crook County,* 58, 69.
66. Bogira, *Courtroom 302,* 183.
67. Bogira, *Courtroom 302,* 58.
68. Laurence Ralph, *The Torture Letters: Reckoning with Police Violence* (Chicago: University of Chicago Press, 2020).
69. Bogira, *Courtroom 302,* 69.
70. Bogira, *Courtroom 302,* 69.
71. Bogira, *Courtroom 302,* 69.
72. Bogira, *Courtroom 302,* 183–84.
73. Butler, *Let's Get Free,* 102.

74. Butler, *Let's Get Free,* 102.
75. Gonzalez Van Cleve, *Crook County.*
76. Bogira, *Courtroom 302,* 155.
77. Gonzalez Van Cleve, *Crook County.*
78. Keith A. Findley and Michael S. Scott, "Multiple Dimensions of Tunnel Vision in Criminal Cases," *Wisconsin Law Review* 2006, no. 2 (2006): 291–397.
79. Tom Geraghty interview.
80. James Baldwin, *The Evidence of Things Not Seen* (New York: Holt, Rinehart, and Winston, 1985).

    Whereas Susan Bandes approaches tunnel vision as occurring within the vantage point of prosecutors, I approach it as a collaboration between the two institutional actors. Police are powerful in exerting pressure and even fear upon prosecutors by applying discretion in charging and, eventually, conviction. In addition, Bandes acknowledges the pressure on prosecutors to obtain convictions but does not elaborate on how police apply pressure on DAs to help close cases with little regard for accuracy. Overall, prosecutors are enormously dependent upon police to get the wins they need to be promoted. Susan A. Bandes, "Loyalty to One's Convictions: The Prosecutor and Tunnel Vision," *Howard Law Journal* 49 (2006): 475. See also Gonzalez Van Cleve, *Crook County.*
81. Bogira, *Courtroom 302,* 163.
82. Bonita Brodt, "Witness, 11, Hysterical at Murder Trial," *Chicago Tribune,* April 8, 1982, 17, cited in Bogira, *Courtroom 302,* 164.

## Chapter 4: Burying the Evidence

1. Unless otherwise noted, material in this section is drawn from Jason Meisner, "Trial to Expose 'Street Files' Used by Police to Hide Evidence Years Ago," *Chicago Tribune,* November 21, 2016, updated May 23, 2019, www.chicagotribune.com/2016/11/21/trial-to-expose-street-files-used-by-police-to-hide-evidence-years-ago/; Frank Laverty, testimony, *Palmer v. City of Chicago,* 562 F. Supp. 1067 (N.D. Ill. before Mar. 31, 1983), rev'd, 755 F.2d 560 (7th Cir. 1985) (hereafter "Laverty Testimony"); Bogira, *Courtroom 302.*
2. Meisner, "Trial to Expose 'Street Files' "; see also Laverty Testimony.
3. On police omitting exculpatory information from police reports and the use of the "double filing" system by the Chicago Police Department, see Stanley Z. Fisher, "Just the Facts, Ma'am: Lying and the Omission of Exculpatory Evidence in Police Reports," *New England Law Review* 28 (1993): 1–66. According to Myron W. Orfield Jr., "Police keep dual sets of investigatory files; official files and 'street files.' Exculpatory material in the street files may be edited from the official record." Orfield Jr., "Deterrence, Perjury, and the Heater Factor," 83.
4. "Twenty-five years ago, in violation of the law, detectives maintained 'street files'—documents that weren't turned over to defense lawyers because they contained inconvenient truths that could hamper the prosecution of the men or women the police had decided were perpetrators." John Conroy, "The Good Cop," *Chicago Reader,* January 4, 2007, https://chicagoreader.com/news/the-good-cop/.
5. "82.2% of people detained at Homan Square were black, compared with 32.9% of the Chicago population." "11.8% of detainees in the Homan Square logs were

Hispanic, compared with 28.9% of the population." Spencer Ackerman, "Homan Square Revealed: How Chicago Police 'Disappeared' 7,000 People," *The Guardian,* October 19, 2015, www.theguardian.com/us-news/2015/oct/19/homan-square-chicago-police-disappeared-thousands.

6. Ackerman, "Homan Square Revealed."
7. *Brady v. Maryland,* 373 U.S. 83, 87 (1963).
8. Laverty Testimony, 287.
9. Laverty Testimony, 287.
10. Laverty Testimony, 288.
11. Bogira, *Courtroom 302,* 158.
12. *Jones v. City of Chicago* et al. 856 F.2d 985, 991 (7th Cir. 1988). See also Bogira, *Courtroom 302,* 159.
13. Jones Street File, 47.
14. Jones Street File, 47.
15. Gonzalez Van Cleve, *Crook County.*
16. Gonzalez Van Cleve, *Crook County,* 391.
17. *Jones v. City of Chicago.*
18. "Michael J. Angarola: Top County Prosecutor," *Chicago Tribune,* October 31, 1987, updated August 9, 2021, www.chicagotribune.com/1987/10/31/michael-j-angarola-top-county-prosecutor/.
19. Laverty Testimony, 308–11.
20. Meisner, "Trial to Expose 'Street Files.'"
21. Flint Taylor, *The Torture Machine: Racism and Police Violence in Chicago* (Chicago: Haymarket Books, 2019), Kindle ed., loc. 59.
22. *United States v. Jon Burge,* Indictment, Count One: Special February 2008-2 Grand Jury, www.justice.gov/archive/usao/iln/chicago/2008/pr1021_01a.pdf.
23. For a high-level overview of interrogations that occurred in Vietnam, see John Kifner, "Report on Brutal Vietnam Campaign Stirs Memories," *New York Times,* December 28, 2003.
24. Taylor, *Torture Machine,* Kindle ed., loc. 67; "Report on the Failure of Special Prosecutors Edward J. Egan and Robert D. Boyle to Fairly Investigate Police Torture in Chicago," April 24, 2007, https://peopleslawoffice.com/wp-content/uploads/2012/02/5.8.07.Final-Corrected-Version-of-Report.pdf, 23–24.
25. Taylor, *Torture Machine,* Kindle ed., loc. 67.
26. Masha Lisitsyna, "The 'Dry Submarino': Police Torture in Kazakhstan," Open Society Foundations, April 26, 2010, www.opensocietyfoundations.org/voices/dry-submarino-police-torture-kazakhstan. See also Jason Payne-James, Anthony Busuttil, and William Smock, eds., *Forensic Medicine: Clinical and Pathological Aspects* (London: Greenwich Medical Media, 2003), 61.
27. Taylor, *Torture Machine;* "Report on the Failure of Special Prosecutors Edward J. Egan and Robert D. Boyle."
28. Natasha Folling, "Blacks Not Shocked by Policemen Murders," *Chicago Metro-News,* February 13, 1982, 1, cited in Baer, *Beyond the Usual Beating,* 99.
29. Taylor, *Torture Machine,* Kindle ed., loc. 60.
30. Taylor, *Torture Machine,* Kindle ed., loc. 60.
31. Taylor, *Torture Machine,* Kindle ed., loc. 60.
32. The investigation of this pervasive torture was done in a manner to obfuscate the truth. For instance, no African American detectives were called to give testimony

around what they saw under Burge's leadership. Many "leads concerning detectives who had witnessed abuse by Burge and privately complained about it were not pursued." "Report on the Failure of Special Prosecutors Edward J. Egan and Robert D. Boyle," 36.

33. Taylor, *Torture Machine.*
34. Taylor, *Torture Machine,* Kindle ed., loc. 64.
35. Taylor, *Torture Machine,* Kindle ed., loc. 463. See also Joey L. Mogul, "The Struggle for Reparations in the Burge Torture Cases: The Grassroots Struggle That Could," *Public Interest Law Reporter* 21, no. 3 (2016): 209; Natalie Y. Moore, "Payback," The Marshall Project, October 30, 2018, www.themarshallproject.org/2018/10/30/payback.
36. In 1982, Andrew Wilson's twenty-one-year-old brother, Jackie, was also tortured into confession and made a co-defendant in the murder of the two White officers William Fahey and Robert O'Brien. After thirty-six years of wrongful imprisonment, he was finally exonerated in 2020. Jackie's exoneration was only secured when, at his third trial, it came to light that Nicholas Trutenko, who had previously prosecuted the Wilson brothers, had later developed a close friendship with William Coleman, the jailhouse informant who had testified against them. Trutenko had even been made godfather of Coleman's daughter. Jackie Wilson has since received nearly $30 million in settlement.

    Megan Crepeau, "Wilson Ruled Innocent in Burge-Related Case—West," *Chicago Tribune,* December 19, 2020, https://digitaledition.chicagotribune.com/tribune/article_popover.aspx?guid=f58af933-dd68-4b2a-9221-0812eb76ea69; Maurice Possley, "Jackie Wilson," National Registry of Exonerations, October 16, 2020, https://exonerationregistry.org/cases/12899; "Jackie Wilson Receives Largest Pre-Trial Settlement of a Wrongful Conviction Case in U.S. History," Loevy + Loevy, July 16, 2025, www.loevy.com/big-wins/jackie-wilson-receives-largest-pre-trial-settlement-of-a-wrongful-conviction-case-in-u-s-history/.
37. U.S. Department of Justice, Civil Rights Division, and U.S. Attorney's Office, Northern District of Illinois, Investigation of the Chicago Police Department, January 13, 2017, https://issues.chicagoreader.com/general/pdfs/chicago_police_department_findings.pdf, 75.
38. Sworn statement of Frank J. Laverty, *Orange v. Burge,* No. 04 C 00168 (N.D. Ill., sworn statement filed before Judge Holderman and Magistrate Brown), 32–34.
39. Meisner, "Trial to Expose 'Street Files.'"
40. Meisner, "Trial to Expose 'Street Files.'"
41. Taylor, *Torture Machine,* Kindle ed., loc. 320.
42. Retaliation is not unique to Chicago. It is a national problem. Daphne Duret, Gina Barton, and Brett Murphy, "Dead Rats, Death Threats, Destroyed Careers: How Law Enforcement Punishes Its Whistleblowers," *USA Today,* November 9, 2021, www.usatoday.com/in-depth/story-series/2021/11/09/cops-report-excessive-force-risk-jobs/8514211002/; Government Accountability Project, "Breaking the Blue Wall of Silence: The Vital Role of Whistleblower Protections for Law Enforcement Officers," May 2022, https://whistleblower.org/wp-content/uploads/2022/05/NewMayGovAcctProj_Blue-Wall-of-Silence-Report231.pdf.
43. An anonymous whistleblower sent letters in official police envelopes to Flint Taylor in 1989; this person's identity has never been revealed. The letters named officers who participated in torture under Burge's command and alleged that Mayor Jane Byrne and Richard M. Daley were aware of the torture and knowingly used confes-

sions given under coercion. Deep Badge (anonymous whistleblower) letters to Flint Taylor, February–June 1989, on file with Flint Taylor, People's Law Office, Chicago.

44. Meisner, "Trial to Expose 'Street Files.'"
45. Laverty broke the brotherhood in policing and the "blue wall of silence," which is a widespread phenomenon helping cover up law enforcement officers' wrongdoings. For example, in Los Angeles, California, "more than 40 local law enforcement agencies have yet to provide the Los Angeles County district attorney's office with names of officers who have histories of dishonesty and other misconduct that could affect their credibility in court," even though that information could help ensure fair trials. See Adam M. Gershowitz and Caroline E. Lewis, "Laundering Police Lies," *Wisconsin Law Review* 2023 (2023): 1200–01; Ben Poston, "Few Police Agencies Have Given L.A. Prosecutors the Names of Dishonest Cops," *Los Angeles Times,* June 20, 2021, www.latimes.com/california/story/2021-06-20/few-la-police-agencies-have-given-gascon-dishonest-cop-names.
46. "In June 2010, a federal court convicted Burge on criminal charges—not for torture but for lying under oath when he denied torturing people in a civil trial brought by one of his victims." Moore, "Payback."
47. Bogira, *Courtroom 302,* 168.
48. Meisner, "Trial to Expose 'Street Files'"; Flint Taylor interview.
49. According to civil rights attorney H. Candace Gorman, the city passed new police reforms in the wake of the George Jones case, ordering officers to turn over their notes or "street files." Police could still keep copies of their written notes, but all originals must be publicly filed. The police department made a common form for note-taking with the goal of standardizing how police recorded their investigations and requiring them to be part of the main file. However, despite these reforms, police continued to view street files as their personal property, and such reforms have been largely symbolic. Author interview with H. Candace Gorman, July 19, 2023.
50. *Palmer v. City of Chicago,* 806 F.2d 1316 (7th Cir. 1986).
51. Meisner, "Trial to Expose 'Street Files.'"
52. Milton B. Deas, Commander-Area 2, memo to Raymond Clark, Acting Chief-Detective Division, April 21, 1982 (Subject "Recommendations"), 2 [capitalization and underlining omitted].
53. "Police are not likely to take the stated rules of the game seriously and are encouraged to operate by their own codes, including those which affirm the necessity for lying wherever it seems justified by the ends." Skolnick, "Deception by Police," 53.

    "Most deceptive police practices are unlikely to stop." Alpert and Noble, "Lies, True Lies, and Conscious Deception," 249.
54. *Brady v. Maryland,* 373 U.S. 83 (1963).
55. Susan Bandes argues that *Brady* violations are a group effort, as well as a reflection of a long-standing office culture of disregard for *Brady.* She discusses how prosecutorial culture in particular and organizational culture in general make training essential for reform. Susan A. Bandes, "The Lone Miscreant, the Self-Training Prosecutor, and Other Fictions: A Comment on *Connick v. Thompson,*" *Fordham Law Review* 80 (2011): 715.
56. The slow violence of waiting has long been wielded against victims of oppression, as Martin Luther King Jr. proclaimed, "For years now I have heard the word 'wait.' It rings in the ear of every Negro with a piercing familiarity. This 'wait' has almost always meant 'never.'" Martin Luther King Jr., "Letter from Birmingham Jail," August 1963, 2.

57. Meisner, "Trial to Expose 'Street Files.'"
58. "People's Law Office 20 Years: Working with People and Their Movements for Justice and Liberation," Chicago Chapter, National Lawyers Guild, and People's Law Office, November 18, 1989, 33, https://freedomarchives.org/Documents/Finder/DOC510_scans/NLG/510.NLG.Peoples.Law.Office.20.Years.pdf.
59. "People's Law Office 20 Years," 22.
60. *Chicago Lawyer,* April 1987, vol. 10, no. 4, quoted in "People's Law Office 20 Years," 33.
61. Bogira, *Courtroom 302,* 170.
62. Bogira, *Courtroom 302,* 170.
63. Bogira, *Courtroom 302,* 169.

    The Supreme Court ruled that the death penalty in criminal sentencing is "qualitatively different" from all other types of punishment and requires extraordinary procedural safeguards. *Callins v. Collins,* 510 U.S. 1141 (1994). Here we see a local prosecutor "turned judge" more concerned about winning rather than doing justice and safeguarding rights in order to be absolutely sure the correct person is convicted. See *Furman v. Georgia,* 408 U.S. 238, 286–89 (1972). Illinois now has a moratorium on the death penalty for these reasons.
64. Moore, "Payback."
65. Moore, "Payback."
66. Beyond the torture that we know about, for over half a century, the Chicago Police have engaged in what can only be described as systemic terror despite their oath to serve and protect communities. This is still an ongoing problem, and no major reforms have been put in place to curb this violence. In 2017, the Department of Justice (DOJ) investigated the Chicago Police Department in the aftermath of the shooting death of Laquan McDonald and the vast cover-up that nearly hid the murder from public scrutiny. In that instance, the DOJ offered definitive evidence of the department's routine civil rights violations, including excessive force. Police shot unarmed citizens who did not pose a threat and used Tasers (even on children). These practices disproportionately affected people of color, and the disciplining of officers was inconsistent and rare. However, what sustained these decades of police torture—both of suspects and community members—was a practice of "coach and conceal." Police were socialized and instructed by legal representatives on how to alter their statements to avoid accountability and punishment. "Coach and conceal" was the professionalization of lying as a regular part of the business of policing but lying that occurred on the "back end"—usually after police practices were exposed to the general public. Coach and conceal required socialization, institutionalized practices, and the threat of violence for those whistleblowers who may have had the propensity to resist this clandestine system of police lies. With reference to the code of silence, "one way to cover up police misconduct is when officers affirmatively lie about it or intentionally omit material facts"; as one sergeant is quoted in the report as saying, "If someone comes forward as a whistleblower in the Department, they are dead on the street." U.S. Department of Justice and U.S. Attorney's Office, Investigation of the Chicago Police Department, Civil Rights Division, U.S. Department of Justice, and U.S. Attorney's Office, Northern District of Illinois, January 13, 2017, https://issues.chicagoreader.com/general/pdfs/chicago_police_department_findings.pdf, 75. This language is similar to the violence faced by Laverty for exposing the street file system.

67. "Report on the Failure of Special Prosecutors Edward J. Egan and Robert D. Boyle," 43.
68. John Conroy, "Blind Justices?," *Chicago Reader,* November 30, 2006, https://chicagoreader.com/news/blind-justices/.
69. "Report on the Failure of Special Prosecutors Edward J. Egan and Robert D. Boyle," 43.
70. Gonzalez Van Cleve, *Crook County,* 74.
71. Gonzalez Van Cleve, *Crook County,* 78. The pseudonyms used in this book are based on Institutional Review Board standards.
72. Beyond the street file system, many judges signed off on torture. See "Report on the Failure of Special Prosecutors Edward J. Egan and Robert D. Boyle."
73. The court system is an insular culture where it pays politically if one complies with the rules of the mostly White, mostly male boys' club. Former prosecutors can get promoted and then elected to the bench. "Nineteen of the twenty-three judges interviewed served as prosecutors. Likewise, nineteen judges were male and only four judges were female. Many judges were former prosecutors, and thus were preselected to the bench as members of the white boys' club." Gonzalez Van Cleve, *Crook County,* 57.
74. Malik had done all the readings, my readings, and he knew exactly who I was. In fact, we had been quoted in the same news article. It was an article on the impossible backlog of torture cases coming from the Chicago Police. I was quoted as an expert; Malik and his case were profiled. He had to remind me of this as well. Abigail Blachman, "Decades After Alleged Torture by Police: Years More Wait to Have Cases Resolved," *Injustice Watch,* September 11, 2019, www.injusticewatch.org/news/2019/decades-after-alleged-torture-by-police-years-more-wait-to-have-cases-resolved/.
75. Free Abdul-Malik Muhammad, Facebook, March 2, 2022, www.facebook.com/photo/?fbid=152009067249929&set=pb.100076832333793.-2207520000.
76. During the preparation of this book, Malik lost a friend and fellow Northwestern graduate, Michael Broadway. He died of "bronchial asthma, with hypertensive cardiovascular disease and heat stress as 'significant contributing conditions.' " In effect, the horrendous prison conditions made preventable medical conditions deadly. Blair Paddock and Brandis Friedman, "Heat Stress 'Significant Contributing Condition' in Death of Michael Broadway, Who Died While Incarcerated at IDOC's Stateville," *WTTW News,* September 13, 2024, https://news.wttw.com/2024/09/13/heat-stress-significant-contributing-condition-death-michael-broadway-who-died-while.
77. Free Abdul-Malik Muhammad, Facebook post.
78. *People v. Abdul Malik Muhammad,* No. 1-22-0372, Plaintiff-Appellant's Brief and Argument in Support of Appeal (Ill. App. Ct. 1st Dist. filed 2023) (No. 00 CR 1357201).
79. *People v. Muhammad,* 2023 IL App (1st) 220372 13.
80. "Survivor Stories: Abdul-Malik Muhammad," Chicago Alliance Against Racist and Political Repression, www.caarpr.org/survivors-1/abdul-malik-muhammad.
81. H. Candace Gorman interview.
82. Before the Illinois Torture Inquiry and Relief Commission, In re: Claim of Abdul M. Muhammad, Case Disposition, TIRC Claim No. 2014.256-M (Relates to Cook County Circuit Court Case 00-CR-13572-01).
83. H. Candace Gorman interview.

84. "Keith Mitchell," National Registry of Exonerations, https://exonerationregistry.org/cases/12332.
85. *People v. Muhammad,* 2025 IL 130470, *People of the State of Illinois, Appellant, v. Abdul Malik Muhammad, Appellee,* Opinion filed July 10, 2025, 4.
86. "Nathson Edgar Fields," National Registry of Exonerations, https://exonerationregistry.org/cases/10448.
87. H. Candace Gorman interview.
88. H. Candace Gorman interview.
89. Kim Janssen, "Ex-Death Row Inmate: Police 'Street Files' Prove I Was Framed by Cops, Prosecutor," *Chicago Sun-Times,* April 20, 2014; H. Candace Gorman interview.
90. H. Candace Gorman interview.
91. H. Candace Gorman interview.
92. H. Candace Gorman interview.
93. H. Candace Gorman interview.
94. H. Candace Gorman interview.
95. H. Candace Gorman interview.
96. Jason Meisner, "Old Police 'Street Files' Raise Question: Did Chicago Cops Hide Evidence?" *Chicago Tribune,* February 14, 2016, updated June 11, 2018, www.chicagotribune.com/2016/02/13/old-police-street-files-raise-question-did-chicago-cops-hide-evidence/.
97. H. Candace Gorman interview. Research assistant Sophia Block's question is paraphrased here. Her specific questions were: "Is there anything you think that could be done to address the street file system. Because, as we've seen, the laws have been altered. But the system hasn't really changed at all. Do you think there's any positive paths forward?"

## Chapter 5: Making Wolf Packs Real

1. Unless otherwise noted, material in this section is drawn from Omar Muhammad, *The Kids Who Cried Wolf: Roscetti Case* (independently published, 2019).
2. The ABLA Homes were a large public housing development including the Jane Addams Homes, Robert Brooks Homes, Loomis Courts, and Grace Abbott Homes.
3. Jodi Wilgoren, "Three Cleared by DNA Tests Enjoy Liberty After 15 Years," *New York Times,* December 6, 2001, www.nytimes.com/2001/12/06/us/three-cleared-by-dna-tests-enjoy-liberty-after-15-years.html.
4. Muhammad, *Kids Who Cried Wolf,* 5.
5. Orfield Jr., "Deterrence, Perjury, and the Heater Factor," 45, 75.
6. Bridgeport, a predominantly White neighborhood where Mayor Richard J. Daley lived, has a dark history of racial violence. Bridgeport was so notorious for its racist violence toward Black Chicagoans that some Black Chicagoans recall police officers intimidating them by dropping them off near the neighborhood in order to fend for themselves and run for their lives to get home. On the history of racism in Bridgeport, see Erica Gunderson, "'You Didn't See Nothin': Podcast Revisits 1997 Bridgeport Hate Crime," *WTTW News,* March 4, 2023, https://news.wttw.com/2023/03/04/you-didn-t-see-nothin-podcast-revisits-1997-bridgeport-hate-crime; Gary Marx and Andrew Martin, "Unwritten Rules Remain in Bridgeport," *Chi-*

*cago Tribune,* March 26, 1997, www.chicagotribune.com/1997/03/26/unwritten-rules-remain-in-bridgeport/; Don Terry, "Chicago Neighborhood Reveals an Ugly Side," *New York Times,* March 27, 1997, www.nytimes.com/1997/03/27/us/chicago-neighborhood-reveals-an-ugly-side.html; Rachel Kim, "In Bridgeport, Past and Present Live Side by Side," *South Side Weekly,* June 9, 2020, https://southsideweekly.com/bridgeport-past-present-live-side-side-vigilantes/.

7. White people were allowed to exercise their First Amendment right to freedom of assembly and descend on a police station. But if Black people exercised the same right, they were criminalized for mob action or met with police violence such as tear gas or batons. It is only deemed a crime if police view it as such. See Jerry Thornton, "Police Go to Public in Medical Student's Slaying," *Chicago Tribune,* October 20, 1986.
8. Maurice Possley and Steve Mills, "New Evidence Stirs Doubt over Murder Convictions," *Chicago Tribune,* May 2, 2001, revised May 13, 2019, www.chicagotribune.com/2001/05/02/new-evidence-stirs-doubt-over-murder-convictions-2/.
9. Gonzalez Van Cleve, *Crook County.*
10. Possley and Mills, "New Evidence Stirs Doubt."
11. Robert K. Ressler and Tom Shachtman, *Whoever Fights Monsters: My Twenty Years Tracking Serial Killers for the FBI* (New York: St. Martin's Press, 1992), 166.
12. Equal Justice Initiative, "The Superpredator Myth, 25 Years Later," *EJI News,* April 7, 2014, https://eji.org/news/superpredator-myth-20-years-later/; "The 'Superpredator' Scare," *The New York Times,* April 6, 2014, video, www.nytimes.com/video/us/100000002807771/the-superpredator-scare.html.

    Carroll Bogert and Lynnell Hancock, "Superpredator: The Media Myth That Demonized a Generation of Black Youth," The Marshall Project, November 20, 2020, www.themarshallproject.org/2020/11/20/superpredator-the-media-myth-that-demonized-a-generation-of-black-youth.
13. Equal Justice Initiative, "The Superpredator Myth, 25 Years Later."
14. Reuters, "Fact Check: Hillary Clinton, Not Joe Biden, Used the Term 'Super Predator' in the 1990s," Reuters, October 26, 2020, www.reuters.com/article/world/fact-checkhillary-clinton-not-joe-biden-used-thetermsuperpredatorin199-idUSKBN27B1PB/.
15. Reuters, "Fact Check."
16. Eduardo Bonilla-Silva, *Racism Without Racists: Color-Blind Racism and the Persistence of Racial Inequality in the United States,* 3rd ed. (Lanham, MD: Rowman & Littlefield, 2010).
17. Elizabeth Hinton, *From the War on Poverty to the War on Crime: The Making of Mass Incarceration in America* (Cambridge, MA: Harvard University Press, 2016).
18. *Lean on Me,* directed by John G. Avildsen (Burbank, CA: Warner Bros., 1989).
19. Harold Garfinkel, "Conditions of Successful Degradation Ceremonies," *American Journal of Sociology* 61, no. 5 (March 1956): 421. See also Gonzalez Van Cleve, *Crook County,* 52–53.
20. In his book *Black in White Space,* Elijah Anderson describes the "iconic ghetto" as more than just a place; it is an imagined space that embodies a host of stereotypes and stigmas related to inner-city poverty, violence, and Blackness. It becomes a shorthand for where Black people live regardless of their social class, education, or background. See Anderson, *Black in White Space: The Enduring Impact of Color in Everyday Life* (Chicago: University of Chicago Press, 2022).
21. On the racial contradictions of public education in America, see Carter Godwin

Woodson, *The Mis-Education of the Negro* (Washington, DC: Associated Publishers, 1969).

22. Despite the moniker the "Central Park Five," there was an additional defendant implicated in this case. Steven Lopez, at fifteen years old, was arrested along with the Central Park Five. Although he was indicted and charged in connection with the rape of Trisha Meili and the robbery of John Loughlin (one of the four male joggers) as well as with attempted murder, sexual abuse, assault, and riot, he took a deal to plead guilty to the robbery of Loughlin and the other charges were dismissed. "Steven Lopez," National Registry of Exonerations, https://exonerationregistry.org/cases/13357.
23. *The Birth of a Nation*.
24. "Wolf Pack's Prey." *New York Daily News,* April 21, 1989, www.nydailynews.com/2013/04/09/central-park-jogger-near-death-after-savage-attack-in-1989/.
25. "Wolf Pack's Prey."
26. "Wolf Pack's Prey."
27. "Wolf Pack's Prey."
28. Elizabeth Hinton and Heather Ann Thompson, "Why Mass Incarceration Matters: Rethinking Crisis, Decline, and Transformation in Postwar American History," *Journal of American History* 97, no. 3 (December 2010): 703–34.
29. "All But One of the Hundreds of Kids Sent to Adult Court by Chicago Prosecutors Are Children of Color," Equal Justice Initiative, May 23, 2014, https://eji.org/news/kids-of-color-disproportionately-sent-to-adult-court-by-chicago-prosecutors/; "The Republic: Study: Illinois Law Requiring Kids to Face Adult Charges for Certain Crimes May Discriminate," ACLU of Illinois, April 22, 2014, www.aclu-il.org/en/news/republic-study-illinois-law-requiring-kids-face-adult-charges-certain-crimes-may-discriminate.
30. "Youth Tried as Adults," Office of Juvenile Justice and Delinquency Prevention, www.ojjdp.gov/ojstatbb//structure_process/qa04107.asp?qaDate=1999; see also David S. Tanenhaus and Steven A. Drizin, "Owing to the Extreme Youth of the Accused: The Changing Legal Response to Juvenile Homicide," *Journal of Criminal Law and Criminology* 92 (2001): 641–705.
31. 720 Ill. Comp. Stat. 5/25-1, Section 25-1 (Mob Action).
32. 720 Ill. Comp. Stat. 5/25-1, Section 25-1 (Mob Action).
33. 730 Ill. Comp. Stat. 5/5-4.5-25 (Class X Felonies).
34. Joe Biden, "User Clip: Joe Biden Speech on 1994 Crime Bill: 'Predators on Our Streets,'" C-SPAN, November 18, 1993, www.c-span.org/clip/senate-proceeding/user-clip-joe-biden-speech-on-1994-crime-bill-predators-on-our-streets/4879694; Andrew Kaczynski, "Biden in 1993 Speech Warned of 'Predators on Our Streets' Who Were 'Beyond the Pale,'" *CNN Politics,* March 7, 2019, www.cnn.com/2019/03/07/politics/biden-1993-speech-predators.
35. Elijah Anderson, "Toward Knowing the Iconic Ghetto," in *The Ghetto: Contemporary Global Issues and Controversies,* ed. Ray Hutchison and Bruce D. Haynes (New York: Routledge, 2018), 67–82.
36. Flint Taylor interview.
37. Faust Rossi, "The Scottsboro Trials: A Legal Lynching," *Cornell Law Forum,* Paper 948, Winter 2002, http://scholarship.law.cornell.edu/facpub/948; "The Scottsboro Boys," National Museum of African American History and Culture, accessed October 3, 2023, https://nmaahc.si.edu/explore/stories/scottsboro-boys.
38. Rossi, "Scottsboro Trials."

39. *Powell v. Alabama,* 287 U.S. 45 (1932).
40. Even the terminology of the "wolf pack," although significantly more common beginning in the 1980s, extends at least as far back as the 1940s. In 1948, for instance, multiple newspapers referred to increasingly common violent and lawless "wolf pack" gangs of boys. See "Police Press Crackdown on Rowdies," *Detroit Free Press,* July 27, 1948, https://freep.newspapers.com/image/98369266/.
41. Ressler and Shachtman, *Whoever Fights Monsters,* 167.
42. Unless otherwise noted, material in this section is drawn from Muhammad, *Kids Who Cried Wolf.*
43. Margaux Joselow, "Promise-Induced False Confessions: Lessons from Promises in Another Context," *Boston College Law Review* 60 (2019): 1641–87.
44. "And Justice for All?," *Dateline NBC,* NBC News, aired December 6, 2002, 22:35–23:30, www.youtube.com/watch?v=T7vsbHKxOxw; Muhammad, *Kids Who Cried Wolf,* Kindle ed., loc. 131.
45. Muhammad, *Kids Who Cried Wolf,* Kindle ed., loc. 145. See also "Calvin Ollins," National Registry of Exonerations, https://exonerationregistry.org/cases/10671.
46. Linnet Myers, "Trial Begins in Medical Student's Slaying," *Chicago Tribune,* February 3, 1988, 3.
47. Possley and Mills, "New Evidence Stirs Doubt," 1.
48. Possley and Mills, "New Evidence Stirs Doubt." See also "And Justice for All?," *Dateline NBC.*
49. "And Justice for All?," *Dateline NBC.*
50. Author interview with Alexa Van Brunt, June 14, 2024.
51. 725 Ill. Comp. Stat. 5/103-2.1 (When statements by accused may be used). Only a handful of states (Delaware, Illinois, Oregon, California, and Utah) have specific laws in place barring police officers from using deceptive tactics when questioning minors.
52. For example, dozens of witnesses have accused former Chicago Police Department Detective Reynaldo Guevara of using coercion and physical violence to force them to make false identifications in cases. At least forty-nine other cases he investigated as a detective have folded under misconduct allegations, though he has not been charged with any crime. He retired from the police department in 2005. Andy Grimm, "Lawyers: City Should Stop Fighting Wrongful Conviction Cases Tainted by CPD Misconduct," *Chicago Sun-Times,* March 21, 2023, https://chicago.suntimes.com/city-hall/2023/3/21/23650709/chicago-police-wrongful-conviction-guevara-lawsuits-misconduct-loevy; Matthew Hendrickson, "50th Murder Case Connected to Disgraced Former Chicago Police Detective Is Overturned by Judge," *Chicago Sun-Times,* March 4, 2025, https://chicago.suntimes.com/crime/2025/03/04/50th-murder-case-disgraced-chicago-police-detective-overturned.
53. Abdon M. Pallasch, "4-Year Probe Clears Prosecutors, Cops in Ford Heights Four Case—No Need to Charge Officials Who Sent Innocent Men to Death Row, Report Says," *Chicago Sun-Times,* August 22, 2003, 3.
54. "Case Summary: Verneal Jimerson," Center on Wrongful Convictions, researched by Rob Warden, last revised January 16, 2001, Northwestern University School of Law, wwws.law.northwestern.edu/legalclinic/wrongfulconvictions/exonerations/documents/iljimersonchart.pdf.
55. "Paula Gray," researched by Maurice Possley, last revised April 8, 2023, National Registry of Exonerations, https://exonerationregistry.org/cases/10660.
56. For more details about the Ford Heights Four case, see David Protess and Rob

Warden, *A Promise of Justice: The Eighteen-Year Fight to Save Four Innocent Men* (New York: Hyperion, 1998).

57. Flint Taylor interview.
58. Samuel R. Gross et al., "Race and Wrongful Convictions in the United States, 2022," National Registry of Exonerations, September 2022, 8. Some official practices, however, are so normalized that they are never called "misconduct." Even in those cases, the average time to exoneration is 12.2 years. For Black exonerees it took 13.3 years; for White exonerees, the number was 11.3 years.
59. See "Dennis Williams," Center on Wrongful Convictions, Bluhm Legal Clinic, Northwestern Pritzker School of Law, www.law.northwestern.edu/legalclinic/wrongfulconvictions/exonerations/il/dennis-williams.html.
60. "And Justice for All?," *Dateline NBC.*
61. Muhammad, *Kids Who Cried Wolf,* 53–54.
62. Joshua A. Tepfer, Craig M. Cooley, and Tara Thompson, "Convenient Scapegoats: Juvenile Confessions and Exculpatory DNA in Cook County, IL," Faculty Working Papers, Paper 221, 2012, 10, http://scholarlycommons.law.northwestern.edu/facultyworkingpapers/221.
63. *Robert Veal v. Tasso J. Kachiroubas* et al., No. 12 C 8342, 2014 WL 321708 at 2 (N.D. Ill. Jan. 29, 2014). See also "Convictions Vacated Against 3 in 1991 Ill. Slaying," *San Diego Union-Tribune,* November 3, 2011, last updated September 3, 2016, www.sandiegouniontribune.com/2011/11/03/convictions-vacated-against-3-in-1991-ill-slaying/.
64. "DNA Evidence Links Man to 1991 Murder, May Clear 5 Convicted in Case," *Chicago Tribune,* April 15, 2011, last updated August 23, 2021, www.chicagotribune.com/2011/04/15/dna-evidence-links-man-to-1991-murder-may-clear-5-convicted-in-case/.
65. Tepfer, Cooley, and Thompson, "Convenient Scapegoats," 11.
66. "Wrongful Conviction: False Confessions," episode 117, "Dixmoor 5," hosted by Laura Nirider and Steven Drizin, podcast, March 4, 2020.
67. Tepfer, Cooley, and Thompson, "Convenient Scapegoats," 55. After being the supervisor of felony review, Robert Milan's career did not stop. He later rose to First Chair Felony Trial Division, First Assistant State's Attorney, and ran for State's Attorney in 2008. See Tara Malone, "Devine Backs Aide as Successor: State's Attorney Breaks Silence with Endorsement," *Chicago Tribune,* January 14, 2008.
68. The half brothers who were defendants in the case had their father as their alibi, and he even had a paystub to show it was true. Tepfer, Cooley, and Thompson, "Convenient Scapegoats."
69. "Robert Taylor," Center on Wrongful Convictions of Youth, Bluhm Legal Clinic, Northwestern Pritzker School of Law, www.law.northwestern.edu/legalclinic/wrongfulconvictions/exonerations/il/the-dixmoor-five.html.
70. Paul Butler, *Chokehold: Policing Black Men* (New York: The New Press, 2017).
71. In 1995, the Englewood Four had five arrests. Jerry Fincher, at eighteen years old, voluntarily informed police of details in Nina Glover's murder, which indicated his participation in the abduction, rape, and murder. He placed Terrill Swift, Harold Richardson, Vincent Thames, and Michael Saunders at the scene. Fincher's statement was determined to be coerced and suppressed as evidence at the pretrial hearing. His charges were dropped after he was in custody for three and a half years. "Michael Saunders," National Registry of Exonerations, https://exonerationregistry.org/cases/11045.

72. Lauren Fitzpatrick, "Four Englewood Men Won't Be Retried for 1994 Rape and Murder," *Chicago Sun-Times,* January 18, 2012, https://chicago.suntimes.com/news/2012/1/18/18532890/four-englewood-men-won-t-be-retried-for-1994-rape-and-murder.
73. There were some differences between the written confessions. For example, Shainne's statement said Robert T. was driving.
74. Tepfer, Cooley, and Thompson, "Convenient Scapegoats."
75. Expert Steven Drizin, Clinical Professor of Law at Northwestern Pritzker School of Law, described the patterned ways that false confessions are written, even how State's Attorneys and police seem to use the same language. The scripts within the confession make it harder for defendants to claim they were coerced. Finally, there are patterned ways that police get suspects to seem as though they are correcting errors in the confession, which makes the confession seem more persuasive and real. Steven Drizin, text exchange with the author, March 6, 2024.
76. "In about a quarter of the cases, forensic witnesses falsely reported that the defendants might have been the source of crime-scene blood, semen or fingerprints, while concealing forensic tests that had already shown that was impossible. . . . For example, in 1988 Calvin and Larry Ollins, Omar Saunders and Marcellius Bradford, ages 14 through 18, were convicted of rape and murder in Chicago. At their trial, forensic analyst Pamela Fish testified that semen found on the victim's body and undergarments could have come from three of the four defendants. In fact, she knew from blood tests that she had conducted and hidden that none of the defendants could have been the source of the semen." Samuel R. Gross et al., "Government Misconduct and Convicting the Innocent," National Registry of Exonerations, September 1, 2020, 66, www.law.umich.edu/special/exoneration/Documents/Government_Misconduct_and_Convicting_the_Innocent.pdf.

    While it is true that no court ever found Pam Fish guilty of perjury, this evidence shows that "shading" her testimony had crossed the boundaries into what many would see as overt lying. Organizations like the National Registry of Exonerations directly claim that Fish testified to one thing on the stand when she knew it to be false. This occurred in the Roscetti case but also in ten other cases in Chicago. See Gross et al., "Government Misconduct and Convicting the Innocent," 67.

    In one case, a man named John Willis was sentenced to one hundred years in prison for two rapes that he did not commit. Fish's testing showed that John was excluded as the source of the semen from the victim but then she testified that her testing was "inconclusive."

    See both: Gross et al., "Government Misconduct and Convicting the Innocent"; Steve Mills, "Crime Lab Analyst Moved," *Chicago Tribune,* May 13, 2019, www.chicagotribune.com/2001/08/16/crime-lab-analyst-moved-2/.
77. "At present, forensic science is virtually unregulated—with the paradoxical result that clinical laboratories must meet higher standards to be allowed to diagnose strep throat than forensic labs must meet to put a defendant on death row." Eric S. Lander, "DNA Fingerprinting on Trial," *Nature* 339 (1989): 501–5, cited in Paul C. Giannelli, "Wrongful Convictions and Forensic Science: The Need to Regulate Crime Labs," *North Carolina Law Review* 86, no. 1 (2007): 165.
78. Gonzalez Van Cleve, *Crook County.*
79. Forensic science first rose to prominence in the second half of the nineteenth century, among self-certified experts that were not part of the large scientific commu-

nity. Many professionals built their careers on testifying as expert witnesses, often dismissing errors as near impossible, with little to no scientific proof of such accuracy.

A 2009 report represented the first attempt to evaluate whether there is any scientific proof to suggest these techniques are reliable. See National Research Council, *Strengthening Forensic Science in the United States: A Path Forward* (Washington, DC: National Academies Press, 2009). Of the forensic techniques studied, the report found that *only* DNA can accurately identify the source of evidence at a crime scene. In 2016, Obama's Presidential Council of Advisors on Science and Technology came to the same conclusion. See "Forensic Science in Criminal Courts: Ensuring Scientific Validity of Feature-Comparison Methods," President's Council of Advisors on Science and Technology, Executive Office of the President, September 2016, https://obamawhitehouse.archives.gov/sites/default/files/microsites/ostp/PCAST/pcast_forensic_science_report_final.pdf; see also M. Chris Fabricant, *Junk Science and the American Criminal Justice System* (Brooklyn: Akashic Books, 2022).

80. Pam Fish is an actor across various cases, although junk science itself is a pervasive practice across cases and jurisdictions. Following her misconduct in the Roscetti case, the accuracy of her work was called into question again. In another wolf pack case, she "testified that the results of her DNA tests of semen from Lewis' [the victim's] body were inconclusive, leaving open the possibility that Williams [the defendant] might be its source. Later DNA testing, however, excluded Williams and his codefendants as the sources of the semen." Scientific evidence is not solely objective, and Pam Fish is an example of one person in the system perpetuating wrongful conviction. See Steve Mills, "Controversial Ex-Forensic Lab Analyst Focus of Another Inmate's Appeal," *Chicago Tribune,* January 31, 2017, updated May 22, 2019, www.chicagotribune.com/2017/01/31/controversial-ex-forensic-lab-analyst-focus-of-another-inmates-appeal/; Mills, "Crime Lab Analyst Moved."
81. Steve Mills and Maurice Possley, "Report Alleges Crime Lab Fraud: Scientist Is Accused of Providing False Testimony," *Chicago Tribune,* January 14, 2001, 1.1.
82. Rosalind Rossi, "Jury Tours Roscetti Murder Site," *Chicago Sun-Times,* May 7, 1988, 7.
83. Laura H. Nirider, Joshua A. Tepfer, and Steven A. Drizin, "Combating Contamination in Confession Cases (Reviewing *Convicting the Innocent: Where Criminal Prosecutions Go Wrong* by Brandon L. Garrett)," *University of Chicago Law Review* 79, no. 2 (2012): 7.
84. Elijah Anderson, "The Iconic Ghetto," *Annals of the American Academy of Political and Social Science* 642, no. 1 (2012): 8–24.
85. Rossi, "Teen Guilty in Lori Killing."
86. In another instance, the "iconic ghetto" was used as a piece of evidence, similar to the Roscetti Four case. According to Ben Austen, during closing arguments in Johnnie Veal's parole proceedings—after decades in prison for the murder of two police officers, a crime he has always maintained he did not commit—prosecutors contended that releasing him would not only affect residents of Cabrini-Green, a predominantly Black housing project, but could also have ripple effects extending into White suburban communities where most jurors lived—playing on the racial fears that violence or disorder from the "ghetto" could spread beyond its boundaries. Ben Austen, *Correction: Parole, Prison, and the Possibility of Change* (New York: Flatiron Books, 2023), 195.

87. Rossi, "Teen Guilty in Lori Killing."
88. Closing argument transcript from Robert Taylor's trial, 51–52.
89. Rossi, "Teen Guilty in Lori Killing."
90. Rossi, "Teen Guilty in Lori Killing." See also Linnet Myers, "Trial Begins in Medical Student's Slaying," *Chicago Tribune,* February 3, 1988, 3; "No Satisfaction in Roscetti Case," *Chicago Tribune,* February 10, 2002, 2.8; Possley and Mills, "New Evidence Stirs Doubt"; Sharon Cohen, "Jailed at 14, Youth Refused to Surrender Hope," *Los Angeles Times,* June 9, 2002, www.latimes.com/archives/la-xpm-2002-jun-09-adna-calvin-story.html.
91. Rossi, "Teen Guilty in Lori Killing."
92. "And Justice for All?," *Dateline NBC.*
93. Gonzalez Van Cleve, *Crook County.*
94. Gonzalez Van Cleve, *Crook County,* 43.
95. Gonzalez Van Cleve, *Crook County,* 164.
96. "And Justice for All?," *Dateline NBC.*
97. Gonzalez Van Cleve, *Crook County,* 164.
98. "15-Year-Old Gets Life Sentence for Rape, Murder," *Chicago Tribune,* March 11, 1988, updated August 8, 2021, www.chicagotribune.com/1988/03/11/15-year-old-gets-life-sentence-for-rape-murder/.
99. Rossi, "Teen Guilty in Lori Killing."

## Chapter 6: The Danger in the Mirror

1. The only upside was that Daniel was able to see things beyond "the hood," the impoverished side of Chicago which started as his home. "An Impossible Crime," episode 208, *Criminal* podcast, aired February 24, 2023, https://thisiscriminal.com/episode-208-an-impossible-crime-2-24-2023/, 2:43.
2. Deon Patrick, Daniel Taylor, Paul Phillips, and Lewis Gardner, *The Hazel Boyz: The Trials of Four Innocent Men* (Atlanta: Get It Done Publishing, 2024).
3. Nicole Gonzalez Van Cleve, "How Does It Feel to Be the Problem? A Call for Du Boisian Criminology and Theorizing Racial Punishment," in *The Oxford Handbook of W.E.B. Du Bois,* ed. Aldon D. Morris et al. (Oxford: Oxford University Press, 2025).
4. "An Impossible Crime," 5:50.
5. "An Impossible Crime," 9:40.
6. *Daniel Taylor v. City of Chicago,* No. 14 C 737 (N.D. Ill. Oct. 3, 2018), 2018 WL 6167636.
7. Akia Philips, Joseph Brown, and Rodney Mathews were the remaining teenagers wrongfully arrested alongside Daniel Taylor, Lewis Gardner, Dion Patrick, Dennis Mixon, and Paul Phillips.
8. "An Impossible Crime"; Steve Mills, Maurice Possley, and Ken Armstrong, "When Jail Is No Alibi in Murders: New Evidence Undercuts State Case," *Chicago Tribune,* north sports final edition, *Cops and Confessions* series, last of four parts, December 19, 2001.
9. *Daniel Taylor v. City of Chicago.*
10. *Daniel Taylor v. City of Chicago.*
11. The following details about Ms. McCoy are from Steve Bogira, "They Came in Through the Bathroom Mirror," *Chicago Reader,* September 3, 1987, https://chicagoreader.com/news/they-came-in-through-the-bathroom-mirror/.

12. *Candyman,* directed by Bernard Rose (Los Angeles: TriStar Pictures, 1992).
13. "An Impossible Crime," 23:55.
14. "An Impossible Crime," 24:02.
15. "And jurors in excessive force cases reported that, videos or no videos, 'they had been swayed most of all by officers' [own] assertions that they feared for their lives.' In jurors' view, if the police officers say they felt threatened, they felt threatened. If they felt threatened, their actions must have been reasonable." Bandes, "Video, Popular Culture, and Police Excessive Force," 11–12, quoting Julie Bosman, Mitch Smith, and Michael Wines, "Jurors Find Video Isn't Providing 20/20 Vision in Police Shootings," *New York Times,* June 25, 2017, www.nytimes.com/2017/06/25/us/police-shootings-trials-video-body-cam.html.
16. "An Impossible Crime," 24:45.
17. Gonzalez Van Cleve, *Crook County,* ch. 5.
18. Gonzalez Van Cleve, *Crook County,* 147. On testilying, see Slobogin, "Testilying."
19. "An Impossible Crime," 27:37.
20. "An Impossible Crime," 28:03.
21. *In re Gault,* 387 U.S. 1 (1967). The rights guaranteed by this case included notice of charges, right to counsel, right to remain silent, and right to confrontation.
22. *In re Gregory W., In re Gerald S.,* 19 N.Y.2d 55 (1966).
23. *In re Gregory W., In re Gerald S.* "deals with a dramatic and, it is to be hoped, extreme example. Two 12-year-old Negro boys were taken into custody for the brutal assault and rape of two aged domestics, one of whom died as the result of the attack." *In re Gault,* 387 U.S. 1 (1967).
24. There are other cases in which individuals who have airtight alibis have been charged. For example, in 1999 there was an instance in Chicago in which a student was charged for a murder supposedly committed while he was in school as a student. See "Murder Case Dropped, Teen Still Held," *Chicago Tribune,* May 18, 1999, updated August 11, 2021, www.chicagotribune.com/1999/05/18/murder-case-dropped-teen-still-held/. Lee Hester was in school, but the alibi given by his Black teacher was insufficient to save him from conviction.
25. *In re Gregory W., In re Gerald S.,* 19 N.Y.2d 55, (N.Y. Dec. 30, 1966).
26. "After a single request, the odds of signing were 4.5 times higher for the sleep-deprived participants than for the rested participants." Steven J. Frenda et al., "Sleep Deprivation and False Confessions," *Proceedings of the National Academy of Sciences* 113, no. 8 (2016): 2047.
27. Another such defendant in Chicago charged with murder while in police custody was a man named Mario Hayes. According to police, he confessed to a murder that he committed while in the Cook County Jail. See Maurice Possley and Steve Mills, "Little Adds Up in Murder Case," *Chicago Tribune,* March 21, 1999, 1, 15.
28. Bandes, "It Is an Open Secret."
29. Ken Armstrong, Maurice Possley, and Steve Mills, "Coercive and Illegal Tactics Torpedo Scores of Cook County Murder Cases," *Chicago Tribune,* December 16, 2001, updated August 20, 2021, www.chicagotribune.com/2001/2/16/coercive-and-illegal-tactics-torpedo-scores-of-cook-county-murder-cases/.
30. Armstrong, Possley, and Mills, "Coercive and Illegal Tactics Torpedo Scores of Cook County Murder Cases."
31. Patrick et al., *Hazel Boyz,* 108.

32. Justina Giglio, "Dr. Yusef Salaam of the 'Exonerated Five' on the Power of Narrative and His Path to Justice," Kresge Foundation, July 28, 2025, https://kresge.org/news-views/dr-yusef-salaam-of-the-exonerated-five-on-the-power-of-narrative-and-his-path-to-justice/.
33. "An Impossible Crime," 31:30.
34. Free Abdul-Malik Muhammad, Facebook, photo post, March 2, 2022, www.facebook.com/photo/?fbid=152009067249929&set=pb.100076832333793.-2207520000. Christopher Seeds comes to a similar conclusion. See Seeds, *Death by Prison: The Emergence of Life Without Parole and Perpetual Confinements* (Oakland: University of California Press, 2022).
35. Daniel tried to commit suicide three weeks after he was first sent to prison. "Something happened that I haven't really shared in many interviews. I tried to take my own life. I wasn't one of those people who just talked about it. I really meant to end it. One night . . . I just lay there, hoping to bleed out, to escape this hell. I thought I would just fade away, but obviously, that didn't happen. The guy in the cell next to me noticed the blood. I lost so much that it leaked through the mattress onto the floor. He saw it and called the guards." Patrick et al., *Hazel Boyz,* 88.
36. Reporter Steve Mills "saw something in our case that others had overlooked, and he made it his mission to tell the world what was happening. . . . His articles brought our case to the attention of people who could help, people who could make a difference. And in the end, that attention is what led to Daniel's release in 2013." Patrick et al., *Hazel Boyz,* 77.
37. Daniel Taylor recounts the disbelief he felt during the closing argument at his trial: "In closing argument at trial, the prosecutors carefully chose which police paperwork to believe. One asserted, 'paper-work is not foolproof. But I'll tell you what is foolproof. And what is foolproof are the defendant's own words.' The jury bought it." Patrick et al., *Hazel Boyz,* 145.
38. Daniel Taylor's fight from inside prison was similar to Omar's, and eventually Daniel obtained his GED. "I started my appeal process right away, but every appeal I filed was denied. My direct appeal, the one that was supposed to be the most straightforward, was not even reconsidered. It was just denied. Then I filed a post-conviction petition and was denied again. It felt like a never-ending cycle of rejection. . . . Here I was, not educated enough to defend myself properly, but with no other choice. After your direct appeal, everything—every motion or petition that you file at different stages—you have to do it yourself. So I had to learn how to file a petition, how to put it in legal format, and how to look up case law to argue different points where I believed my rights were violated." Patrick et al., *Hazel Boyz,* 85–86.
39. Michael L. Walker, *Indefinite: Doing Time in Jail* (New York: Oxford University Press, 2022).
40. "Uniform Crime Report for Homicides: 1965–2023," *Murder Accountability Project,* www.murderdata.org/p/blog-page.html; "Victim Characteristics 1976–2023," *Murder Accountability Project,* www.murderdata.org/p/victims.html.
41. Muhammad, *Kids Who Cried Wolf,* 54.

## Chapter 7: The Final Question

1. James Baldwin, "Notes on the House of Bondage," *The Nation,* November 1, 1980, 439–43, www.thenation.com/article/archive/notes-house-bondage/.
2. The Honorable R. Eugene Pincham, interviewed by Adele Hodge, May 5, 2003, The HistoryMakers Digital Archive, A2002.176, session 2, tape 9, story 1.
3. The Honorable R. Eugene Pincham, interviewed by Adele Hodge, May 5, 2003, The HistoryMakers Digital Archive, A2002.176, session 2, tape 9, story 1.
4. The Honorable R. Eugene Pincham, interviewed by Adele Hodge, May 5, 2003, The HistoryMakers Digital Archive, A2002.176, session 2, tape 8, story 1.
5. "Long Live Anthony Porter," Chicago Torture Justice Center, September 2024, www.chicagotorturejustice.org/newsandevents/long-live-anthony-porter; AP, "Anthony Porter, Whose Case Helped End Death Penalty in Illinois, Dies," *Chicago Sun-Times,* July 8, 2021, https://chicago.suntimes.com/politics/2021/7/8/22568299/anthony-porter-illinois-death-penalty-dies.
6. H. Candace Gorman interview; "Long Live Anthony Porter"; "Exonerated Death-Row Inmate Charged with Theft," NBC Chicago, September 25, 2011, www.nbcchicago.com/news/local/exonerated-death-row-inmate-charged-with-theft-anthony-porter-arrested-illinois/1911900/.
7. AP, "Exonerated Illinois Inmate Charged with Theft," *Daily Herald* (Arlington Heights, Ill.), September 26, 2011, www.dailyherald.com/20110926/news/exonerated-illinois-inmate-charged-with-theft/.
8. "Exonerated Death Row Inmate Going Back to Prison for Stealing Deodorant," CBS Chicago, August 2, 2012, www.cbsnews.com/chicago/news/exonerated-death-row-inmate-going-back-to-prison-for-stealing-deodorant/.
9. The Honorable R. Eugene Pincham, interviewed by Adele Hodge, May 5, 2003, The HistoryMakers Digital Archive, A2002.176, session 2, tape 9, story 1.
10. The Honorable R. Eugene Pincham, interviewed by Adele Hodge, May 5, 2003, The HistoryMakers Digital Archive, A2002.176, session 2, tape 9, story 1.
11. The Honorable R. Eugene Pincham, interviewed by Adele Hodge, May 5, 2003, The HistoryMakers Digital Archive, A2002.176, session 2, tape 9, story 1.
12. Brown, "Accused," 8.
13. Derrick K. Baker, "'Power Rangers' Rescue Boys in Harris Murder Case," *N'Digo,* April 1–7, 1999, 6–8, 20.
14. Baker, "'Power Rangers' Rescue Boys in Harris Murder Case."
15. Elijah Henderson Civil Case, 71.
16. Brown, "Accused," 8.
17. Brown, "Accused."
18. Wrongful conviction *is* police brutality but happening within the police station and in more clandestine places rather than on the streets. See Susan Bandes, "Patterns of Injustice: Police Brutality in the Courts," *Buffalo Law Review* 47, no. 3 (Fall 1999): 1275–342.
19. The Honorable R. Eugene Pincham, interviewed by Adele Hodge, May 5, 2003, The HistoryMakers Digital Archive, A2002.176, session 2, tape 9, story 1.
20. The Honorable R. Eugene Pincham, interviewed by Adele Hodge, May 5, 2003, The HistoryMakers Digital Archive, A2002.176, session 2, tape 9, story 1.
21. The Honorable R. Eugene Pincham, interviewed by Adele Hodge, May 5, 2003, The HistoryMakers Digital Archive, A2002.176, session 2, tape 9, story 1.

22. The Honorable R. Eugene Pincham, interviewed by Adele Hodge, May 5, 2003, The HistoryMakers Digital Archive, A2002.176, session 2, tape 9, story 1.
23. The Honorable R. Eugene Pincham, interviewed by Adele Hodge, May 5, 2003, The HistoryMakers Digital Archive, A2002.176, session 2, tape 8, story 6.
24. The Honorable R. Eugene Pincham, interviewed by Larry Crowe, January 17, 2007, The HistoryMakers Digital Archive, A2002.176, session 3, tape 13, story 7.
25. The Honorable R. Eugene Pincham, interviewed by Adele Hodge, May 5, 2003, The HistoryMakers Digital Archive, A2002.176, session 2, tape 9, story 1.
26. The Honorable R. Eugene Pincham, interviewed by Adele Hodge, May 5, 2003, The HistoryMakers Digital Archive, A2002.176, session 2, tape 9, story 2.
27. Baker, " 'Power Rangers' Rescue Boys in Harris Murder Case."
28. Unless otherwise noted, the following information comes from Catherine Ferguson interview; author interview with Maurice Possley, September 12, 2023.
29. "Although PR spending in all three cities makes up a tiny share of their multi-billion-dollar budgets, the portion of its budget Chicago pays for PR staff salaries is nearly double the portion budgeted in Los Angeles, and more than eight times the portion budgeted in New York." Geoffrey Cubbage, "Analysis: Chicago Outspends and Outstaffs NYC, LA, on Communications and Public Relations," Better Government Association, October 18, 2022, www.bettergov.org/2022/10/18/analysis-chicago-outspends-and-outstaffs-nyc-la-on-communications-and-public-relations/.
30. For 2023, the proposed budget numbers were used. See Cubbage, "Analysis." More recently, the Chicago Police Department has increased the number of public relations (PR) employees (police officers, part-timers, and citizens) over the years to protect its image. This allows crime cases to be covered up and sway public perception of events. The cover-up of Laquan McDonald's shooting by a Chicago officer in 2014 led to increased spending on PR to spin their misconduct. "As the city fought in court to keep evidence of the child's murder secret and then later to control the uproar when a judge ordered it to release a video of the shooting, Chicago increased its police budget to pay for twenty-five full-time public relations positions. As of early 2023, Chicago's cops had forty-eight full-time positions devoted to manipulating public information. The 2024 budget funded fifty-five." Alec Karakatsanis, *Copaganda: How Police and the Media Manipulate Our News* (New York: New Press, 2025), 59.
31. Cubbage, "Analysis."
32. Alongside the Chicago Police Department's increase in their public relations (PR), other U.S. cities have experienced copaganda, starting with feeding news outlets, which may be underfunded and understaffed to conduct a full investigation, taking advantage of this weakness. "The Los Angeles sheriff has 42 full-time PR people. LAPD has another 25. New York has 90 or so, right? These are just a few police departments, right? So, we're talking about, over the course of the country, tens of thousands of people working full-time on curating and producing the news. So, when a local news outlet has to fill 22 minutes of coverage at 6:30 and 7 and 10:30 and 11:00 PM, the police not only send them, you know, snippets of who they've arrested, but they send them video, audio, charts, graphs, people to quote, experts to identify, right? So, they basically produce the news for people. So, that's a huge factor—this sort of like bureaucratic workflow of news organizations, and the sort of political economy of how these organizations are set up makes it very easy to manipulate if you have a large PR propaganda apparatus." "What Is

Copaganda, and How Do We Fight It?," *NYCLU,* podcast, season 4, episode 6, July 3, 2025, featuring Alec Karakatsanis, www.nyclu.org/podcast/what-is-copaganda-and-how-do-we-fight-it. See also Maya Lau, "Police PR Machine Under Scrutiny for Inaccurate Reporting, Alleged Pro-Cop Bias," *Los Angeles Times,* August 30, 2020, www.latimes.com/california/story/2020-08-30/police-public-relations.

33. Reporters are often too busy to fact-check thoroughly and sometimes inadvertently contribute to the dissemination of propaganda. "Police PR units literally produce content for the news, in a format that allows reporters, editors, and producers to exert as little work as possible. The replication and replacement by police PR officials of traditional journalist functions is particularly important given the prolonged and steep decline in the number of reporters and budgets in local newsrooms." Karakatsanis, *Copaganda,* 69. See also Yona TR Golding, "Q&A: Alec Karakatsanis on the Media's Role in Spreading 'Copaganda,'" *Columbia Journalism Review,* April 16, 2025, www.cjr.org/the_media_today/qa_alec_karakatsanis_copaganda.php.
34. Alec Karakatsanis points to the San Francisco Police Department as an example of the extent to which manipulation of public perception through media has led to staging details of a press conference: "Mayor London Breed . . . collaborated with cops to stage a press conference in front of Louis Vuitton . . . a trove of police text messages argued, 'that's the visual for where the rule of law needs to make its stand.'" Karakatsanis, *Copaganda,* 63.
35. In his classic 1979 book *The Process Is the Punishment,* Malcolm Feeley details the arduous nature of pretrial punishment. Rather than punishment meted out by judges, the accusation made by police and prosecutor sets a whole series of punishments in motion prior to adjudication and a determination of guilt. See Feeley, *The Process Is the Punishment: Handling Cases in a Lower Criminal Court* (New York: Russell Sage Foundation, 1979).
36. Kotlowitz, "Unprotected."
37. Cassidy, "Ugliness of Being a Kid."
38. Pam Belluck, "Chicago Boys, 7 and 8, Charged in the Brutal Killing of a Girl, 11," *New York Times,* August 11, 1998.
39. On August 2 and 3, 2018, a "bait truck" filled with Nike shoes was deliberately left near West 59th Place and South Princeton Avenue in Englewood, Chicago, as part of a joint sting operation between the Norfolk Southern Railroad and the Chicago Police. The tactic was to lure and arrest people attempting to steal from the truck, relying on the racist belief that Black people are thieves. Emma G. Fitzsimmons, "A Truckload of Nike Shoes, Left as 'Bait,' Stings Chicago," *New York Times,* August 24, 2018.
40. Kotlowitz, "Unprotected."
41. Carpenter and Forte, "Killed for Her Bike," 1. See also Kotlowitz, "Unprotected."
42. Kotlowitz, "Unprotected," 43.
43. Kotlowitz, "Unprotected," 43.
44. Police knew "within hours" that the confession was false and that there were no stab wounds on the body, but they proceeded with the case anyway. For Eddie, he was lucky enough to be acquitted by a judge but spent over a year in jail being punished just for being accused. James Hill and Steve Mills, "Judge Rejects 'Confession' of Teen to Murder Youth Is Freed; Evidence Undermines State's Case," *Chicago Tribune,* Chicagoland final edition, April 30, 1999, 1. See also Possley and Mills, "Little Adds Up in Murder Case," 1.
45. Kotlowitz, "Unprotected," 43.

46. Kotlowitz, "Unprotected."
47. Kotlowitz, "Unprotected," 44.
48. Carpenter and Forte, "Killed for Her Bike."
49. If the state's evidence meets this low threshold, the next question the judge must answer is whether or not to keep the boys locked up pending their trials or whether to allow them to go home with their families. When children are held in custody, these hearings must occur quickly. In Chicago that is supposed to happen no later than forty hours after their arrest.
50. Elijah Henderson Civil Case, 57, citing transcript of August 10, 1998, 13–14. *Henderson v. City of Chicago,* Plaintiffs' Complaint at Law, filed by Elijah Akbar Henderson through Rosetta Crawford and Sonja Crawford, against the City of Chicago, the Chicago Police Department, and Officers Allen Nathaniel and James Cassidy.
51. Paradoxically, Oppenheimer is now a civil rights attorney who represented one of the Marquette Park Four and who touts his national acclaim from his work as a prosecutor on this case.
52. Elijah Henderson Civil Case, 60.
53. Butler, *Let's Get Free.*
54. Gonzalez Van Cleve, *Crook County.*
55. Illinois Juvenile Court Act of 1987, 705 Ill. Comp. Stat. 405/5-501.
56. Carpenter and Forte, "Killed for Her Bike."
57. Gonzalez Van Cleve, *Crook County,* 52–55. See also Nicole Gonzalez Van Cleve, "Due Process and the Theater of Racial Degradation: The Evolving Notion of Pretrial Punishment in the Criminal Courts," *Daedalus* 151, no. 1 (2022): 135–52.
58. Butler, *Let's Get Free.*
59. "I am still proud of my men, let there be no doubt about it." Taylor, *Torture Machine,* Kindle ed., loc. 113.
60. Butler, *Let's Get Free.*
61. From an interview with Assistant State's Attorney Terence Johnson that was later unsealed from an FBI report: "During the motion to suppress hearing CASSIDY and Detective PALIDINO circulated a document that detailed what the detectives and ASAs should say when questioned regarding the circumstances of the GLOVER investigation. CASSIDY passed the document to JOHNSON and VALENTINI and told them to read it before they testified. CASSIDY told them, 'this is what we do' and that the document would help if they are asked certain questions. The document was used so that they all would provide a consistent statement. During breaks the detectives told JOHNSON and VALENTINI what the defense attorneys were asking and focusing on and what their responses should be. The detectives told them to follow the time line so they would be on the same page. They were concerned the judge would throw out the statements." Exhibit no. 1, Federal Bureau of Investigation Transcript with Terence Johnson, FD-302 (Rev. 10-6-95), 5, dated March 14, 2012, filed under seal pursuant to Local Rule 26.2, Case: 1:12-cv-09158, Document no. 461 (filed February 24, 2017). See also Jon Seidel, "Unsealed FBI Report Alleges Police Fed Statements to 'Englewood Four,'" *Chicago Sun-Times,* July 20, 2017; *Saunders v. City of Chicago,* Nos. 12-cv-9158, 12-cv-9170, 12-cv-9184 (N.D. Ill. July 19, 2017), 2017 WL 3082036.
62. Gonzalez Van Cleve, *Crook County.*
63. Elijah Henderson Civil Case, 11. See also *Saunders v. City of Chicago,* Nos. 12-cv-9158, 12-cv-9170, 12-cv-9184 (N.D. Ill. July 19, 2017), 2017 WL 3082036, Exhibit no. 1, FBI Transcript with Johnson, FD-302, March 14, 2012.

64. *Doe et al. v. Cassidy et al.*, Condensed Transcript and Concordance, Continued Deposition of Allen Nathaniel, vol. 3, PM session, May 9, 2001, 646.
65. Andrew Abbott, "Status and Status Strain in the Professions," *American Journal of Sociology* 86, no. 4 (1981): 819–35; John P. Heinz, Robert L. Nelson, Rebecca L. Sandefur, and Edward O. Laumann, *Urban Lawyers: The New Social Structure of the Bar* (Chicago: University of Chicago Press, 2005).
66. Possley, "Anguish Grips Mom," 1.
67. Kotlowitz, "Unprotected," 50.
68. The Honorable R. Eugene Pincham, interviewed by Adele Hodge, May 5, 2003, The HistoryMakers Digital Archive, A2002.176, session 2, tape 9, story 2.
69. The Honorable R. Eugene Pincham, interviewed by Adele Hodge, May 5, 2003, The HistoryMakers Digital Archive, A2002.176, session 2, tape 9, story 2.
70. Kotlowitz, "Unprotected," 50.
71. Kotlowitz, "Unprotected," 50.
72. Kotlowitz, "Unprotected," 50.
73. Catherine Ferguson interview. Also see Peter F. Nardulli, "Insider Justice: Defense Attorneys and the Handling of Felony Cases," *Journal of Criminal Law and Criminology* 77, no. 2 (1986): 379–417.
74. Author interview with Darron Bowden, October 30, 2023.
75. Kotlowitz, "Unprotected," 50.
76. Gonzalez Van Cleve, *Crook County*, ch. 2 and p. 70.
77. Shaun L. Gabbidon, "W.E.B. Du Bois: Pioneering American Criminologist," *Journal of Black Studies* 31, no. 5 (2001): 581–99.
78. Kotlowitz, "Unprotected," 50.
79. Gonzalez Van Cleve, *Crook County*.
80. Gonzalez Van Cleve, *Crook County*, 72. See also Rudyard Kipling, "The White Man's Burden," *McClure's Magazine* 12, no. 4 (1899): 290–91.
81. Maurice Possley and Teresa Puente, "Young Suspects Sent Home Wearing Small Monitoring Bracelets: A 7- and 8-Year-Old Accused of Murder Return to Their Relatives, Under 24-Hour House Confinement," *Chicago Tribune*, August 14, 1998.
82. Kotlowitz, "Unprotected," 50.
83. Possley and Puente, "Young Suspects Sent Home."
84. Possley and Puente, "Young Suspects Sent Home."
85. Kotlowitz, "Unprotected," 50.
86. Kotlowitz, "Unprotected"; Brown, "Accused," 2.
87. Maurice Possley, "Boys Framed, Lawyer Charges Perjury: Issue Raised in Ryan Harris Case," *Chicago Tribune*, September 3, 1998, 1.
88. Bandes, "It Is an Open Secret."
89. Author interview with Alexa van Brunt, June 14, 2024.
90. Daniel Medwed persuasively articulates this principle of finality: "The system runs like a conveyor belt in a factory. A conviction is manufactured at the trial level before it travels up the assembly line. Judges and prosecutors quickly check its components at various workstations before putting a lid on the case for good and dispatching it to the annals of case law." Medwed, *Barred: Why the Innocent Can't Get Out of Prison* (New York: Basic Books, 2022), 10.
91. Charisse Jones, "Shock Turns to Doubt in Chicago," *USA Today*, August 14, 1998, final edition, 3A.
92. Legendary columnist Mike Royko played this role in the Lee Hester case and lion-

ized Sergeant Sheldon Teller, who was central to framing Lee but would later be convicted of dealing drugs. John Gorman, "Pizza Exec's Widow Is Questioned," *Chicago Tribune,* northwest sports final, NW edition, December 5, 1991, 1; Michael Royko, "Detective's Story Like Movie Script," *Chicago Daily News,* April 22, 1961, 3.

93. Richard Roeper, "Too Soon to Take Sides in Child Murder Case," *Chicago Sun-Times,* August 17, 1998.
94. Richard Devine, "Former Prosecutor Defends Cook County's Criminal Justice System," *Crain's Chicago Business,* July 1, 2016, www.chicagobusiness.com/article/20160701/OPINION/160639983/richard-devine-writes-in-defense-of-cook-county-s-criminal-justice-system.
95. Roeper, "Too Soon to Take Sides."
96. "Editorial," *Chicago Sun-Times,* August 17, 1998, 28.
97. Kotlowitz, "Unprotected," 52.
98. Maurice Possley and Steve Mills, "Charges Dropped Against 2 Boys: Prosecutors Give Up Their Murder Case Against a 7-Year-Old and an 8-Year-Old, but Questions Persist About How Police Handled the Investigation of Ryan Harris' Death; Tests Find Semen on Girl's Clothes," *Chicago Tribune,* September 5, 1998, 1, www.chicagotribune.com/1998/09/05/charges-dropped-against-2-boys/.
99. Possley and Mills, "Charges Dropped."
100. Kotlowitz, "Unprotected," 52.
101. Possley and Mills, "Charges Dropped."
102. Maurice Possley, "Murder Case Against Boys 7 and 8 Dropped: Crime Lab Finds Semen on Victim's Undergarments," *Chicago Tribune,* September 4, 1998, 1; see also Possley and Mills, "Charges Dropped."
103. Steve Mills and Maurice Possley, "Cops Ignored Clues That Case Was Weak," *Chicago Tribune,* September 6, 1998, 1.
104. Possley and Mills, "Charges Dropped."
105. Possley and Mills, "Charges Dropped."
106. Possley and Mills, "Charges Dropped."
107. Cassidy has a long history of coercing false confessions, most notably in the case of the Marquette Park Four, in which he and his fellow officers coordinated unconstitutional coercive interrogations on the young Black men, resulting in their wrongful convictions. See Andy Grimm, "'Marquette 4' Defendants Sue City over Wrongful Convictions," *Chicago Sun-Times,* February 12, 2018; *McCoy v. Cassidy* (#2027) et al., No. 1:2018-cv-01068, Document 95 (N.D. Ill. 2024).
108. Kotlowitz, "Unprotected," 53.
109. Burke in a 1999 *Nation* magazine article, as reported by Chip Mitchell, "A Cook County State's Attorney Candidate Once Helped Convict a Boy Whose Murder Confession Was Found to Be Coerced," WBEZ Chicago, December 19, 2023, www.wbez.org/criminal-justice/2023/12/19/eileen-oneill-burke-tied-to-a-black-boys-wrongful-conviction.
110. A. D. Quig and Charles Sam, "State's Attorney Candidate Prosecuted Boy Whose Murder Conviction Was Overturned Because Police Coerced Confession," *Chicago Tribune,* December 21, 2023.
111. Cassidy, "Ugliness of Being a Kid," 19.
112. Max Blaisdell, "Cook County State's Attorney Stops Maintaining Lists of Discredited Cops," *Chicago Reader,* 2025, https://chicagoreader.com/news/reader-investigative-reports/brady-list-eileen-oneill-burke-cook-county/.

113. Elijah Henderson Civil Case, 11.
114. Elijah Henderson Civil Case, 11.
115. Elijah Henderson Civil Case, 54. On work crimes, see Abraham S. Blumberg, "The Practice of Law as Confidence Game: Organizational Cooptation of a Profession," *Law and Society Review* 1, no. 2 (1967): 15–39.
116. Roeper, "Too Soon to Take Sides."
117. Sadovi, "Mother Tearfully Recalls."
118. Peter J. Vilkelis, "A Trustworthy Cop," *Chicago Tribune,* September 22, 1998, 14.
119. Vilkelis, "Trustworthy Cop," 14.
120. Teresa Puente and Janita Poe, "Emotion Washes Englewood," *Chicago Tribune,* September 6, 1998, 14.
121. Puente and Poe, "Emotion Washes Englewood," 14.
122. Puente and Poe, "Emotion Washes Englewood."
123. Puente and Poe, "Emotion Washes Englewood."
124. Puente and Poe, "Emotion Washes Englewood."
125. Carlos Sadovi, "Ryan Harris' Slaying Haunts Mother and City; 7 Years After Death, Boy's Suit Set for Trial," *Chicago Tribune,* August 1, 2005, 2C.1.
126. Sadovi, "Ryan Harris' Slaying."
127. Sadovi, "Ryan Harris' Slaying."
128. Daniel Taylor, text exchange with the author, October 2, 2025.
129. "Freed Inmate Accuses Off-Duty Cops of Battery," *Chicago Tribune,* April 2, 2002, updated August 20, 2021, www.chicagotribune.com/2002/04/02/freed-inmate-accuses-off-duty-cops-of-battery/.
130. Letter from Kathleen T. Zellner to Monroe G. Milstein, April 2, 2022, re: Larry Ollins.
131. Possley, "Ex-Murder Suspect Is Busy Being a Boy."
132. Possley, "Ex-Murder Suspect Is Busy Being a Boy."
133. Darron Bowden interview.
134. Mayor Richard M. Daley continued his support of his officers, as did top prosecutor Richard Devine, even though more incriminating details revealed themselves. For instance, the police produced adult sketches of possible suspects based on witness interviews and then buried them. See Pam Belluck, "Chicago Boys, 7 and 8, Charged in the Brutal Killing of a Girl, 11," *New York Times,* September 5, 1998, N1; Teresa Puente and Gary Washburn, "Cops Admit Discounting Witnesses' Descriptions," *Chicago Tribune,* September 10, 1998, 32.
135. Catherine Ferguson interview.
136. Possley, "Ex-Murder Suspect Is Busy Being a Boy."
137. Possley, "Ex-Murder Suspect Is Busy Being a Boy."
138. Possley, "Ex-Murder Suspect Is Busy Being a Boy."
139. Catherine Ferguson interview.
140. Carlos Sadovi, "Court Told of Threats in Harris Case; Family Fears Mounted After Boy Was Charged," *Chicago Tribune,* September 1, 2005, 2NS.4.
141. Teresa Puente and Gary Washburn, "Cops Admit Discounting Witnesses' Descriptions," *Chicago Tribune,* September 10, 1998, updated August 11, 2021, https://www.chicagotribune.com/1998/09/10/cops-admit-discounting-witnesses-descriptions/.
142. Puente and Washburn, "Cops Admit Discounting."
143. Terry Wilson, "Police Say Apartment House Fire Fatal to 6 Was Deliberately Set," *Chicago Tribune,* June 4, 1999, 4.
144. Wilson, "Police Say Apartment House Fire."

145. Wilson, "Police Say Apartment House Fire."
146. Steve Patterson, "Boy in Harris Case Harmed by Arrest—or Family Life?," *Chicago Sun-Times,* September 1, 2005, 24.
147. Steve Patterson and Fran Spielman, "$6.2 Mil. Settlement in Ryan Harris Case: Boy Was Wrongfully Accused of Slaying," *Chicago Sun-Times,* September 19, 2005, 1.
148. "Officers Accused of Excessive Force," ABC7 Chicago, May 1, 2008. www.abc7chicago.com/archive/6115614/; "Mother and Son Convicted over Melee with Police," CBS Chicago, April 7, 2011, www.cbsnews.com/chicago/news/mother-and-son-convicted-over-melee-with-police/.
149. "Officers Accused of Excessive Force."
150. "Mother and Son Convicted over Melee with Police."
151. "Officers Accused of Excessive Force."

## Conclusion

1. James Baldwin, *No Name in the Street* (New York: Dial Press, 1972), 149.
2. Melanie Newport, *This Is My Jail: Local Politics and the Rise of Mass Incarceration* (Philadelphia: University of Pennsylvania Press, 2022), 21.
3. Newport, *This Is My Jail,* 31.
4. Newport, *This Is My Jail,* 33.
5. Anthony M. Platt, *The Child Savers: The Invention of Delinquency* (Chicago: University of Chicago Press, 1977); Geoff K. Ward, *The Black Child-Savers: Racial Democracy and Juvenile Justice* (Chicago: University of Chicago Press, 2012).
6. Romarr Gipson interview.
7. Catherine Ferguson interview.
8. Samuel R. Gross, "What We Think, What We Know, and What We Think We Know About False Convictions," *Ohio State Journal of Criminal Law* 14 (2016): 753; Samuel R. Gross et al., "Rate of False Conviction of Criminal Defendants Who Are Sentenced to Death," *Proceedings of the National Academy of Sciences* 111, no. 20 (2014): 7230–35.
9. Steve Mills, "Daniel Taylor Was Innocent. He Spent Decades in Prison Trying to Fix the State's Mistake," *ProPublica,* May 25, 2022, www.propublica.org/article/wrongful-conviction-murder-chicago-police-daniel-taylor.
10. Gonzalez Van Cleve, *Waiting Room,* 4.
11. Gonzalez Van Cleve, *Waiting Room,* 4.
12. Javier Auyero, *Patients of the State: The Politics of Waiting in Argentina* (Durham, NC: Duke University Press, 2012), cited in Gonzalez Van Cleve, *Crook County,* 31. See also Lara-Millán and Gonzalez Van Cleve, "Interorganizational Utility."
13. Blair Paddock, "'Egregious Delays' and No Attorney Assistance: How Those Incarcerated Fight Their Convictions," *WTTW News,* May 27, 2025, https://news.wttw.com/2025/05/27/egregious-delays-and-no-attorney-assistance-how-those-incarcerated-fight-their.
14. Author interview with intake staff at Loevy + Loevy.
15. Since the nationwide average time to exoneration is sixteen years, innocence firms are forced to triage these claims of innocence. See "By the Numbers," Innocence Project, July 8, 2025, https://innocenceproject.org/exonerations-data/; Innocence Project Evaluation Criteria, accessed July 25, 2025, https://lawweb.colorado.edu/law/centers/innocence/EvaluationCriteria.pdf; "Wrongful Convictions for Lesser

Crimes Often Fall Through the Cracks," Innocence Project, February 9, 2015, accessed July 25, 2025, https://innocenceproject.org/news/wrongful-convictions-for-lesser-crimes-often-fall-through-the-cracks/.

16. Pretrial punishment shifts power to prosecutors and police even before a defendant is found guilty. See Feeley, *Process Is the Punishment*.
17. The National Registry of Exonerations, "25,000 Years Lost to Wrongful Convictions," June 14, 2021, https://exonerationregistry.org/sites/exonerationregistry.org/files/documents/25000%20Years.pdf.
18. The National Registry of Exonerations, accessed January 13, 2026, https://exonerationregistry.org/.
19. Invisible Institute data from the Citizens Police Data Project (CPDP) regarding police misconduct in Chicago show that from 1988 to 2023, "there have been 259,827 allegations of misconduct against Chicago police officers." An astounding "8% of those allegations were disciplined." CPDP also has limitations due to what is made available to the public. For instance, a citizen complaint against an officer may have egregious elements like improper use of force or allegations of illegal search, but it also may have small violations like incorrect paperwork. It's possible for an officer to be found in violation of a paperwork complaint while not being in violation of the more egregious offenses. In the data, the entire complaint would be marked as sustained, which would make it seem that more officers are held accountable than they actually are. For more information, explore data from the CPDP here: https://invisible.institute/police-data.
20. *United States v. Burge,* United States Court of Appeals for the Seventh Circuit, April 2013; People's Law Office Archive, https://chicagopolicetorturearchive.com/documents. See also Jon Burge Torture Index, https://torturememorial.wordpress.com/wp-content/uploads/2011/06/jonburgetortureindex-icat.pdf; "U.S. Indicts Former Chicago Police Cmdr. on Perjury, Obstruction of Justice Charges Related to Alleged Torture and Physical Abuse," U.S. Department of Justice, October 21, 2008, www.justice.gov/archive/opa/pr/2008/October/08-crt-938.html.
21. Taylor, *Torture Machine,* Kindle ed., loc. 409.
22. Elijah Henderson Civil Case, 11.
23. This is the only case in which I anonymized a subject, to prevent any unintended disclosure that could identify a child or other vulnerable person who is unable to consent.
24. Steve Schmadeke, "Defense Questions Appointment of Former Prosecutor to Handle Burge Cases," *Chicago Tribune,* May 11, 2017, updated May 23, 2019, https://www.chicagotribune.com/2017/05/11/defense-questions-appointment-of-former-prosecutor-to-handle-burge-cases/.
25. Amy Wooten, "Election 2008: Bob Milan," *Windy City Times,* January 30, 2008, https://windycitytimes.com/2008/01/30/election-2008-bob-milan/.
26. Robert J. Milan, "Preventing and Addressing Wrongful Convictions," *The Practical Prosecutor,* 2005, cited in Tepfer, Cooley, and Thompson, "Convenient Scapegoats."
27. Milan, "Preventing and Addressing Wrongful Convictions," 35.
28. Schmadeke, "Defense Questions Appointment."
29. Robert J. Milan, "Call in the National Guard to Protect Chicago's South and West Sides," *Chicago Tribune,* June 30, 2015, updated May 11, 2019, https://www.chicagotribune.com/2015/06/30/call-in-the-national-guard-to-protect-chicagos-south-and-west-sides/.
30. James Cassidy, "The Ugliness of Being a Kid of the '90s," *Chicago Tribune,* December 28, 1994.

31. Nicole Gonzalez Van Cleve, "Why Trump's Threat to 'Send in the Feds' Won't Help Chicago," *CNN,* updated June 30, 2017, https://www.cnn.com/2017/01/04/opinions/real-help-for-chicago-van-cleve-opinion.
32. Schmadeke, "Defense Questions Appointment of Former Prosecutor."
33. "12 Years Behind Bars, Now Justice at Last," *Chicago Tribune,* February 1, 2005, updated August 22, 2021, https://www.chicagotribune.com/2005/02/01/12-years-behind-bars-now-justice-at-last-2/.
34. Clarissa Palermo, Assistant State's Attorney, letter to Robert J. Milan, Supervisor, Felony Review Unit, Re: The Oral Statement of Duel Thomas Concerning the Murder of Quinton Kirkwood, March 29, 1999.
35. David Jackson, "Appellate Ruling Gets Personal in Back-and-Forth Fight with Special Prosecutor," Injustice Watch, February 6, 2024, https://www.injusticewatch.org/judges/2024/special-prosecutor-appellate-decision-carl-walker-michael-hyman/.
36. *People v. Muhammad,* 2023 IL App (1st) 220372, 1-22-0372, 5, 80.
37. Illinois Torture Inquiry and Relief Commission Act, 775 ILCS 40/1 (Ill. 2009). For example, see: *In re Claim of Adrian Thomas,* TIRC Claim No. 2012-120-T (Illinois Torture Inquiry and Relief Commission), related to Cook Cnty. Cir. Ct. Case No. 94-CR-1229, 17; "Report on the Failure of Special Prosecutors Edward J. Egan and Robert D. Boyle," 3.
38. *People v. Muhammad,* 2023 IL App (1st) 220372, 1-22-0372, 5. See also Defendant's Exhibit 2, page 2 of 21, in *People of the State of Illinois v. Abdul Malik Muhammad,* No. 1-22-0372 (Ill. App. Ct. 1st Dist.), Plaintiff-Appellant's Brief and Argument in Support of Appeal, filed by H. Candace Gorman electronically on September 8, 2022.
39. Defendant's Exhibit 2, page 11 of 21, *People v. Muhammad,* No. 1-22-0372 (Ill. App. Ct. 1st Dist.).
40. *People v. Muhammad,* No. 1-22-0372 (Ill. App. Ct. 1st Dist.).
41. *People v. Muhammad,* 2023 IL App (1st) 220372, 1-22-0372.
42. *People v. Muhammad,* 2023 IL App (1st) 220372, 1-22-0372, para. 20.
43. *People v. Muhammad,* 2023 IL App (1st) 220372, 1-22-0372, para. 20.
44. *People v. Muhammad,* 2023 IL App (1st) 220372, 1-22-0372, para. 7, 8.
45. *People v. Muhammad,* 2023 IL App (1st) 220372, 1-22-0372, 125.
46. Feeley, *Process Is the Punishment.*
47. Medwed, *Barred.*
48. Blachman, "Decades After Alleged Torture by Police."
49. Jackson, "Unsealed Records Reveal New Details."
50. Laurence Ralph, "This Is America—The Torture Letters: Reckoning with Police Violence," lecture, Brown University, YouTube video, posted by Brown University, www.youtube.com/watch?v=FarcQdCRL3o.

## Epilogue

1. James Baldwin, interview by Jordan Elgrably, "The Art of Fiction," *The Paris Review,* 91, no. 78 (1984), https://www.theparisreview.org/interviews/2994/the-art-of-fiction-no-78-james-baldwin.
2. Shaquil Manigault, "'The Kids Who Cried Wolf' Is Rockford Man's Story of Wrongful Conviction," *Rockford Register Star,* March 7, 2020, www.rrstar.com/story/entertainment/books/2020/03/07/kids-who-cried-wolf/1568270007/.

3. Jim Hagerty and B. J. Lutz, "Man Cleared in Chicago Homicide Teaches Civics After Spending 14 Years in Prison," WGN-TV, July 29, 2024, updated July 29, 2024, https://wgntv.com/news/omar-muhammad-civics-classes-chicago-homicide-exoneration/.
4. Eli Faber, *The Child in the Electric Chair: The Execution of George Junius Stinney Jr. and the Making of a Tragedy in the American South* (Columbia: University of South Carolina Press, 2021).
5. Omar Saiahadin, Facebook post, September 26, 2020.
6. Author interview with Omar Muhammad, March 23, 2024.

# Wrongful Conviction as an Empirical Site of Investigation: Author's Notes on Research and Analysis

I am trained as an empirical researcher in the field of sociology. Rather than examining one case of a phenomenon, I am interested in what numerous cases—a whole sample of cases—tell us about the social norms and institutions we take for granted.

Each of the many wrongful convictions described in this book is particular unto itself, but collectively they dramatize the criminal justice system's most clandestine techniques of racial abuse, which, until now, have been mostly dismissed as a series of unrelated "accidents" related to police corruption or incompetence.

As a social scientist, I take these mistakes and make them into a sample of cases where one can see systemic patterns and build a theory of how wrongful convictions have related features that comprise an institutional pathway in the criminal justice system. The heaviest burden of research such as this is building theories about the social world by inferring causal relationships from observed patterns and narratives. This work requires careful scaffolding of data over long periods of time, with close attention to patterns and points of convergence in narratives and other defining features of cases.

A strong sample of cases is important because this study is concerned with practices that are meant to be hidden from outsiders. This is what Professor Laurence Ralph calls the "open secrets" of institutions, what people in power know but refuse to admit or acknowledge as true.* The goal is to use a sample of cases to show the patterns of these so-called open secrets that create a type of wrongful conviction system in the United States.

Sociologist Brittany Friedman argues that "truth-telling" is a type of method of data-driven inquiry. A practice of "discovery, of rebuilding that which has been attacked," or vanished. A process that requires digging and revealing what was intended to be hidden. Without such an orientation, the state can prevent us from "fully theorizing the reality of racist intention."† Examining the social meaning around cover-ups, clandestine activities, and the bending and breaking of laws by law enforcement actors is essential to understanding the criminal justice system, broadly, and its impact on the most vulnerable among us.

For those curious about the research process, below I detail my research design in service of this "truth telling" objective. It required rebuilding and reconstructing cases from multiple sources to retell the process and logics of wrongful conviction.

## Summary of Approach

From a methodological standpoint, this is a work of historical ethnography that integrates archival research with traditional ethnography or

* Laurence Ralph, *The Torture Letters: Reckoning with Police Violence* (Chicago: University of Chicago Press, 2020), ix–xxiv.

† Brittany Friedman, *Carceral Apartheid: How Lies and White Supremacists Run Our Prisons (Justice, Power, and Politics)* (Chapel Hill: University of North Carolina Press, 2025), Kindle edition, loc. 261.

embedded fieldwork. I examine cases of wrongful conviction as having their own "life history," starting with arrest, extending over decades of time, and traveling across legal systems (lower courts, appeals courts, the Supreme Court, and even the civil courts). By adding layers of data, I "rebuild" wrongful conviction cases from the ground up. This includes: interviews with key actors in the cases, archival materials, official reports, news media coverage, oral histories, legal documents from both criminal and civil cases, years of ethnographic observation from being embedded in the court system, and historical ethnographic techniques to revisit old crime scenes, neighborhoods, and police stations where past drama unfolded.*

This research could not have been completed without the foundation of my past major study of Cook County–Chicago's Criminal Court System which was published in the book *Crook County*. In that research, I was embedded in the criminal court system and conducted an ethnography of the courtrooms in the largest unified court system in the nation. I lay out this data collection in great detail in the Methods Appendix in the book. "Over the course of seven years (1997–2004), I completed three ethnographic visits of the field site, amounting to nine months of observations. In order to incorporate both participant and observer roles, I worked as a law clerk for the Cook County State's Attorney's Office (six months in 1997–1998) and for the Cook County Public Defender's Office (three months in 2004)."† This position allowed for access to both front-stage and backstage environments including judges' chambers for plea bargains, courtrooms, lock-ups, and the respective offices of prosecutors and public defenders. It also gave me proximity to police officers working with prosecutors. This study also included 104 interviews with private attorneys, public defenders, prosecutors, and judges. Beyond my field-

* Marcus Anthony Hunter, *Black Citymakers: How The Philadelphia Negro Changed Urban America* (New York: Oxford University Press, 2015).

† Gonzalez Van Cleve, *Crook County*, 196.

work, I collected an additional one thousand hours of observations of all twenty-five courtrooms in the main courthouse with the help of one hundred thirty court watchers. The sum total of this data was crucial to understanding the culture of the courts and the police as they create and process cases in the system.

As this research began, I focused considerable attention on the issue of false confessions because they are the most common type of evidence used in serious cases like murder. They are important indicators of how police and prosecutors craft criminal cases with "contaminating narratives" used to incite anti-Black racial animus with juries. I inductively coded the false confessions in nearly fifty exoneration cases from Chicago. Inductive coding is a process of looking for patterns and themes that emerged from a sample of cases. What I found in the confessions was a type of "narrative contamination" or extralegal narratives that leverage racial tropes and transform an innocent person into a criminal "monster" through their confession.

Through interviews with seasoned attorneys who worked on these cases, I realized that the false confessions were necessary but insufficient to understanding the vast array of processes that led to the gendered and raced patterns of who gets accused, interrogated, and charged while innocent. I began treating the false confession as a narrative starting point. The micro-scenes in the false confessions often gained flight and resonance in the news media as well as in the trial itself, with prosecutors "performing" for the jury. I interrogated how racist logics became a type of "evidence" despite contradicting physical evidence of innocence. To understand the force of the racial contamination of false confessions, it required examining the beliefs, social relationships, institutional norms of practice in police and prosecution, and the media coverage that gives rise to the pattern of Black youth being targeted by the police.

Rebuilding the media footprint for these cases was essential to understanding wrongful conviction. The media acts as unintentional collaborators in disseminating the police's crime fiction narratives on cases. As such, sustained media coverage of criminal cases is an important indicator of our collective understanding of crime, victimization, criminality, and race as well as the police's framing of guilt around an alleged suspect. In all the cases mentioned in the book, we conducted a comprehensive media search and analysis of all local and national reporting on each case.

Developing uniform search criteria that could gather all reporting on these cases presented a challenge. In some cases, the defendants were too young to be named in the media and privacy rules protected their identity. For instance, for Romarr Gipson, his name was not included in local or national media until he was 18 years old. In other cases, like the Englewood Four, there were numerous defendants and the media used a notorious moniker (rather than the legal names of all the defendants) to report on the case. Often, it was important to search under the victim's name in order to get the full breadth of coverage on a particular case. For instance, in the case of the Dixmoor Five, the young victim was missing for seven months while the police received media coverage (and pressure) to name a suspect, resulting in the arrest of five innocent boys.

For all cases, we started searching on the victim's name on the day prior to the murder and kept the search inclusive into the present day. This allowed us to see how the case was often still "ongoing" with victims' families, defendants, civil suits, and the like still in the news. Using the victim's name allowed us to see all media coverage prior to the police naming a suspect and regardless if the suspect was a minor and their identity hidden from the public. Because naming conventions varied—some defendants were minors and unnamed, others were identified by monikers—we layered search terms using victims' names, defendants' names (including common misspellings), and case nicknames.

In these key cases, we pulled all the media coverage for two of the largest news franchises for the city of Chicago: the *Chicago Tribune* and the *Chicago Sun-Times*. They are the top two Illinois daily newspapers by circulation (data as of July 2021). To ensure that we included Black voices and journalists, we included the *Chicago Defender,* which "cover the interests of the urban African American community with culturally relevant content not regularly serviced by mainstream media."* In effect, the *Chicago Defender* is considered the Black newspaper for Black people in the city of Chicago and often provided counter-narratives of these high-profile crimes. We also ensured that we did a national search to see how these high-profile cases migrated into the national imagination. For high-profile cases like the Ryan Harris case, we searched under "Ryan Harris," "Romarr Gipson," "Romarr Gibson," (a common misspelling) and "Elijah Henderson."

Below we detail the number of articles obtained from each newspaper publication and how many were relevant to the case.

In our search of the *Chicago Tribune,* we yielded 472 articles, 385 of which were relevant.

When searching the *Chicago Sun-Times,* we found 655 articles, 268 of which were relevant.

The *Chicago Defender* had an output of 356 articles, 227 of which related to the case.

Lastly, our national search consisted of 199 articles, 52 of which were relevant. In total, our searches on the case yielded 1,458 articles, 832 being relevant.

All searches were replicated and cross-checked by research assistants and reference librarians to ensure consistency and reliability. Beyond this general strategy, we layered additional search criteria that reflected the unique features of the case. For the police, prosecutors, and other actors who were instrumental to these cases, we conducted media searches on their names which allowed us to see other cases of wrongful conviction or misconduct in which they were involved. Two examples were Detective James Cassidy and Pamela Fish. Once their other cases were identified, we gathered legal documents and investigated how those cases unfolded as well. In all, we created a web of cases by following the officers and other key actors as they moved across cases, precincts, or time.

* *Chicago Defender*, "About Us," https://chicagodefender.com/about-us/ (accessed February 2, 2026).

My researchers and I often felt like we were falling down the proverbial rabbit hole because the abundance of cases was vast. This was not about following "bad apples" but about finding institutional patterns and practices across cases to see the techniques unfolding on defendants that were unrelated.

Through this myriad of data, I reconstructed each case of wrongful conviction and compared the individual case to other cases of wrongful conviction. There, I could see the patterns that collectively represent the techniques of wrongful conviction as a process in the criminal justice system. I also could see the racist logics that justified these clandestine processes prior to the case reaching the courts.

As I unearthed findings related to Chicago, I compared these cases to other national cases. For instance, claims about Daniel Taylor "escaping" prison to commit murder matched the same narrative in the *In re Gault,* 387 U.S. 1 (1967) ruling, which described a child only referred to as Gregory W. by the Court escaping a locked security ward to commit a murder and sexual assault. The case and its description of the crime also paralleled Lee Hester. In another example from our research, Chicago's street file system is parallel to one reported in Detroit.* It also has parallel practices coming out of New Orleans (see *Connick v. Thompson,* 563 U.S. 51 (2011)). Indeed, Justice Ruth Bader Ginsburg called these practices a tinder box where so-called *Brady* violations of evidence disclosure were "nigh inevitable."†

Beyond comparing Chicago cases to each other and other national corollaries, I began this research by examining two famous historical cases of wrongful conviction: George Stinney in South Carolina (the youngest child to be executed in the United States) and the "wolf pack case" of the Scottsboro Boys. These historic cases provided a road map

* Steve Neavling, "Detroit Police Buried Evidence, and Innocent Men Paid the Price," *Metro Times,* October 2, 2024.

† See Ruth Bader Ginsburg's dissent in *Connick v. Thompson:* "This case is one such instance. Connick, who himself had been indicted for suppression of evidence, created a tinderbox in Orleans Parish in which *Brady* violations were nigh inevitable." *Connick v. Thompson,* 563 U.S. 51 (2011).

of practices and cultural justification for the more modern cases profiled in this book.

## Notes on the Jurisdiction: The Wrongful Conviction Capital of the Nation

Of all the jurisdictions represented in the National Registry of Exonerations, one stands out by far. Since 1989, Chicago's Cook County alone has 499 wrongful convictions that have been exonerated, with Harris County, Texas (233 exonerations), and Los Angeles County, California (141) in a distant second, and third place, respectively.* There are two plausible reasons for this dubious distinction. As I have documented in past research, Chicago has a sordid history of police brutality and systemic cover-ups of those patterns and practices by judges, prosecutors, and elected officials. In the court system, I showed systemic violations of due process that were normalized as part of the everyday workings of the court. Taken together, these informal ways of bringing cases in and through the system could lead to such high numbers of wrongful convictions. This was my original hypothesis. Another explanation for why Chicago is the wrongful conviction capital of the nation is that Chicago has a well-developed exonerations movement. Northwestern University and the University of Chicago, for example, have their own clinics to review cases, and they have the resources and students to scrutinize some cases coming out of the local court system. Compared with other jurisdictions around the nation, this legal community has had some success exonerating and then getting civil settlements for people wronged by wrongful conviction. As such, we have myriad cases to see the process of wrongful conviction from a robust sample coming out of Chicago. With so many cases that are well litigated, we know convincingly that the former defendants are

* The National Registry of Exonerations. Accessed February 9, 2026. https://exonerationregistry.org/

innocent. As "settled history," these cases provide a significant paper trail of archives and media coverage. Within these archival documents are the names of essential players in these cases: defendants, parents, journalists, police, prosecutors—an entire social web of actors who shaped or were impacted by the outcome. In some cases, these actors are still available for interviews.

Finally, Chicago is a city that I know well. I have been embedded and researching in the criminal justice system there for over a decade, doing fieldwork in the prosecutor's office and the public defender's office, which was well documented in my first book, *Crook County*. I had proximity to the Chicago police and have reported on the pervasiveness of police perjury. I have embedded in and around Chicago's Cook County jail, a behemoth carceral structure the size of over seventy-two American football fields, and an institution often used by the Chicago police as a place of terror and a tool for silencing witnesses.

Chicago has remained resistant to reform and has thwarted federal oversight even after the vast cover-up of Laquan McDonald's murder, which was a national scandal. Their compliance to a consent decree* has been more symbolic than substantive. It is a city nearly frozen in time from a series of high-profile cases that helped bring wrongful conviction to national attention in the 1980s to the most recent occurrences in this decade.

Chicago is an "elegant case" to examine how a jurisdiction—the largest unified court system in the nation—can be so successful in convicting innocent Black boys and young men.† It also shows how Chicago, like so many other places across the nation, has normalized this "ordinary dysfunction."‡

So many of Chicago's cases have corollaries in history and across

* Sam McCann, "Everything You Need to Know about Consent Decrees," *Vera* https://www.vera.org/news/everything-you-need-to-know-about-consent-decrees#:~:text=The%20court%20approves%20the%20agreement,affected%20by%20the%20unlawful%20practices (accessed October 23, 2025).

† *Crook County*, 22.

‡ *Crook County*, 21.

jurisdiction, showing that wrongful conviction has generalizable features beyond a single location, place in time, local political administration, or the police's national talking point about "bad actors" as "bad apples." This is a system, profiled in Chicago, that has cultural endurance and reach well beyond its borders.

One final note: selecting the cases profiled in this book was difficult. Actually, it was heart-wrenching. Each case and each kid could have been a centerpiece of this book and the conclusions would have remained the same. Indeed, as my research assistants and I vetted the cases, there was guilt that we had to eliminate some cases and kids from having their stories profiled in an in-depth manner for the book, but their stories are collectively told in this work. The sample reached "saturation" where, in case after case, patterns became predictable and even repetitive. In the end, we looked for "elegant cases" or cases that could help crystallize the techniques of wrongful conviction for the reader to understand. Overall, this is a collective story that is no longer invisible.

## Final Notes on Fact-Checking

While researchers frequently rely on peer review, they often do not use professional fact-checkers as newsrooms like *The New York Times*, *The Atlantic*, and *The Washington Post* require. It is my intention that this work passes both standards of excellence and accuracy. The following represents an overview of the detailed fact-checking that was conducted for this book. At present, there are 1,033 distinct saved files that were used during fact-checking the book. The sources supporting this book extend far beyond academic journal articles. They include legal case law, trial transcripts, appellate briefs, Supreme Court filings, archival documents, newspaper reporting, government records, oral histories, video and audio recordings of interviews, and investigative materials, among other primary and secondary sources. This figure does not include hard-copy books consulted and electronic books that could not be downloaded or archived, but are cited in the notes of this book. This number also does not include large database searches that are counted as a single file. For example, a ProQuest search of the *Chicago Tribune* related to the Harris cases yielded 322 separate articles, yet this search is counted as a single saved file within the 1,033-file total.

In addition, this count does not reflect the hundreds of sources independently located and reviewed by twenty-three research assistants, nor the numerous targeted verifications conducted in authoritative sources that did not generate separate saved files (e.g., confirming spellings, titles, and dates). This research acted as essential background and verification for cases profiled in the book and was foundational for the process of case selection in this study. For these reasons, the 1,033-file figure should be understood as an extremely conservative accounting of the documentation and research that underlies the manuscript. A substantial body of research remains on the proverbial "cutting room floor," and was not explicitly profiled in this book. This remaining data represents opportunities for future academic articles and possibly a new book project. However, it does not escape me that the abundance of data in this book is also an indication of the shear enormity of victims of wrongful conviction and their suffering.

This book was fact-checked in three distinct stages. First, there was a legal fact-check of case law, prosecution procedure, and relevant U.S. Supreme Court rulings. Second, there was an academic and journalistic fact-check done by a professional fact-checker who has extensive experience fact-checking both academic books and trade books as well as publications of the National Academies of Sciences, Engineering, and Medicine. Finally, there was a final read conducted by a veteran practicing lawyer and clinical law professor. Through this process, we became acutely aware that the lies that were seeded by police in these cases often traveled across sources, media coverage, and legal filings. For instance, the duration of a child's confession, as in the Lee Hester case, differed in the media, in the Illinois Supreme Court files, and the U.S. Supreme Court filings. This made it all the more important that we used multiple sources to confirm the accuracy of each detail in each of the cases profiled in the book. In a sense, police lies were like contaminants, traveling quickly even in legal arenas where legal documents, transcripts, and filings are often assumed to be a settled set of facts. Because such contradictions are frequent and often cumulative, it was not feasible to document every instance without dramatically expanding the length of the book. Instead, representative examples are noted in the footnotes to illustrate how factual distortions propagate through a case's life cycle.

# Index

## About the Author

Nicole Gonzalez Van Cleve is Associate Professor of Sociology at Brown University and an affiliated scholar with the American Bar Foundation in Chicago, Illinois. She is the award-winning author of *Crook County* and has contributed articles to *The New York Times, The Atlantic, NBC News, Crain's Chicago Business,* and CNN. Her legal commentary has been featured on NPR, *NBC News,* and MS Now's *The Rachel Maddow Show.*